GLOBAL TALENT MANAGEMENT AND STAFFING IN MNES

INTERNATIONAL BUSINESS & MANAGEMENT

Series Editor: **Pervez N. Ghauri**

Published:

Related journals – sample copies available on request:

INTERNATIONAL BUSINESS & MANAGEMENT VOLUME 32

GLOBAL TALENT MANAGEMENT AND STAFFING IN MNES

EDITED BY

YING GUO
Xi'an Jiaotong-Liverpool University, Jiangsu, China

HUSSAIN G. RAMMAL
University of Technology Sydney, NSW, Australia

PETER J. DOWLING
La Trobe University, Victoria, Australia

Emerald

United Kingdom — North America — Japan
India — Malaysia — China

Emerald Group Publishing Limited
Howard House, Wagon Lane, Bingley BD16 1WA, UK

First edition 2016

Copyright © 2016 Emerald Group Publishing Limited

Reprints and permissions service
Contact: permissions@emeraldinsight.com

British Library Cataloguing in Publication Data
A catalogue record for this book is available from the British Library

ISBN: 978-1-78635-354-2
ISSN: 1876-066X (Series)

Printed and bound by CPI Group (UK) Ltd, Croydon, CR0 4YY

ISOQAR certified
Management System,
awarded to Emerald
for adherence to
Environmental
standard
ISO 14001:2004.

Certificate Number 1985
ISO 14001

INVESTOR IN PEOPLE

Contents

List of Contributors

Ramudu Bhanugopan	School of Management and Marketing, Charles Sturt University, New South Wales, Australia
Zoltan Buzady	Central European University Business School, Budapest, Hungary
Peter J. Dowling	Department of Management and Marketing, La Trobe University, Victoria, Australia
Joao Ferreira	Management and Economics Department, University of Beira Interior, Covilhã, Portugal
Ying Guo	International Business School Suzhou, Xi'an Jiaotong-Liverpool University, Jiangsu, China
Charlotte Jonasson	Aarhus University, Aarhus, Denmark
Haiying Kang	Australian Institute of Business, Adelaide, Australia
Jakob Lauring	Aarhus University, Aarhus, Denmark
Yvonne McNulty	RMIT University, Sentosa Cove, Singapore
Snejina Michailova	University of Auckland Business School, Auckland, New Zealand
Yoko Naito	School of Political Science and Economics, Department of Business Administration, Tokai University, Kanagawa, Japan
Dana L. Ott	University of Auckland Business School, Auckland, New Zealand
Hussain G. Rammal	UTS Business School, University of Technology Sydney, NSW, Australia
Vanessa Ratten	La Trobe Business School, La Trobe University, Victoria, Australia

Jan Selmer   Aarhus University, Taby, Sweden

Jie Shen   Shenzhen International Business School,
                              Shenzhen University, Guangdong, People's
                              Republic of China

Justin Williams   School of Business and Management, Niagara
                              College, Niagara on the Lake Ontario,
                              Canada

Ling Eleanor Zhang   King's College London, School of
                              Management & Business, London,
                              United Kingdom

About the Editors

Ying Guo is Lecturer in Human Resource Management at Xi'an Jiaotong-Liverpool University, Suzhou, China. She received her PhD from the UniSA Business School, University of South Australia in Adelaide, Australia. Her research interests include expatriate management, global talent management and staffing, cross-cultural management, knowledge transfer and leadership. She is an active member of the Academy of International Business (AIB), and Australia and New Zealand International Business Academy (ANZIBA).

Hussain G. Rammal is Senior Lecturer in International Business Strategy at University of Technology Sydney (UTS), Australia. He is co-editor of *Review of International Business and Strategy* and Area Editor of *Journal of Asia Business Studies*. Previously, he was a faculty member at the University of Adelaide and University of South Australia, and has held visiting positions at the University of Aberdeen Business School in Scotland, and Aalto University in Finland. Hussain's current research interests include internationalization of service firms; international business negotiations; international entrepreneurship; and knowledge transfer in MNEs.

Peter J. Dowling (Ph.D, The Flinders University of South Australia) is Professor of International Management & Strategy at La Trobe University, Melbourne, Australia. He has held visiting appointments in the United States at Cornell University and Michigan State University and in Germany at the University of Paderborn and the University of Bayreuth. He has co-authored a number of books including Dowling, Festing & Engle *International Human Resource Management* (6th Ed., 2013), Cengage, UK. He was Founding Editor of *Asia Pacific Journal of Human Resources* and an Editor of *International Journal of Human Resource Management*.

About the Authors

Ramudu Bhanugopan is Associate Professor of human resource management at the School of Management and Marketing, Charles Sturt University, Australia. His research focuses on human resource management practices across borders, HR metrics in MNEs, global leadership development, and cross border business collaborations.

Zoltan Buzady is a Hungarian who grew up in Germany. Zoltan earned his first degree in Law at the London School of Economics (UK) and completed a Global MBA at CASS Business School (UK). The focus of his PhD was on the strategic challenges in transition economies. His interest in cross-cultural aspects of people management drove him to write new teaching materials (twice global-award-winner of the CEEMAN Case Writing Competition). He has published on and is involved in international comparative studies on aspects of managing people in Central Europe and Central Asia. His current research focuses on Leadership and Flow Theory, combining these concepts with the process of Self-Development and Change Management, aiming to further Leadership Development that is applicable in different cultural and situational contexts.

Joao Ferreira is Associate Professor at the University of Beira Interior (UBI), Portugal. He completed the European Doctoral Programme of Entrepreneurship and Small Business Management at the Autonomous University of Barcelona (UAB), Spain. He is currently the Scientific Coordinator of NECE — Research Unit of Business Sciences, UBI. Since 2013, he has been a member of the A3Es agency evaluator group, responsible for evaluating management, marketing, and entrepreneurship degrees in Portugal. He has published various articles in international journals and is editor of some international books. His areas of interest are strategy, competitiveness, and entrepreneurship.

Charlotte Jonasson is Assistant Professor at Department of Psychology, Aarhus University. Her research interests are cross-cultural management and institutional work. She also conducts research on distributed leadership and organizational change. Charlotte Jonasson has published international articles in journals such as *Organization studies* and *British Journal of Management*.

Haiying Kang is Lecturer at School of Management, RMIT University. Her research interests include international HRM, HRM, and international business. She has published a number of journal articles in *International Journal of Human*

Resource Management, Asia Pacific Business Review and *Thunderbird International Business Review*. Her papers have also been accepted by many conferences, such as Academy of International Business, Australian and New Zealand Academy of Management and Australian and New Zealand Academy of International Business. She has been teaching HRM-related courses at both undergraduate and postgraduate level since 2010.

Jakob Lauring is Professor at Department of management, Aarhus University. Jakob Lauring research interests are focused on different themes within international and cross-cultural management. One of his main interests is expatriate management and expatriate adjustment. Jakob Lauring also conducts research on multicultural teams as co-located or and virtual. Here a central theme has been language management. Jakob Lauring has published more than 100 international articles in outlets such as *Journal of Worlds Business*, *British Journal of management*, *Human Resource Management Journal*, and *International Business Review*.

Yvonne McNulty is Associate Faculty at RMIT University, Singapore. She earned her PhD in International Business from Monash University in Melbourne, Australia. Her research focuses on global mobility and expatriation, global careers and global families, and has been published in the *Journal of World Business*, *Management International Review* and *International Journal of Intercultural Relations*. She is Associate Editor at the *Journal of Global Mobility* and *The International Journal of Human Resource Management*, and serves on the EAB of *Global Business and Organizational Excellence, Journal of Multinational Corporation Strategy* and *International Journal of Business and Emerging Markets*. Yvonne is co-author (with Kerr Inkson) of *Managing Expatriates: A Return on Investment Approach* (Business Expert Press, 2013), *The Handbook of Expatriate Marriage* (with Andrea Kennedy; Marshall Cavendish, 2016), and the *Research Handbook of Expatriates* (with Jan Selmer; Edward Elgar, 2016). She is a retired veteran of five years full-time service in the Royal Australian Navy.

Snejina Michailova (PhD from Copenhagen Business School, Denmark) is Professor of International Business at The University of Auckland Business School, New Zealand. Her research is in the areas of International Management and Knowledge Management. Her work has appeared in *Academy of Management Review, Academy of Management Executive, Journal of Management Studies, Journal of International Business Studies, Journal of World Business, Management International Review, International Business Review, The International Journal of Human Resource Management, Journal of International Management, critical perspectives on international business, California Management Review, Long Range Planning, Management Learning, Journal of Knowledge Management, Organizational Dynamics, Technovation, Employee Relations, European Management Journal*, and other journals. She has co-edited books on cross-cultural management (Routledge), knowledge governance (Oxford University Press), women in international management

(Edward Elgar), HRM in Central and Eastern Europe (Routledge) and research methodologies in non-Western contexts (Palgrave Macmillan). She is currently Associate Editor of *Critical Perspectives on International Business*.

Yoko Naito is Associate Professor of Human Resource Management in the Department of Business Administration, School of Political Science and Economics at Tokai University, and an adjunct researcher at the Institute for Transnational Human Resource Management at Waseda University, Japan. She obtained her PhD in 2013 and was awarded the Ohtsuka memorial Award in 2014 from Hokkaido University. Her research interests are HRM strategies in multi-national enterprises, with a focus on management of international repatriates and foreign employees, their knowledge sharing/transfer, socialization/adjustment, career effectiveness, and work life balance. Before she joined academia, she worked in the manufacturing and banking industries.

Dana L. Ott is a PhD candidate in the Department of Management and International Business at the University of Auckland Business School, New Zealand. She holds a MS in Management with a specialization in Human Resource Management from the University of Maryland University College, USA, and a BA in Psychology from the University of Nebraska, USA. Her research interests include the outcomes of international experiences and the development of skills to enhance expatriates' performance and success during international assignments. More specifically, her work examines the relationship between study abroad programs and the development of cultural intelligence.

Vanessa Ratten is Associate Professor at the La Trobe University, Australia. She completed her PhD at the UQ Business School, The University of Queensland, Australia, which is rated as one of the highest ranked in the Asia-Pacific region. She currently is the Program Coordinator of the Entrepreneurship and Innovation degrees at the La Trobe Business School and teaches innovation, entrepreneurship, marketing, and management courses. She has previously been on the business faculties of Deakin University, The University of Queensland, Queensland University of Technology and Duquesne University, USA. Her research interests are international entrepreneurship, technology innovation, and sport entrepreneurship.

Jan Selmer is Professor, Department of Management at Aarhus BSS – School of Business and Social Sciences, Aarhus University, Denmark. He received his Doctorate from Stockholm University, Sweden and has held various positions at universities, mostly in Asia. His research interest lies in cross-cultural management with a special focus on global mobility and expatriation. He is the Founding Editor-in-Chief of the *Journal of Global Mobility: The home of expatriate management research* (Emerald). His academic production includes nine books and numerous journal articles in international peer-reviewed academic journals. His book, *Expatriate Management: New Ideas for International Business*, published in 1995 by

Quorum Books, has become a classic text about the topic. He is the co-editor of the *Research Handbook of Expatriates* (Edward Elgar).

Jie Shen is currently Professor of Human Resource Management at Shenzhen University in Shenzhen City, Guangdong Province, China. Previously, he held positions of Professor of HRM at Curtin University, Associate Professor at Monash University and University of South Australia in Australia. Professor Jie Shen's research interests are HRM, international HRM and international business. He has published more than 150 academic and research thesis with seven monographs. His work appears in *Journal of Management, Human Resource Management, Journal of Business Ethics, International Business Review, International Journal of Human Resource Management, Personnel Review,* and *Thunderbird Business Review.*

Justin Williams has over two decades of experience in industry and as an international educator. With an industry background in Human Resources, Employee Relations and Strategic Planning, Justin found his passion for education while teaching at Royal Roads University in Victoria, Canada. As an educator at the undergraduate and graduate level in organizational behavior and leadership, Justin leveraged his industry experience to apply theoretical knowledge in the classroom. Justin continued his passion for travel and education in Iran with Royal Roads University and then in the Emirate of Qatar with the College of the North Atlantic and then the University of Calgary. A strong supporter of applied theory and interactive learning, Justin is also an advocate of the intrinsic value of using international experience to build valuable 21st century skills. Justin is the Chair (Outreach) of the Academy of International Business (MENA) and a regular peer reviewer for AOM and AIB, as well as several academic journals. Justin is the Associate Dean for the School of Business at Niagara College, Canada.

Ling Eleanor Zhang is Research and Teaching Fellow at School of Management and Business, King's College London. A key focus of her research is interaction across boundaries, which is manifested in contexts such as boundary spanning of multicultural employees, social categorisation and conflict management between expatriates and host country employees, and language challenges employees face at subsidiaries of multinational corporations. Her work on bicultural expatriates has been nominated for the British Academy Nayef Al-Rodhan Prize for Transcultural Understanding 2016. She has published in outlets such as the *International Journal of Human Resource Management* and *Cross Cultural Strategic Management.*

Global Talent Management and Staffing in MNEs: An Introduction to the Edited Volume of International Business and Management

Effective management of human resources can facilitate the creation of specific knowledge and building of social relations within the organization (Barney, 1991; Lado & Wilson, 1994). The international human resource management literature highlights the importance of attracting, recruiting, and retaining suitable workforce that contributes to the multinational enterprises' (MNEs) sustainable competitive advantage (Collings & Mellahi, 2009; Tarique & Schuler, 2008, 2010). MNEs are now more focused on developing and obtaining capabilities from their global talent pool rather than sending expatriates for specific tasks (Sparrow, Scullion, & Tarique, 2014). In this volume, we consider global talent management as an activity that involves managing employees' development in a global context, such as the activities relating to the management of talented employees at key positions and employees' global career development (Collings, 2014; Collings & Mellahi, 2009; Farndale, Scullion, & Sparrow, 2010; Mellahi & Collings, 2010; Sidani & Al Ariss, 2014).

Global staffing is the primary focus of talent management and is concerned with whether MNEs' overseas subsidiary is staffed and managed by parent country nationals, third country nationals, or host country nationals (Cerdin & Brewster, 2014; Collings, Morley, & Gunnigle, 2008; Tarique & Schuler, 2008). Parent country national staffing and its contribution to individual and organizational level outcomes has been the key focus of studies found in the global staffing literature (Gong, 2003). Traditionally, international expatriate assignments were for a period of three to five years. However, the high cost associated with using expatriates coupled with rapid expansion of MNEs' foreign operation had led to an imbalance between the demand for, and supply of parent country nationals, and has forced MNEs to use short-term international staffing arrangements (Collings, Scullion, & Morley, 2007; Reiche, Kraimer, & Harzing, 2011). These alternative arrangements include short-term assignments, commuter assignments, international business travel, and virtual assignments (Collings et al., 2007; Dowling, Festing, & Engle, 2013). In addition, the use of host and third country nationals in MNEs' global operations is another important component of global talent management that requires further investigation (Collings, McDonnell, Gunnigle, & Lavelle, 2010; Tarique, Schuler, & Gong, 2006).

The identification of talent and knowledge, which resides in an individual, is perhaps the first step of the global talent management process. The other areas of concern for the organization are the management of the expatriate and repatriation process.

1. Tacit Knowledge Held by Individuals

Talent management involves identifying the key skills and knowledge held by individuals in the organization, and managing its transfer across within the organization's global network. However, this knowledge that resides in the individuals is inherently difficult to transfer. Part of the difficulty lies in trying to convert this tacit knowledge into an explicit form that can be understood and applied globally. Nonaka and Takeuchi (1995) provided perhaps the most comprehensive and widely used knowledge transfer model. This model, known as the SECI (Socialization, Externalization, Combination and Internalization), details how organizations can transfer tacit knowledge by making it explicit through various steps (Li & Scullion, 2010). The first of these is socialization where individuals meet and work with each other to learn. This knowledge is then made explicit by documenting it. This process continues until the tacit knowledge is absorbed by the other individual and becomes part of their tacit knowledge.

While transfer of knowledge between individuals can be difficult, it is considered to be even harder when attempted between individuals from different countries. Differences in cultural norms, learning, hierarchy, and other contextual issues can act as hindrance, and can lead to miscommunication and other issues. It is therefore important for organizations to identify and select those individuals who are able to adapt to different working conditions.

2. Staffing Approach

To staff their global operations, organizations can use various staffing options (Michailova, Mustaffa, & Barner-Rasmussen, 2016). These options include ethnocentric, polycentric, regiocentric, and geocentric staffing. Ethnocentric staffing philosophy is appropriate for firms that wish to maintain strong control over the subsidiary, and usually would result in a parent country manager staffing the overseas subsidiary. Polycentric staffing philosophy supports a decentralized structure, where the host-country nationals are given the responsibilities of managing the operations. The rise of regional trade agreements, and regional integration at the common and economic union levels has helped inter-regional mobility of individuals, allowing organizations to select an individual from within the subsidiary's regional location to manage their operations. And finally, organizations can ignore the geographic location of the individual by taking a geocentric approach, where the best person for the job is selected regardless of their country of origin.

Whilst much has been made about organizational culture, and the need for control being among the key factors that influence the decision of an organization to employ either a parent, host, or third country national to staff their global operations, in reality the organization's staffing is also influenced by the regulatory environment (Sekiguchi, Froese, & Iguchi, 2016). The movement of individuals and their ability to work around the world can be limited by national-level policies relating to work permits, movement of professionals, and mutual recognition of educational qualification and experience. This is especially a concern in professional services firms, where the individual may need to register with the local accrediting body in order to carry out their duties in the country. As Rammal and Rose (2014) discuss, the limitations on movement of professionals can create hurdles for firms attempting to transfer knowledge within the organizational network, and force them to use an individual from the host country or host region to manage operations. These staffing philosophies and how they are influenced by country-level policies and expectations are illustrated in Figure 1.

To address this limitation and to facilitate the transfer of knowledge through the socialization process, organizations can utilize the option of providing training course in the parent country, where the manager of the subsidiary can interact and work with the experienced individuals, or exploring the possibility of utilizing the inpatriation option where individuals from the host countries are brought in to the parent country of the organization to work (Harzing, Pudelko, & Reiche, 2015).

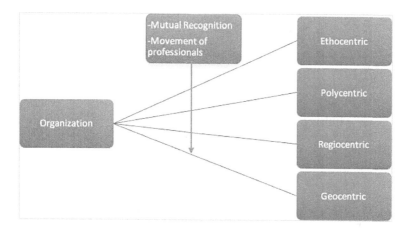

Figure 1: Staffing philosophies and country-level influences on selection.

3. Selection Criteria

The identification of talent within organizations is the first of many steps that an effective human resources department has to take. Working within the national-level requirements of a country, an organization needs to select individuals who can not only manage operations in the subsidiaries but also can identify talent and facilitate the knowledge transfer beyond national boundaries. The selection of such individuals requires much thought, and consideration of factors beyond individual skills and talent.

To improve the chances of achieving the outcomes expected from an expatriate assignment, an organization has to ensure that it invests in provide appropriate training and support to the selected individual. However, the selection process itself can be complex, and may include a number of issues to consider, including: motivation of their employee; experience; remuneration; family considerations; and nationality. The motivation of the individual to accept an expatriate assignment and work away for home for an extended period of time is sometimes overlooked by organizations. An individual may want to accept the task for intrinsic reasons: such as to further their learning, and gain relevant experience; and/or for more extrinsic reasons: such as increase in salary, or a promotion, or living in a city that is seen to be more desirable for their lifestyle (Caligiuri, Baytalskaya, & Lazarova, 2016). If the task for which the individual is selected only fulfills their extrinsic desires, then the long-term job satisfaction may not be there and can affect the individual's motivation.

Similarly, the experience of the individual also has to be relevant to the task, and may in some cases be an external pressure that organizations may face (Mäkelä, Suutari, Brewster, Dickmann, & Tornikoski, 2016). For example, during the 1980s and early part of the 1990s, there was an expectation that managers posted to the subsidiaries in Japan and other Asian country would fit a specific profile when it came to age and seniority. The selection of these managers went beyond just their skills and abilities, as the conditions in the local environment demanded that senior staff be given the task of managing the offices. Recent studies have also suggested a link between the age of the expatriates and their adjustment to a new work environment (see for example, Wechtler, Koveshnikov, & Dejoux, 2015).

Another key issue in the selection of expatriates is the role of family. The importance of family adjustment has been recognized as a key element in the success of the expatriate. A large number of studies conducted on expatriate adjustment have shown that the failure of the family to adjust to a new environment can result in the expatriate returning before the completion of the assignment (Baker & Ciuk, 2015; Cole & Nesbeth, 2014; Welch & Bjorkman, 2015). This failure is due to the culture shock that the family can face in unfamiliar surroundings, and is often a result of limited exposure to the host country culture prior to the acceptance of the assignment. Some organizations tend to extend pre-departure training to the family as well, but often the limited time between the selection of the expatriate and commencement of the assignment makes it difficult for the family to plan in advance for issues such as schooling, medical needs and other activities.

Delving further into the family adjustment issue, some researchers have highlighted the issues faced by the trailing spouse (Lazarova, McNulty, & Semeniuk, 2015; McNulty, 2012), and dual-career (Känsälä, Mäkelä, & Suutari, 2015) or dual-income couples (Hughes, 2013). The potential loss of an income for such couples if they decide to move to the host country should be a consideration for the organization, and an appropriate strategic response should be provided. But perhaps an area that remains under researched in the expatriate and talent management literature is the use of dual-nationality or dual-citizenship held by an individual.

As discussed earlier, the movement of professionals can be limited due to nationality requirements and work permits. To address this issue, MNEs are increasingly relying on their human resource department to also identify talent from the self-initiated expatriates in different countries. These expatriates in many cases can hold dual-citizenship or dual-nationality, which allows them to work in different countries without facing mobility restriction. Similarly, organizations would need to look within their global network to identify dual-national/dual-citizen individuals from their talent pool, and identify opportunities to use them to overcome the nationality requirements placed. In Figure 2, we highlight some of the key considerations for expatriate selection.

4. Repatriation and Career Management

A well-managed repatriation program should ideally follow a successful expatriate assignment. The talent management process is often focused and limited to the

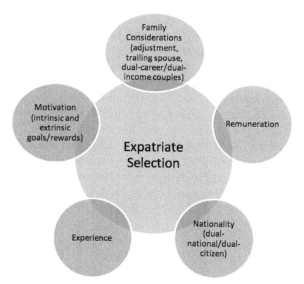

Figure 2: Key considerations in expatriate selection.

expatriate assignment, which can result in poor planning for the repatriation process. Failure to plan for how the returning expatriate would be utilized means that not only does the organization miss out on the knowledge that the individual gained during their expatriate assignment, but also risk losing the individual to a competitor (Baruch, Aitman, & Tung, 2016; Greer & Stiles, 2016). Research in this area suggests that organization can experience a high percentage of repatriate turnover due to poor repatriation process and lack of career planning for the individuals (Black & Gregersen, 1999; Harzing & Christensen, 2004).

If properly managed, not only can organizations apply the knowledge gained by the individuals during their assignment but can also utilize their experience to mentor other expatriates in the organization. Another benefit of successful repatriation is that organizations can access the networks that these individuals have built during their interactions with local buyers, suppliers, and government organizations. Johanson and Vahlne (2009) highlight the benefits of networks or the advantage of being an "insider" in the internationalization process. Individuals build these networks on behalf of organizations, and managing these networks should be part of the consideration when it comes to managing the knowledge transfer across national boundaries. Figure 3 illustrates this process from selection of the expatriate, through to the repatriation process and the application of new skills and knowledge and use of networks.

5. Overview of Chapters in This Volume

The chapters of this edited volume cover a wide range of issues related to global talent management. The first six chapters explore global talent management and staffing options from the individual level, and base it in different research contexts. The issues discussed in these chapters relate to various expatriate management activities and global staffing in MNEs such as recruitment, selection, compensation, repatriation, learning, training and career development. Focusing on the starting point for expatriation assignment, Chapter 1 by Ott and Michailova provide an historical overview of expatriate selection. The chapter provides a critical review of the expatriate selection related literature over the past five decades. It identifies five expatriate selection criteria at the organizational, individual, and contextual levels. These include organization philosophy, technical competence, relational abilities, personal characteristics, and spouse and family situation. The authors argue that the identified expatriate selection criteria are not only applied to the traditional international assignments but also can be helpful for the alternative assignment patterns.

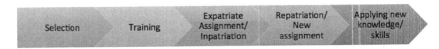

Figure 3: Managing the knowledge transfer process.

In Chapter 2, Kang and Shen provide empirical evidence for how expatriate recruitment and selection process takes places in a MNEs' overseas operation. The authors conducted semi-structured interviews with the employees working in South Korean MNEs' subsidiaries operating in China, and find that "one-way selection" (rather than open recruitment) approach is employed by South Korean MNEs in relation to expatriate recruitment and selection. The criteria of recruitment and selection practices in South Korean MNEs' subsidiary are adjusted to suit the local environment, and helps attract host country nationals. The authors also suggest that South Korean MNEs should pay more attention to expatriate career development, individual and family issues in expatriate and repatriation process.

Chapters 3 and 4 focus on the use of alternative expatriate assignment options in MNEs. In Chapter 3, Selmer, Lauring, Zhang, and Jonasson highlight the trend of using self-initiated expatriates (SIEs) to perform at high level management position, a role which in the past was only given to organizational assigned expatriates (OEs). The chapter compares SIE CEOs and OE CEOs from the perspectives of demography, expatriate personality and job performance in Chinese context and finds that SIE CEOs are more experienced, tend to have less self-control, have different temperament, and tend to rate lower on job performance compared to their OE counterparts. Guo, Rammal and Dowling in their study (Chapter 4) focus on the career capital development of SIEs in China. The chapter reviews the empirical studies which comparing SIEs and OEs, and using the career capital theory, the authors discuss SIEs' career capital accumulation and development through international assignment in China. The study provides three propositions for career capital development of SIEs in China through knowing-how, knowing-why and knowing-whom. Understanding these elements and linking it to the individual expatriates' motivations for the assignment can help MNEs design relevant training programs, and provide adequate learning and development opportunities for SIEs employed in China.

Chapter 5 focuses on the topic of repatriation, which is a key area in post expatriation period. In this chapter, Naito present the survey findings with the managers who have successfully completed their assignment and repatriated back to their parent country, Japan. This chapter discusses the multiple aspects of repatriation adjustment from the perspectives of work and personal life, and identifies three influencing factors of readjustment. Investigating the repatriation process and readjustment can help MNEs identify and apply the knowledge held by repatriates, and retain these skilled and talent employees after repatriation.

The issue of expatriate compensation and global talent management is the focus of the study by McNulty presented in Chapter 6. The author reviews the expatriate compensation literature over the past 10 years, and discuss the home- and host-based approaches to expatriate compensation. The study identifies the challenges and opportunities that MNEs face in attempting to use these two approaches, and proposes a "global compensation" host-based compensation approach that is based on performance and can help avoid overpayment and unfairness.

Chapters 7, 8, and 9 discuss the global talent management and staffing options by linking with human resource management practices, policies and company strategy. In Chapter 7, Ratten and Ferreira look at the links between global talent management and corporate entrepreneurship strategy. Discussing the role of human capital, innovative recruitment practice, cross-cultural staffing policies, and this chapter highlights the importance of global talent management on increasing an entrepreneurial organizations' global competitiveness and organizational performance. The authors highlight the importance of selecting, recruiting and retaining talent in MNEs, and explain that incorporating these elements as part of the human resource policies can help organizations develop and sustain innovation in products, services and processes.

Williams and Bhanugopan in Chapter 8 address the issue of localization of human resources in the Middle East. Using the human capital theory, the authors conducted a survey of expatriate managers undertaking an international assignment in Qatar, and examined the relations between work values, organizational commitment, and human resource localization. The findings of the study suggest a positive relationship between human resource localization and organizational commitment, and a negative relationship between human resource localization and work values.

The last chapter by Buzady looks at the trends in relation to global talent management in the Central and Eastern Europe (CEE) region, which includes Bulgaria, Czechia, Hungary, Poland, Romania, and Slovakia. The chapter focuses on the findings of surveys conducted with the expatriates and local mangers in CEE region to seek their perception and opinions on talent management practices and policies. The author highlights significant differences in perceptions and opinions of expatriate versus local mangers, and argues that the adoption of regional specific talent management and staffing practices can help MNEs exploit the value-added opportunities in the CEE region.

Ying Guo
Hussain G. Rammal
Peter J. Dowling

References

Baker, C., & Ciuk, S. (2015). "Keeping the family side ticking along": An exploratory study of the work-family interface in the experiences of rotational assignees and frequent business travellers. *Journal of Global Mobility*, *3*(2), 137−154.

Barney, J. (1991). Firm resources and sustained competitive advantage. *Journal of Management*, *17*(1), 99−120.

Baruch, Y., Aitman, Y., & Tung, R. L. (2016). Career mobility in a global era. *The Academy of Management Annals*, *10*(1), 841−889.

Black, J. S., & Gregersen, H. (1999). The right way to manage expats. *Harvard Business Review, 77*(2), 52–59.

Caligiuri, P., Baytalskaya, N., & Lazarova, M. B. (2016). Cultural humility and low ethnocentrism as facilitators of expatriate performance. *Journal of Global Mobility, 4*(1), 4–17.

Cerdin, J. L., & Brewster, C. (2014). Talent management and expatriation: Bridging two streams of research and practice. *Journal of World Business, 49*(2), 245–252.

Cole, N., & Nesbeth, K. (2014). Why do international assignments fail? *International Studies of Management & Organization, 44*(3), 66–79.

Collings, D. G. (2014). Integrating global mobility and global talent management: Exploring the challenges and strategic opportunities. *Journal of World Business, 49*(2), 253–261.

Collings, D. G., McDonnell, A., Gunnigle, P., & Lavelle, J. (2010). Swimming against the tide: Outward staffing flows from multinational subsidiaries. *Human Resource Management, 49*(4), 575–598.

Collings, D. G., & Mellahi, K. (2009). Strategic talent management: A review and research agenda. *Human Resource Management Review, 19*(4), 304–313.

Collings, D. G., Morley, M. J., & Gunnigle, P. (2008). Composing the top management team in the international subsidiary: Qualitative evidence on international staffing in US MNCs in the Republic of Ireland. *Journal of World Business, 43*(2), 197–212.

Collings, D. G., Scullion, H., & Morley, M. J. (2007). Changing patterns of global staffing in the multinational enterprise: Challenges to the conventional expatriate assignment and emerging alternatives. *Journal of World Business, 42*(2), 198–213.

Dowling, P. J., Festing, M., & Engle, A. D. (2013). *International human resource management* (6th ed.). London: Cengage Learning.

Farndale, E., Scullion, H., & Sparrow, P. (2010). The role of the corporate HR function in global talent management. *Journal of World Business, 45*(2), 161–168.

Gong, Y. (2003). Toward a dynamic process model of staffing composition and subsidiary outcomes in multinational enterprises. *Journal of Management, 29*(2), 259–280.

Greer, T. W., & Stiles, A. C. (2016). Using HRD to support repatriates a framework for creating an organization development strategy for repatriation. *Human Resource Development Review, 15*(1), 101–122.

Harzing, A.-W., & Christensen, C. (2004). Expatriate failure: Time to abandon the concept? *Career Development International, 9*(7), 616–626.

Harzing, A.-W., Pudelko, M., & Sebastian Reiche, B. (2015). The bridging role of expatriates and inpatriates in knowledge transfer in multinational corporations. *Human Resource Management.* doi:10.1002/hrm.21681

Hughes, J. L. (2013). Persisting problems with operationalizing dual-career couples: A proposal to use the term dual-income couples. *Marriage & Family Review, 49*(8), 694–716.

Johanson, J., & Vahlne, J.-E. (2009). The Uppsala internationalization process model revisited: From liability of foreignness to liability of outsidership. *Journal of International Business Studies, 40*(9), 1411–1431.

Känsälä, M., Mäkelä, L., & Suutari, V. (2015). Career coordination strategies among dual career expatriate couples. *The International Journal of Human Resource Management, 26*(17), 2187–2210.

Lado, A. A., & Wilson, M. C. (1994). Human resource systems and sustained competitive advantage: A competency-based perspective. *Academy of Management Review, 19*(4), 699–727.

Lazarova, M., McNulty, Y., & Semeniuk, M. (2015). Expatriate family narratives on international mobility: Key characteristics of the successful moveable family. In L. Mäkelä & V. Suutari (Eds.), *Work and family interface in the international career context* (pp. 29–51). Switzerland: Springer International Publishing.

Li, S., & Scullion, H. (2010). Developing the local competence of expatriate managers for emerging markets: A knowledge-based approach. *Journal of World Business, 45*(2), 190–196.

Mäkelä, L., Suutari, V., Brewster, C., Dickmann, M., & Tornikoski, C. (2016). The impact of career capital on expatriates' perceived marketability. *Thunderbird International Business Review, 58*(1), 29–40.

McNulty, Y. (2012). 'Being dumped in to sink or swim': An empirical study of organizational support for the trailing spouse. *Human Resource Development International, 15*(4), 417–434.

Mellahi, K., & Collings, D. G. (2010). The barriers to effective global talent management: The example of corporate elites in MNEs. *Journal of World Business, 45*(2), 143–149.

Michailova, S., Mustaffa, Z., & Barner-Rasmussen, W. (2016). Subsidiaries of multinational corporations: A framework for analyzing employee allegiances. *Journal of Leadership & Organizational Studies, 23*(2), 116–127.

Nonaka, I., & Takeuchi, H. (1995). *The knowledge creating company: How Japanese companies create the dynamics of innovation.* New York, NY: Oxford University Press.

Rammal, H. G., & Rose, E. L. (2014). New perspectives on the internationalization of service firms. *International Marketing Review, 31*(6), 550–556.

Reiche, S. B., Kraimer, M. L., & Harzing, A.-W. (2011). Why do international assignees stay? An organizational embeddedness perspective. *Journal of International Business Studies, 42*(4), 521–544.

Sekiguchi, T., Froese, F. J., & Iguchi, C. (2016). International human resource management of Japanese multinational corporations: Challenges and future directions. *Asian Business & Management, 15*(2), 83–109.

Sidani, Y., & Al Ariss, A. (2014). Institutional and corporate drivers of global talent management: Evidence from the Arab Gulf Region. *Journal of World Business, 49*(2), 215–224.

Sparrow, P., Scullion, H., & Tarique, I. (2014). *Strategic talent management: Contemporary issues in international context.* Cambridge: Cambridge University Press.

Tarique, I., & Schuler, R. (2008). Emerging issues and challenges in global staffing: A North American perspective. *The International Journal of Human Resource Management, 19*(8), 1397–1415.

Tarique, I., Schuler, R., & Gong, Y. (2006). A model of multinational enterprise subsidiary staffing composition. *The International Journal of Human Resource Management, 17*(2), 207–224.

Tarique, I., & Schuler, R. S. (2010). Global talent management: Literature review, integrative framework, and suggestions for further research. *Journal of World Business, 45*(2), 122–133.

Wechtler, H., Koveshnikov, A., & Dejoux, C. (2015). Just like a fine wine? Age, emotional intelligence, and cross-cultural adjustment. *International Business Review, 24*(3), 409–418.

Welch, D., & Bjorkman, I. (2015). The place of international human resource management in international business. *Management International Review, 55*(3), 303–322.

Acknowledgements

This volume would not have been possible without the support and encouragement of a number of individuals. We would like to thank the authors of the chapters for their contribution. The authors not only answered our call to address contemporary issues related to global talent management, but have also identified a research agenda for the future. We also thank the reviewers for providing timely and insightful comments on the chapters.

We thank Professor Pervez Ghauri, the editor of the International Business and Management Series for giving us the opportunity to edit this volume, and for the support and guidance he has provided. And finally, we would like to thank Dr. Martyn Lawrence from Emerald publishing for his encouragement and support for the completion of this volume.

Chapter 1

Expatriate Selection: A Historical Overview and Criteria for Decision-Making

Dana L. Ott and Snejina Michailova

Abstract

Purpose — The International Human Resource Management literature has paid less attention to the selection of expatriates and the decision-making criteria with regard to such selection, than to issues relating to expatriates' role, performance, adjustment, success, and failure. Yet, before expatriates commence their assignments, they need to be selected. The purpose of this book chapter is to provide an overview of issues related specifically to expatriate selection. In particular, the chapter traces the chronological development of selection over the last five decades or so, from prior to 1970 until present. The chapter subsequently identifies five expatriate selection criteria that have been applied in regard to traditional international assignments, but are also relevant to alternative assignments.

Methodology/approach — We begin by reviewing expatriate selection historically and its position within expatriate management based on changing business environments. Then, drawing from over five decades of literature on international assignments, we identify and discuss five organizational, individual, and contextual level criteria for selecting expatriates.

Findings — Emphasis on different issues tends to characterize expatriate selection during the various decades since the literature has taken up the topic. The chapter describes those issues, following a chronological perspective. In addition, the chapter organizes the various selection criteria in five clusters: organization philosophy, technical competence, relational abilities, personal characteristics, and spouse and family situation.

Global Talent Management and Staffing in MNEs
International Business & Management, Volume 32, 1–24
Copyright © 2016 by Emerald Group Publishing Limited
All rights of reproduction in any form reserved
ISSN: 1876-066X/doi:10.1108/S1876-066X20160000032001

Research limitations and practical implications – While there are studies on expatriate selection, there is more to be understood with regard to the topic. Provided all other expatriation phases are subsequent, if selection is not understood in detail, the foundations of studying phases and processes that take place once expatriates are selected may not be sound. While the scholarly conversations of other expatriate-related issues should continue, the international human resource management literature can absorb more analyses on selection. A better understanding of expatriate selection will assist its better management. The chapter provides a basis for human resource management professionals to be able to map the various criteria for selection, and decide, under particular circumstances, which ones to prioritize and why.

Originality/value – The chapter brings clarity to a topic that has remained less researched when compared to other areas of interest related to expatriates and their international assignments by tracing the historical development of this important phase of the expatriation process. In addition, the chapter organizes a number of selection criteria along five core areas and discusses each of them to gain insights that help explain expatriate selection in greater detail.

Keywords: Expatriates; international assignments; selection criteria; international human resource management; literature review

As an essential part of international business (IB), expatriates and international assignments have been a significant topic in multiple streams of literature for decades. Expatriates' role, performance, adjustment, success, and failure, as well as their family's adjustment, are just some of the themes discussed (Caligiuri, Tarique, & Jacobs, 2009; Harvey & Moeller, 2009). An expatriate is an individual temporarily or permanently residing outside their native country. Historically, business expatriates were managers from the headquarters of a multinational enterprise (MNE) who relocated to a foreign country for the purposes of managing and controlling a subsidiary. More recently the term expatriate has expanded to include any employee working for business concerns outside their home country. These individuals typically work in multiple countries and cultural environments, interact with and adapt to many different cultures, and use cross-cultural skills at home and overseas over the course of their careers (Hurn, 2006).

One of the first stages of the International Human Resource Management (IHRM) process for global staffing within MNEs is the selection of expatriate managers (Collings, Scullion, & Morley, 2007; Harvey & Moeller, 2009). Expatriate selection is "the process of gathering information for the purposes of evaluating and deciding who should be employed in particular jobs" (Shen & Edwards, 2004, p. 816). Expatriate selection includes educating candidates, evaluating candidates, and selecting who should be sent on international assignments.

Traditional international assignments include the relocation of an individual and his/her family to a foreign country for approximately three to five years (Meyskens, Von Glinow, Werther, & Clarke, 2009). There are many challenges associated with traditional international assignments (Collings et al., 2007). The most prominent is the need for these individuals and their families to adjust to living in a new culture when they relocate. Recently, increased possibilities offered by technology and the ease of international travel (Shankaran, Murray, & Miller, 2011) has led organizations to use alternative forms of international assignments (Collings et al., 2007; Dowling, Festing, & Engle, 2013). These alternative assignments include short-term, international commuter and business traveler, and virtual assignments (Collings et al., 2007). When utilizing these types of assignments, expatriates no longer need to relocate for extended periods of time or become immersed in the foreign culture to play an active role in the business dealings of subsidiaries. Furthermore, their success is dependent on their abilities to work effectively with members of multiple cultures and within many different foreign business environments (Earley, 2002; Tarique & Schuler, 2010).

Irrespective of the type or characteristics of the international assignment, expatriates still need to be selected. Before considering the criteria for those selection decisions, it is important to briefly outline the key historical developments of expatriate selection. We consider the main themes within the expatriate selection literature from a historical perspective, including the use and importance of selection, and key drivers within the business environment. Then we identify and discuss the five selection criteria that have been validated in the traditional expatriate literature, which are still relevant to changes in global staffing and alternative forms of international assignments.

1.1. Historical Overview of Expatriate Selection

Expatriate selection has evolved over a number of decades. In Figure 1.1 we depict a historical overview of this development. The focus of expatriate selection during the different decades, shown in the figure, provides a snapshot of the importance of selection and the challenges associated with it. In addition, it identifies the key points related to the business environment that were influencing the role and use of expatriate selection.

While expatriates have always been chosen in some way, in the recent Brookfield Global Relocation Services survey (2014) many MNEs reported that they still do

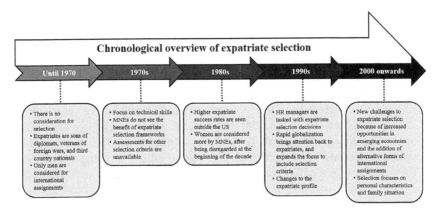

Figure 1.1: Historical evolution of the main expatriate selection themes from prior to 1970 until present.

not have formal candidate assessment programs and instead primarily rely on employees expressing a willingness to take an international assignment to make selection decisions. Furthermore, although in the 1990s organizations reasoned that the absence of easily accessible assessment tools prevented them from applying formal selection processes (Ones & Viswesvaran, 1999; Tung, 1998; Wederspahn, 1992), only 20% of surveyed organizations responded that they currently use assessments to make selection decisions even though these tools are now readily available (Brookfield, 2014).

Originally, expatriate selection was not considered because many MNEs simply focused on recruiting the sons of diplomats and military members who had lived the majority of their lives outside of the United States (Hays, 1971). MNEs believed that these men would be able to represent their organizations outside the headquarters the best. They were usually able to speak foreign languages and were accustomed to differences among cultures. Domestic business operations, at this time, were far more important than IB operations, resulting in this pool of candidates being able to fulfill the overseas needs of MNEs (Harris & Kumra, 2000). Following the end of World War II, international expansion increased rapidly and this pool of candidates could not satisfy the expatriation needs of MNEs. As a result, corporations moved toward selecting veterans of foreign wars, as they had spent a large amount of time in a foreign culture and consisted of an eager pool of potential candidates (Hays, 1974). Unfortunately, many of these expatriates were not equipped with the business knowledge necessary to head operations within the foreign subsidiaries.

Demand for expatriates continued to increase and MNEs began recruiting business executives who had never worked abroad. Alarming numbers of these expatriates were failing in the foreign cultures while at the same time governments in these countries were putting pressure on MNEs to hire locally (Hays, 1974). Initially, companies began to seek out local host country executives to run their operations abroad. MNEs began offering compensation and bonus plans that gained the attention of qualified local nationals, but two problems quickly arose. First, corporations found that these employees did not have the organizational philosophy and headquarters knowledge to lead these projects (Tung, 1981). Second, when opening subsidiaries in less developed countries, MNEs had a hard time finding qualified candidates (Tung, 1982). This led MNEs back to selecting their highest performing and most technically qualified managers for international assignments (Hays, 1974). The belief was that since these employees were the top performers within the organization domestically, they would also be top performers internationally. Their leadership skills were assumed to be easily transferable to foreign environments.

The majority of international assignments in the 1960s consisted of spending two to three years located in a developed country outside of the United States, where the majority of MNEs were headquartered (Lee, 2007). Top performing men were selected to fill the role and relocated along with their spouse and children (Hays, 1971). They were sent to command and control the foreign subsidiary and often portrayed an ethnocentric viewpoint of headquarters over the subsidiary (Harris & Kumra, 2000). Adapting to and understanding the local culture was deemed unnecessary beyond a minimal level. If IHRM provided any training or advice to these expatriates, it was focused on practical living considerations and performance expectations (Harris & Kumra, 2000).

During the 1970s it is clear that MNEs focused solely on the technical skills when making expatriate selection decisions (see Figure 1.1). Although studies at this time found that relational abilities (Hays, 1971, 1974; Miller, 1972; Newman, Bhatt, & Gutteridge, 1978) and family situation (Hays, 1971; Howard, 1974; Miller, 1972) were also areas that should be considered when selecting an expatriate, the tools for assessing these criteria did not exist. Therefore, MNEs did not see the benefit of having expatriate selection frameworks within the organization. They simply told a top performer of their need to send him overseas for a couple of years and what his function would be within the foreign country (Harris & Kumra, 2000). In addition, the international assignment usually included a promotion and additional financial benefits to the expatriate, thus they were unlikely to refuse the opportunity.

In the 1980s, women were included as possible candidates for international assignments and research began to focus more clearly on female expatriates (see Figure 1.1). At the beginning of the decade, scholars found that although women were not specifically seen as incapable of taking international assignments, MNEs did not give them any consideration. Izraeli, Banai, and Zeira (1980) reported that host country managers held a clear preference for interacting with male business executives and managers described many dysfunctions in appointing females into international executive roles. In a later multisource study comparing the opinions of host country organization employees, expatriate managers, and headquarters employees regarding desired expatriate selection criteria, gender was not considered as a relevant selection criterion by any of the respondents (Zeira & Banai, 1985). In addition to considering female expatriates, scholars also demonstrated that success rates were higher among expatriates who were from countries outside the United States (Murray & Murray, 1986; Tung, 1982, 1987). This led to the expansion of expatriate selection research into multiple countries and to comparisons of expatriate selection related practices between different countries.

The 1990s business environment of rapid globalization brought attention once more to internationalization and finding individuals who could work effectively outside their home country. The focus, however, shifted because more MNEs were entering into cross-border joint ventures and as a result expatriates needed the skills necessary to interact with members of foreign cultures more than before (Harris & Kumra, 2000; Tung, 1998). In addition, the economic conditions of global business forced MNEs to re-evaluate the costs associated with international assignments. Furthermore, expatriates were needed mainly in developed countries as trade expansions also called for more international assignments between countries in Europe and the United States (Harris & Kumra, 2000). The expatriate profile also changed. A younger, higher educated, and more gender-diverse workforce showed interest in taking international assignments to gain international experience and expand their career opportunities (Stone, 1991; Tung, 1998). At the same time, dual-career couples were becoming more common making the costs and benefits of relocating internationally more significant.

The literature during the 1990s also focused on selection criteria and found that although expatriates identified adaptation abilities to be paramount, MNEs were reluctant to consider them in actual selection (see Figure 1.1). Stone (1991), for example, concluded that: "it is apparent that while firms may be aware of their importance, these adaptation factors are not in fact given much weight in the actual selection decision-making process" (p. 10). It was also revealed that the activities used for making selection decisions involved IHRM more than in the past. However, many of these HR professionals did not have the training and background to assess a candidate's appropriateness for overseas assignments (Haslberger & Stroh, 1992). This lack of ability was compounded by the fact that reliable, valid, and cost-effective assessments to measure an expatriate's abilities were still missing (Mendenhall & Oddou, 1988; Ones & Viswesvaran, 1999; Tung, 1998; Wederspahn, 1992).

The absence of assessments to measure expatriates' adaptation abilities and appropriateness for international assignments led to an increase in training before international assignments in the early 2000s. In addition, MNEs still focused almost wholly on technical skills to make selection decisions (Anderson, 2005; Caligiuri et al., 2009; Harris & Kumra, 2000; Selmer, 2001). Expatriate selection was grouped with training instead of being identified as a separate set of activities within expatriate management (Morris & Robie, 2001; Romero, 2002). The selection criteria family situation and individual differences were researched (Bauer & Taylor, 2001; Harris & Kumra, 2000; Harvey & Moeller, 2009). Having previously been unconsidered, common expatriate traits in the form of personal characteristics such as age, gender, foreign language ability, and marital status were identified (Guthrie, Ash, & Stevens, 2003; Holopainen & Björkman, 2005; Selmer, 2001; Selmer, Lauring, & Feng, 2009). Expatriate failure was also redefined in the 2000s, leading to studies that questioned previously reported high rates of failure and new reports of reduced failure rates (Harzing, 2002; Harzing & Christensen, 2004; Lee, 2007).

The current business environment continues to keep the topic of expatriation at the forefront of IB research and practice. One of the trends observed has been an increase in IB opportunities in emerging economies, where it has been anticipated that seven-eighths of the population will be located by 2025 (Webb & Wright, 1996). Expansion into these new markets adds greater economic and cultural distance between the home and host culture of expatriates. These new challenges may potentially lead to higher failure rates, increasing the need for expatriate selection (Harvey & Moeller, 2009). Understanding these business environments and selecting expatriates with the skills and abilities to succeed in these more diverse locations is an ongoing challenge. To deal with this, MNEs have begun using alternative forms of international assignments that allow individuals to be involved in subsidiaries, but do not require them to relocate to the country where the subsidiary is based. While overcoming some of the challenges related to traditional international assignments, these alternative international assignments still require an individual to be capable of working constructively with members of other cultures.

A large amount of research has focused on identifying expatriate selection criteria and best practices for IHRM to consider when making expatriate selection decisions for traditional expatriates. More recently, scholars have explored the selection criteria specific to a country or culture (Fischlmayr & Kollinger, 2010; Graf, 2004; Lee, 2007), considered the effects of gender and gender roles on the success of international assignments (Cole & McNulty, 2011; Guthrie et al., 2003; Tharenou, 2010), identified the new challenges of expatriate adjustment (Holopainen & Björkman, 2005; Mäkelä, Känsälä, & Suutari, 2011), and focused on re-defining the key terms involved in expatriation (Harris, 2002; Hurn, 2006; Meyskens et al., 2009; Shankaran et al., 2011).

1.2. Expatriate Selection Criteria

The expatriate selection literature aims to provide practical implications, which is common across the selection field in general. "One of the defining characteristics of the selection field has been that it is a science-based professional practice. This is true internationally and it is a distinguishing feature of our discipline that we could ill afford to lose" (Anderson, Lievens, van Dam, & Ryan, 2004, p. 495). Although it has been argued that because of the changing purposes of international assignments, the expatriate selection criteria need to be adjusted (Scullion & Collings, 2006), many of the criteria originally recommended for selecting traditional expatriates are still appropriate (Tahvanainen, Welch, & Worm, 2005). We identify five expatriate selection criteria that include organizational, individual, and contextual level factors from the traditional international assignment literature that are still relevant to alternative forms of international assignments. The relevancy of the criteria is based on the similar nature of the policies and practices driving selection, cultural competence requirements, and family situation challenges, which are applicable to all international assignments. The expatriate selection criteria that we discuss have been validated and determined from research that includes the opinions of expatriates, HRM, headquarters management, and host country management. Of these criteria, technical competence is the only *given* factor that has historically been utilized when making selection decisions (Tahvanainen et al., 2005). However, organization philosophy, relational abilities, personal characteristics, and spouse and family situation have all been cited more often as reasons for expatriate failure. Figure 1.2 depicts the five expatriate selection criteria and is followed by a discussion of each.

Figure 1.2: Expatriate selection criteria clustered by organization philosophy, technical competence, relational abilities, personal characteristics, and spouse and family situation.

1.2.1. Organization Philosophy

Organization philosophy is included as a selection criterion because it drives the selection approach and practices of MNEs. It is the only organizational level criterion for making selection decisions. Zeira and Banai (1985) identified that MNEs utilize either an open or closed system approach towards selection. In a closed system approach only the opinions of headquarters are considered, selected managers fit the headquarters' managerial and personal behavioral expectations, and selections are made without input from the foreign subsidiary (Zeira & Banai, 1985). They recommended that organizations instead have an open system approach where the expectations of the host environment, managers and stakeholders of the foreign subsidiary, and those of the headquarters are all considered when making selection decisions.

Drawing from Perlmutter (1969), organizations tend to implement one of three basic approaches to expatriate selection: (1) an ethnocentric approach by selecting only parent-country nationals for international positions; (2) a polycentric approach where only host country nationals are selected to manage all aspects of the subsidiary and parent-country nationals only occupy corporate headquarters positions; or (3) a geocentric approach where the MNE seeks to select the best person for the position regardless of nationality. In a later article, Heenan and Perlmutter (1979) added regiocentrism as an intermediary attitude preceding geocentrism where the MNE divides its operations into geographic regions and then selects staff within these regions. Each of these selection approaches has advantages and disadvantages for the MNE and dependent on the approach utilized, can help HR managers to narrow the potential pool of candidates when making selection decisions. Additionally, these approaches also drive alternative international assignment selection decision-making, with the geocentric approach being suggested as the most effective for global talent management (Collings, 2014; Dowling et al., 2013).

A final important aspect of organization philosophy is the level of internationalism throughout the MNE. Tung (1987) found the spirit of internationalism of an MNE, defined as its international orientation and outlook, was a unique factor of European MNEs, which encouraged managers to take international assignments. She also determined that it affects the practices of HRM regarding the level of value that management acknowledges in overseas experiences, the focus of HR to recruit graduates with travel experience, and the multinational composition of management teams within the organization to ensure an international perspective in all aspects of operations (Tung, 1987). Mendenhall and Oddou (1988) expanded on this idea by recommending that future expatriates determine the strategic importance of the international assignment within the MNE, the degree of incorporation of HR in strategic planning, the amount of international experience in senior management, and the degree of formalization and rigor of the selection systems, before allowing themselves to be selected for an international assignment. Furthermore, Gertsen (1990) found that employees are cognizant of the negative effects of failed international assignments resulting in only a few willing candidates if the MNE does not portray a high level of internationalism within their everyday functions. Organizations continue to struggle to meet their global talent demands required to effectively operate in the international context (Farndale, Scullion, & Sparrow, 2010) where a limited candidate pool can negatively impact the success of foreign expansion. Thus, organizations must consider and utilize all types of international assignments as development opportunities, and show support for them throughout the MNE.

1.2.2. Technical Competence

Technical competence is perhaps the most critical expatriate selection criterion because it is the only factor that is considered as a prerequisite for success and a determinant of failure. Traditionally, executives believe that MNEs have reliable mechanisms for evaluating technical ability and, as a result, failure is rarely associated with a lack of job-related technical abilities (Hays, 1971). Technical competence continues to be the most common selection criterion used and it is relied on across multiple countries (Anderson, 2005; Caligiuri et al., 2009; Enderwick & Hodgson, 1993; Haslberger & Stroh, 1992; Shen & Edwards, 2004; Stone, 1991; Zeira & Banai, 1985). When utilizing alternative forms of international assignments, technical competence remains as the first and most essential criterion for making selection decisions (Tahvanainen et al., 2005). It is also viewed as the easiest criterion to identify as many MNEs already have processes and assessments available to evaluate candidates' technical abilities.

Historically, pressure to select the right person, in order to protect their own careers, caused many HR managers to focus on individuals with the highest level of technical skills because it was assumed that since they were able to perform the requirements of their jobs they would likely succeed (Haslberger & Stroh, 1992; Miller, 1972). Thus, all other factors besides technical competence became secondary, and often times unnecessary. HR professionals believed that "proper training can give the candidate the appropriate attitudes for cross-cultural interaction" and they believed that training would "bring about remarkable changes in the attitudes and hence the behavior of individuals" (Tung, 1981, p. 70).

A number of scholars, however, argue that technical competence should not be the only criterion for decision-making because an effective domestic manager is not necessarily able to transfer their success to the international context (Anderson, 2005; Gertsen, 1990; Newman et al., 1978; Scullion & Collings, 2006; Stone, 1991; Welch, Worm, & Fenwick, 2003). Furthermore, this type of selection strategy lacks comprehensiveness and does not benefit the MNE, the subsidiary or the expatriate (Mendenhall & Oddou, 1988; Miller, 1972). According to Mendenhall and Oddou (1988, p. 82): "technical competence has nothing to do with one's ability to adapt to a new environment, deal effectively with foreign coworkers, or perceive and if necessary imitate the foreign behavioral norms."

The importance of technical competence as a decision-making criterion should be related to the specific job of the expatriate. Hays (1974) suggested that there are four categories of international jobs: CEO — responsible for overseeing and directing the entire operation; Functional Head — establishes functional departments in a foreign affiliate; Trouble Shooter — analyzes and solves specific operational problems; and Element Employees — serve similar functional roles as at the headquarters organization. Tung (1981) and Shen and Edwards (2004) have relied on these categories to suggest contingency frameworks for expatriate selection. They suggest identifying the requirements of the role and tasks of the expatriate before determining what additional skills and abilities are necessary to increase the probability of success. Performance has also been recommended as a factor to consider in relation to technical competence, such that an MNE employs a non-compensatory rather than compensatory selection strategy (Newman et al., 1978). In a non-compensatory selection strategy MNEs determine and require minimum standards on all performance dimensions before selecting the expatriate. Finally, Harzing and Christensen (2004) also suggest that using a performance strategy leads to role clarity for the potential expatriate, which positively influences selection decisions. It is important that an individual being considered for any type of international assignment has the required technical competence needed for the job, however, this should not remain as the only criterion utilized for making expatriate selection decisions.

1.2.3. Relational Abilities

Hays (1971) originally used the term relational abilities to refer to an individual's capabilities to relate to and work with local nationals and adapt to the host culture, in order to perform effectively and achieve success. Relational abilities have emerged as a crucial decision-making criterion because the absence of these capabilities is a regularly cited reason for expatriate failure. Howard (1974, p. 139) stated: "the ability of the multinational executive to adapt to local cultural, physical, economic, and political conditions without going completely native is as crucial to his success abroad as air is to his very survival." Tung (1981, p. 69) further clarified: "it is not limited to knowledge of another culture, but includes the ability to relate to, live with and work among people whose value systems, beliefs, customs, manners, and ways of conducting business may be greatly different from one's own."

What skills and capabilities are included under the term relational abilities continues to evolve. Originally it mostly encompassed psychological traits (Graf, 2004; Howard, 1974; Stone, 1991) and coping skills (Murray & Murray, 1986). Later, contextual level factors related to differences in host country culture and the need for expatriates to constructively interact with members of other cultures, led to the addition of cultural competence (Bird, Mendenhall, Stevens, & Oddou, 2010; Graf, 2004; Johnson, Lenartowicz, & Apud, 2006), emotional intelligence (Gabel, Dolan, & Cerdin, 2005; Mayer, Salovey, & Caruso, 2004), cultural intelligence (Earley & Ang, 2003; Thomas et al., 2008), and a number of other abilities. While some scholars have suggested that many abilities are inherent in a successful expatriate (Graf, 2004; Harvey & Moeller, 2009; Shen & Edwards, 2004; Tung, 1987), others have demonstrated that they can be developed through targeted training (Eschbach, Parker, & Stoeberl, 2001; Harris & Kumra, 2000; Shen & Edwards, 2004).

An individual's requisite level of relational abilities should be dependent on the amount of exposure to and interaction with host nationals is necessary in order to perform their specific job within the foreign location (Tung, 1981). More and higher amounts of relational abilities are necessary when the duties of an expatriate require more interaction with host nationals, host country government officials, and subsidiary employees, which greatly influences the level of importance of relational abilities as a decision-making criterion. It is also important to note that some relational abilities, which are viewed as positive traits in one culture, may actually be wholly inappropriate in other cultures (Harris & Kumra, 2000). For example, being a high achiever, task-oriented, ethnocentric, time-driven, aggressive, problem-centered, and viewing social interaction as a *waste* of time, may lead to success in some cultures, but may be reasons for failure in others.

Relational abilities are an unusual criterion of expatriate selection because, regardless of the amount of literature that encourages their consideration or demonstrates their importance for making selection decisions, MNEs rarely use them in practice. Furthermore, HR professionals also know the importance of relational abilities, but frequently report that they are unable to detect them within individuals because such skills and capabilities are not easy to identify (Graf, 2004; Harvey & Moeller, 2009; Tung, 1981). Howard (1974) listed a battery of psychological tests to identify relational abilities, and suggested that they should be given to potential expatriates before making selection decisions. The list included the Minnesota Multiphasic Personality Inventory, the Guilford-Zimmerman Temperament Survey, the F-Test, and full psychiatric evaluations. He also recommended an extensive seven-level selection process where a specified score at each stage must be attained before a candidate can move forward to potentially being selected for an international assignment. Although it may be more useful to employ such tests and inventories to develop candidate profiles before making selection decisions, it is impractical to believe that MNEs can allocate the financial and time-consuming means necessary for this type of approach to decision-making.

In contrast to Howard's (1974) recommendations, Mendenhall and Oddou (1988) found that psychological assessments were unnecessary, but emphasized that expatriates should evaluate their own cross-cultural adaptation skills before accepting an international assignment. These skills include personal skills (techniques that facilitate mental and emotional well-being), people skills (skills to interact effectively with others), and perception skills (abilities to understand why foreigners behave the way they do) (Mendenhall & Oddou, 1988). Gertsen (1990) expanded this line of thinking by suggesting that an expatriate should not be introverted, self-conscious, or otherwise uncomfortable when interacting with foreigners, and Harvey and Moeller (2009) argued that expatriates should be empathetic, respectful, flexible, tolerant, open-minded, sociable, and show an interest in foreign cultures. Furthermore, Graf (2004) suggested that inter-cultural competence (or knowledge about other cultures), the desire to act in a competent way, and skills to manage situations were particularly important for expatriate selection decisions. Finally, Wills and Barham (1994) concluded that expatriates' success can be attributed to their operating with a holistic core competence, rather than just having specific behavioral abilities. The core competence includes three inter-linking parts: cognitive complexity (which includes cultural empathy, a sense of humor, and active listening abilities); psychological maturity (including curiosity to learn and a "present" orientation to time and personal morality); and emotional energy (that includes emotional self-awareness, risk acceptance, and emotional resilience).

Some assessments have been developed, which can be easily scored and which provide information for IHRM regarding two specific aspects of relational abilities — emotional stability and cultural competence. These two aspects of relational abilities have received increasing attention because of their use in research investigations and the development of assessments to measure emotional intelligence (Mayer et al., 2004) and cultural intelligence (Ang et al., 2007; Thomas et al., 2015). Individuals high in emotional intelligence are described as being better able to perceive emotions, use them, understand their meaning, and manage their own emotions, as well as being more agreeable and open, all of which allows them to interact with others in a more effective way (Gabel et al., 2005). Cultural intelligence is an individual's ability to adapt to and interact within culturally diverse environments (Earley & Ang, 2003; Thomas et al., 2008). Both of these types of intelligence can be measured; thus they are suggested as very helpful tools when selecting expatriates (Bücker, Furrer, Poutsma, & Buyens, 2014; Gabel et al., 2005; Graf, 2004; Huff, Song, & Gresch, 2014; Lee, Veasna, & Sukoco, 2014; Mayer et al., 2004).

It is clear that relational abilities consist of multiple components, making it difficult for MNEs to determine which specific abilities need to be present in an expatriate. This is likely the reason why MNEs continue to look past relational abilities and focus on more measurable abilities such as technical competence when selecting expatriates, be it for traditional or alternative forms of international assignments (Lin, Lu, & Lin, 2012; Sparrow, Brewster, & Harris, 2004; Tahvanainen et al., 2005). However, the importance of an individual's relational abilities should not be disregarded when making expatriate selection decisions. In addition, these capabilities and skills are necessary for anyone who needs to constructively interact with members of other cultures, making them highly applicable, not only to traditional, but also to alternative forms of international assignments.

1.2.4. Personal Characteristics

Personal characteristics are frequently used to profile expatriates to identify commonalities among them, and to determine their influence on willingness to accept an international assignment, cross-cultural adjustment, and job performance. This selection criterion is particularly interesting because scholars have uncovered contrasting information about the importance of these characteristics for decision-making. In addition, personal characteristics, such as personality, previous international experience, foreign language ability, and gender and age, continue to gain attention among scholars in relation to both traditional and alternative forms of international assignments.

1.2.4.1. Personality Characteristics

The Big Five personality characteristics are generally thought to be stable and situation-neutral traits within an individual, and as such, can be used as a taxonomy of differences among individuals. Although the terminology used to refer to these characteristics varies, it is widely accepted that they refer to openness, extraversion, emotional stability, agreeableness, and conscientiousness. In relation to expatriates, scholars recommend that the Big Five be used as a typology for selection (Andresen & Margenfeld, 2015; Caligiuri, 2000a; Ones & Viswesvaran, 1999) based on their role as predictors of expatriate effectiveness and adjustment (Huff et al., 2014; Shaffer, Harrison, Gregerson, Black, & Frezandi, 2006), and expatriate job performance (Bruning, Sonpar, & Xiaoyun, 2012; Caligiuri, 2000b; Mol, Born, Willemsen, & Van Der Molen, 2005). Certain personality characteristics have also been demonstrated to be antecedents to some of the relational abilities previously discussed. For example, openness or an individual's curiosity, creativity, and flexibility, and extraversion a common trait among individuals who are social and outgoing, both significantly predict cultural intelligence (Ang, Van Dyne, & Koh, 2006; Harrison, 2012; Şahin, Gurbuz, & Köksal, 2014). Given the demonstrated impact of personality characteristics on the abilities of individuals to effectively interact with culturally different others, they are important when making selection decisions related to traditional, as well as, alternative international assignments.

1.2.4.2. Previous International Experience

Church (1982) originally explored the relationship between prior cultural exposure and sojourner adjustment, and suggested that exposure to a culture allows an individual to develop accurate expectations about that culture. He argued that previous international experience in a particular culture would be influential to the adjustment of an expatriate returning to that same culture. Black (1988) examined this assumption and found that country-specific previous overseas work experience had a positive and significant relationship with work adjustment, but not with general adjustment. Black, Mendenhall, and Oddou (1991) proposed a model of international adjustment and suggested that any previous international experience facilitates expatriate adjustment because it provides accurate predictions of future stressors. Furthermore, the authors predicted that the more accurate the expectations about the foreign environment, the more likely they are to assist the expatriate when they relocate. Based on this argument, previous international experiences should have a positive relationship with adjustment, such that work-related experiences facilitate work expectations and non-work-related experiences facilitate non-work expectations (Black et al., 1991). However, Black and Gregersen (1991) tested this proposition and found that previous international experience was not related to any facet of adjustment.

Takeuchi, Tesluk, Yun, and Lepak (2005) differentiated previous international experiences to include non-work, work, and culture-specific experiences. Based on this operationalization, they found that previous international experience was positively associated with cross-cultural adjustment. Additionally, they concluded that culture-specific previous international experience is a significant moderator of the relationship between current assignment tenure and general adjustment (Takeuchi et al., 2005). A meta-analysis by Bhaskar-Shrinivas, Harrison, Shaffer, and Luk (2005) also confirmed that international experience has a significant and positive relationship with both interaction and work adjustment. The strength of the relationship, however, was much weaker than anticipated, leading the authors to state: "the theoretical proposition about experience is supported, but the practical upshot of previous assignments is almost nil" (Bhaskar-Shrinivas et al., 2005, p. 272). Contrary to this, however, Caligiuri et al. (2009) demonstrated that previous international experience is a predictor of expatriates' success and recommended its inclusion as an expatriate selection criterion. Although the exact influence of previous international experience and the role of culture-specific experiences on expatriate success are still unclear, it is known that previous international experience does not negatively impact expatriates and may also lead to the development of some relational abilities (Earley & Ang, 2003; Şahin et al., 2014; Thomas et al., 2008), confirming its inclusion for making all types of expatriate selection decisions.

1.2.4.3. Foreign Language Ability

While often times assumed to be necessary, the importance of expatriates mastering the host country language has resulted in contradictory findings when investigated. In a multicountry study, Zeira and Banai (1985) compared the selection criteria expectations of host country organization representatives, expatriate managers, and headquarters organization representatives. All three groups identified proficiency in the host country language as absolutely necessary and vital to an expatriate manager's success within the subsidiary. However, in contrast to these findings, Stone (1991) found that headquarters managers, expatriates, and host country managers all rated knowledge of the host country language as the least important criterion when making selection decisions. In a later study, Shen and Edwards (2004) concluded that expatriates, executive managers, and HR managers all felt that foreign language ability should be included as a criterion for any selection program to be effective. It is worth noting that all three of these studies surveyed individuals from MNEs with subsidiaries located in Asia. Fluency in the host country language may not be a requirement, but some level of proficiency greatly assists expatriates in building relationships with host country nationals, and with their adjustment and acceptance inside and outside of the workplace.

Two meta-analytic studies (Bhaskar-Shrinivas et al., 2005; Mol et al., 2005) found that host country language ability is a predictor of both expatriate adjustment and job performance. However, Bhaskar-Shrinivas et al. (2005) found that this ability is not related to work adjustment and therefore should not be seen as a prerequisite. Additionally, the importance of foreign language ability has also been found to be dependent on both the location of the international assignment and the native language of the expatriate. Members of countries where English is not the native language, for example, tend to be more accommodating to expatriates who do not speak the native language compared to members of countries where English is the native language (Bhaskar-Shrinivas et al., 2005). Mol et al. (2005) demonstrated that local language ability predicts expatriate job performance, and suggested that additional research is needed on moderators that are likely to influence this relationship. Finally, Caligiuri et al. (2009) recommended that language ability be assessed when selecting expatriates, but stipulated that the level of language competence needs to be based on the role of the expatriate. Some level of host country language proficiency cannot be seen as a hindrance to success, and will definitely assist an expatriate when working with individuals from other cultures during traditional and short-term international assignments, thereby supporting its consideration when making expatriate selection decisions.

1.2.4.4. Gender and Age

The gender of expatriates is a more recent addition to the list of selection decision-making criteria. As mentioned earlier, scholars did not originally evaluate the impact of gender differences, as mainly male expatriates were employed. Once female expatriates started being regularly considered, host country managers made it clear that they did not find women as appropriate for international assignments due to the view that women will face prejudices while abroad (Adler, 1984; Mayrhofer & Scullion, 2002; Stone, 1991). When given the choice of whether they would select a male or female for an international assignment, managers and expatriates interviewed by Stone (1991) responded: "I would not work for a woman — foreign or Japanese" and "it is better to choose an older man. Female expatriates, especially if young, may find it difficult" (p. 16). However, more recently it has been argued that gender should receive more attention (Michailova & Hutchings, 2016; Tharenou, 2010) and that the belief that gender roles impact the ability of female expatriates to be effective overseas is unfounded (Fischlmayr & Kollinger, 2010). Additionally, some studies have found that women should actually be preferred because they have already overcome the challenges of gender prejudice and, therefore, are better able to accept and surmount cultural differences (Cole & McNulty, 2011; Guthrie et al., 2003). Although gender bias in selection decisions is not appropriate, it can be concluded that women should be evaluated equally for international assignments and should not be excluded from being considered based on gender. Additionally, more women are anticipated to be interested in and participate in alternative international assignments (Meyskens et al., 2009).

Age has also more recently gained attention within expatriate selection literature, mainly due to a general decrease in the age of expatriates, but also because of supply issues that have required younger individuals to participate in international assignments. Selmer (2001) recommended that age be incorporated in expatriate selection decisions and be utilized as "a proxy characteristic for maturity" (p. 1228) based on the positive association between age and both sociocultural and psychology adjustment. Additionally, a meta-analysis of the influence of age on adjustment demonstrated that it has a positive influence on work adjustment, but negative relationships with general and interaction adjustment (Hechanova, Beehr, & Christiansen, 2003). Furthermore, an investigation of the association between expatriate age and performance concluded that, within the Chinese context, increased age results in higher performance (Selmer et al., 2009). Finally, Wechtler, Koveshnikov, and Dejoux (2015) demonstrated that "age is a facilitator of regulation and utilization of emotions on general living adjustment and of regulation of emotions on interactional adjustment" (p. 415). Again, although age should not be used as the only criterion for selecting an individual for expatriation, it should be considered along with other criteria.

1.2.5. Spouse and Family Situation

Often overlooked in the selection decisions of many MNEs is the spouse and/or family who will relocate with an expatriate or also be impacted because of alternative forms of international assignments. The inability of an expatriate's spouse or a family member to adjust to the foreign location is one of the reasons most commonly given by expatriates for their premature return from traditional international assignments (Tung, 1981). Although this reason for expatriate failure was identified very early in the expatriate selection literature (Hays, 1971), research investigations considering spouse and family adjustment did not come until much later (Black & Stephens, 1989; Punnett, Crocker, & Stevens, 1992). Although some MNEs interviewed spouses as part of the selection decision-making processes to determine their attitude toward a prospective overseas move, this was not possible in some countries because it was a legal liability to include interviews with spouses as part of selection decisions (Howard, 1974; Tung, 1981).

Bauer and Taylor (2001) reported that spouse adjustment includes three dimensions: how well the spouse builds relationships with host country nationals, how well the spouse adjusts to local customs and the culture in general, and the extent to which the spouse has a sense of becoming part of or feeling at home in the foreign country. In addition, the authors found that the foreign language abilities of spouses were the most influential factor in their ability to rebuild their sense of identity. Therefore, scholars recommend training and language programs geared directly to spouses in order to facilitate their adjustment (Bauer & Taylor, 2001; Lauring & Selmer, 2010). The literature has also found that there is a decreased willingness among expatriates to accept international assignments when they are a part of a dual-career couple. Gertsen (1990) found that the main reason expatriates turn down international assignments is that their spouse does not want to resign from their current job or they do not want to interrupt their children's education. This has increased the need for MNEs to include the spouse and family situation of a candidate as an important selection criterion. At the same time, HR managers need to carefully consider whether the provision of spousal support programs and assistance for accompanying children are viable (Mäkelä et al., 2011).

Another challenge of expatriate selection, when considering the role of the spouse, is that more females are taking international assignments and relocating with their male spouses. This development represents a change in the traditional gender roles of men and women (Fischlmayr & Kollinger, 2010; Punnett et al., 1992). Cole (2011) demonstrated that female spouses are able to better adapt to foreign cultures and new locations than male spouses, and recommended that male spouses receive networking information to assist them with job searches. Although there is no need to consider spouse adjustment and job placement, or children's education, the disruption of the work-life balance of families caused by alternative assignments can result in stress and burn-out among expatriates (Brewster, Harris, & Petrovic, 2001; Tahvanainen et al., 2005). Furthermore, families frequently need to adjust to the absence of the international manager due to his/her increased work hours and heavy travel schedules (Cappellen & Janssens, 2010). Some expatriates may also seek alternative employment in order to decrease their time spent traveling (Mayerhofer, Müller, & Schmidt, 2010). As a result, spouse and family situation should be considered when making selection decision where the international assignment will impact the work-life balance of individuals.

1.3. Implications and Conclusion

In the spirit of the overall objectives of this edited volume, we sought to contribute by discussing expatriate selection and decision-making criteria. It is hard to justify that selecting the right people for international assignments has attracted less scholarly attention as compared to conversations regarding other expatriate related issues, such as their role, performance, adjustment, success and failure, to mention but a few. We brought together existing studies to trace the chronological development of expatriate selection. Indeed, this complex process has evolved over more than five decades and as such, it has emphasized different aspects in different time periods. In addition, we have identified and presented expatriation selection criteria along five core areas — organization philosophy, technical competence, relational abilities, personal characteristics, and spouse and family situation. We discussed each of them in-depth to gain insights that help the understanding of expatriate selection in greater detail than has been done so far.

Our analysis has potential implications for expatriates, HRM professionals, and MNE executives. Expatriates can benefit from the overview presented in this chapter to get a better understanding of the complexity of selection decisions. They may find it difficult sometimes to interpret and make sense of certain selection activities and decisions and consequently, become frustrated. Knowing more about selection for international assignments is likely to prepare them, such that they can anticipate potential discussions around and decisions regarding their (non)selection. Knowing more about the different selection criteria can be also helpful, as they can prepare to argue their case, whether it is for or against being selected.

HRM professionals may want to take on board the simple, but often compromised fact that the right expatriate selection is the foundation for the potential success of the international assignment and the expatriate. Not paying attention to each of the selection criteria we have specified, individually as well as collectively, can have serious negative consequences for both expatriates and the MNE. The consequences can be heavy and long-standing as careers and families are affected, and MNEs, too, pay high costs, financially and otherwise. Using the five clusters of selection criteria as a system that we have proposed can be a helpful tool that can assist making better expatriate selection decisions.

Being aware of the importance of selection decisions, MNE executives can consider tasking HRM departments to analyze the link between how well the selection decision-making processes are designed and executed, on the one hand, and how successful international assignments are, on the other. To be able to apply appropriate selection criteria and make sound selection decisions, HRM departments need the suitable resources. Senior executives are in the position to allocate resources in a way that does not force these departments to circumvent the rigor of selection, but instead make sure expatriate selection is well supported.

References

Adler, N. J. (1984). Women do not want international careers: And other myths about international management. *Organizational Dynamics, 13*, 66−79.

Anderson, B. A. (2005). Expatriate selection: Good management or good luck? *The International Journal of Human Resource Management, 16*, 567−583.

Anderson, N., Lievens, F., van Dam, K., & Ryan, A. M. (2004). Future perspectives on employee selection: Key directions for future research and practice. *Applied Psychology: An International Review, 53*, 487−501.

Andresen, M., & Margenfeld, J. (2015). International relocation mobility readiness and its antecedents. *Journal of Managerial Psychology, 30*, 234−249.

Ang, S., Van Dyne, L., & Koh, C. (2006). Personality correlates of the four-factor model of cultural intelligence. *Group & Organization Management, 31*, 100−123.

Ang, S., Van Dyne, L., Koh, C., Ng, K. Y., Templer, K. J., Tay, C., & Chandrasekar, N. A. (2007). Cultural intelligence: Its measurement and effects on cultural judgment and decision making, cultural adaptation and task performance. *Management and Organization Review, 3*, 335−371.

Bauer, T. N., & Taylor, S. (2001). When managing expatriate adjustment, don't forget the spouse. *Academy of Management Executive, 15*, 135–137.

Bhaskar-Shrinivas, P., Harrison, D. A., Shaffer, M. A., & Luk, D. M. (2005). Input-based and time-based models of international adjustment: Meta-analytic evidence and theoretical extensions. *Academy of Management Journal, 48*, 257–281.

Bird, A., Mendenhall, M., Stevens, M. J., & Oddou, G. (2010). Defining the content domain of intercultural competence for global leaders. *Journal of Managerial Psychology, 25*, 810–828.

Black, J. S. (1988). Work role transitions: A study of American expatriate managers in Japan. *Journal of International Business Studies, 19*, 277–294.

Black, J. S., & Gregersen, H. B. (1991). Antecedents to cross-cultural adjustment for expatriates in Pacific Rim assignments. *Human Relations, 44*, 497–515.

Black, J. S., Mendenhall, M., & Oddou, G. (1991). Toward a comprehensive model of international adjustment: An integration of multiple theoretical perspectives. *The Academy of Management Review, 16*, 291–317.

Black, J. S., & Stephens, G. K. (1989). The influence of the spouse on American expatriate adjustment and intent to stay in Pacific Rim overseas assignments. *Journal of Management, 15*, 529–544.

Brewster, C., Harris, H., & Petrovic, J. (2001). Globally mobile employees: Managing the mix. *Journal of Professional HRM, 25*, 11–15.

Brookfield Global Relocation Services. (2014). *Global relocation trend 2014 survey report.* Retrieved from www.brookfieldgrs.com

Bruning, N. S., Sonpar, K., & Xiaoyun, W. (2012). Host country national networks and expatriate effectiveness: A mixed-methods study. *Journal of International Business Studies, 43*, 444–450.

Bücker, J. J. L. E., Furrer, O., Poutsma, E., & Buyens, D. (2014). The impact of cultural intelligence on communication effectiveness, job satisfaction and anxiety for Chinese host country managers working for foreign multinationals. *The International Journal of Human Resource Management, 25*, 2068–2087.

Caligiuri, P. M. (2000a). Selecting expatriates for personality characteristics: A moderating effect of personality on the relationship between host national contact and cross-cultural adjustment. *Management International Review, 40*, 61–80.

Caligiuri, P. M. (2000b). The big five personality characteristics as predictors of expatriate's desire to terminate the assignment and supervisor-rated performance. *Personnel Psychology, 53*, 67–88.

Caligiuri, P. M., Tarique, I., & Jacobs, R. (2009). Selection for international assignments. *Human Resource Management Review, 22*, 1504–1530.

Cappellen, T., & Janssens, M. (2010). Characteristics of international work: Narratives of the global manager. *Thunderbird International Business Review, 52*, 337–348.

Church, A. T. (1982). Sojourner adjustment. *Psychological Bulletin, 91*, 540–572.

Cole, N. D. (2011). Managing global talent: Solving the spousal adjustment problem. *The International Journal of Human Resource Management, 22*, 1504–1530.

Cole, N. D., & McNulty, Y. (2011). Why do female expatriates "fit-in" better than males? An analysis of self-transcendence and socio-cultural adjustment. *Cross Cultural Management: An International Journal, 18*, 144–164.

Collings, D. G. (2014). Integrating global mobility and global talent management: Exploring the challenges and strategic opportunities. *Journal of World Business, 49*, 253–261.

Collings, D. G., Scullion, H., & Morley, M. J. (2007). Changing patterns of global staffing in the multinational enterprise: Challenges to the conventional expatriate assignment and emerging alternatives. *Journal of World Business, 42*, 198–213.

Dowling, P. J., Festing, M., & Engle, A. (2013). *International human resource management* (6th ed.), London: Cengage Learning.

Earley, P. C. (2002). Redefining interactions across cultures and organizations: Moving forward with cultural intelligence. *Research in Organizational Behavior, 24*, 271–299.

Earley, P. C., & Ang, S. (2003). *Cultural intelligence: Individual interactions across cultures.* Stanford, CA: Stanford University Press.

Enderwick, P., & Hodgson, D. (1993). Expatriate management practices of New Zealand Business. *The International Journal of Human Resource Management, 4*, 407–423.

Eschbach, D. M., Parker, G. E., & Stoeberl, P. A. (2001). American repatriate employees' retrospective assessments of the effects of cross-cultural training on their adaptation to international assignments. *The International Journal of Human Resource Management, 12*, 270–288.

Farndale, E., Scullion, H., & Sparrow, P. (2010). The role of the corporate HR function in global talent management. *Journal of World Business, 45*, 161–168.

Fischlmayr, I., & Kollinger, I. (2010). Work-life balance – A neglected issue among Austrian female expatriates. *The International Journal of Human Resource Management, 21*, 455–487.

Gabel, R. S., Dolan, S. L., & Cerdin, J. L. (2005). Emotional intelligence as predictor of cultural adjustment for success in global assignments. *Career Development International, 10*, 375–395.

Gertsen, C. M. (1990). Intercultural competence and expatriates. *The International Journal of Human Resource Management, 1*, 341–362.

Graf, A. (2004). Screening and training inter-cultural competencies: Evaluating the impact of national culture on inter-cultural competencies. *The International Journal of Human Resource Management, 15*, 1124–1148.

Guthrie, J. P., Ash, R. A., & Stevens, C. D. (2003). Are women "better" than men? Personality differences and expatriate selection. *Journal of Managerial Psychology, 18*, 229–243.

Harris, H. (2002). Strategic management of international workers. *Innovations in International HR, 28*, 1–5.

Harris, H., & Kumra, S. (2000). International manager development: Cross-cultural training in highly diverse environments. *Journal of Management Development, 19*, 602–614.

Harrison, N. (2012). Investigating the impact of personality and early life experiences on intercultural interaction in internationalized universities. *International Journal of Intercultural Relations, 36*, 224–237.

Harvey, M., & Moeller, M. (2009). Expatriate managers: A historical review. *International Journal of Management Reviews, 11*, 275–296.

Harzing, A. (2002). Are our referencing errors undermining our scholarship and credibility? The case of expatriate failure rates. *Journal of Organizational Behavior, 23*, 127–148.

Harzing, A., & Christensen, C. (2004). Expatriate failure: Time to abandon the concept? *Career Development International, 9*, 616–626.

Haslberger, A., & Stroh, L. K. (1992). *Development and selection of multinational expatriates.* Human Resource Development Quarterly, *3*, 287–293.

Hays, R. D. (1971). Ascribed behavioral determinates of success-failure among US expatriate managers. *Journal of International Business Studies, 2*, 40–46.

Hays, R. D. (1974). Expatriate selection: Insuring success and avoiding failure. *Journal of International Business Studies, 5*, 25–37.

Hechanova, R., Beehr, T. A., & Christiansen, N. D. (2003). Antecedents and consequences of employees' adjustment to overseas assignments: A meta-analytic review. *Applied Psychology: An International Review, 52*, 213–236.

Heenan, D., & Perlmutter, H. (1979). *Multinational organizational development: A social architecture perspective*. Reading, MA: Addison-Wesley.

Holopainen, J., & Björkman, I. (2005). The personal characteristics of the successful expatriate: A critical review of the literature and an empirical investigation. *Personnel Review, 34*, 37–50.

Howard, C. G. (1974). Model for design of a selection program for multinational executives. *Public Personnel Management, 3*, 138–145.

Huff, K. C., Song, P., & Gresch, E. B. (2014). Cultural intelligence, personality, and cross-cultural adjustment: A study of expatriates in Japan. *International Journal of Intercultural Relations, 38*, 151–157.

Hurn, B. J. (2006). The selection of international business managers: Part 1. *Industrial and Commercial Training, 38*, 279–286.

Izraeli, D. N., Banai, M., & Zeira, Y. (1980). Women executives in MNC subsidiaries. *California Management Review, 23*, 53–63.

Johnson, J. P., Lenartowicz, T., & Apud, S. (2006). Cross-cultural competence in international business: Toward a definition and a model. *Journal of International Business Studies, 37*, 525–543.

Lauring, J., & Selmer, J. (2010). The supportive expatriate spouse: An ethnographic study of spouse involvement in expatriate careers. *International Business Review, 19*, 59–69.

Lee, H. (2007). Factors that influence expatriate failure: An interview study. *International Journal of Management, 24*, 403–413.

Lee, L. Y., Veasna, S., & Sukoco, B. M. (2014). The antecedents of cultural effectiveness of expatriation: Moderating effects of psychological contracts. *Asia Pacific Journal of Human Resources, 52*, 215–233.

Lin, C. Y.-Y., Lu, T.-C., & Lin, H.-W. (2012). A different perspective of expatriate management. *Human Resource Management Review, 22*, 189–207.

Mäkelä, L., Känsälä, M., & Suutari, V. (2011). The roles of expatriates' spouses among dual career couples. *Cross Cultural Management: An International Journal, 18*, 185–197.

Mayer, J. D., Salovey, P., & Caruso, D. R. (2004). Emotional intelligence: Theory, findings, and implications. *Psychological Inquiry, 15*, 197–215.

Mayerhofer, H., Müller, B., & Schmidt, A. (2010). Implications of flexpatriates' lifestyles on HRM practices. *Management Revue, 21*, 155–173.

Mayrhofer, W., & Scullion, H. (2002). Female expatriates in international business: Empirical evidence from the German clothing industry. *The International Journal of Human Resource Management, 13*, 815–836.

Mendenhall, M. E., & Oddou, G. (1988). The overseas assignment: A practical look. *Business Horizons, 31*, 78–84.

Meyskens, M., Von Glinow, M., Werther, J. B., & Clarke, L. (2009). The paradox of international talent: Alternative forms of international assignments. *The International Journal of Human Resource Management, 20*, 1439–1450.

Michailova, S., & Hutchings, K. (2016). Critiquing the marginalised place of research on women within international business: Where are we now and where should we be going? *Critical Perspectives on International Business*, forthcoming

Miller, E. L. (1972). The selection decision for an international assignment: A study of the decision maker's behavior. *Journal of International Business Studies, 3*, 49–65.

Mol, S. T., Born, M. P., Willemsen, M. E., & Van Der Molen, H. T. (2005). Predicting expatriate job performance for selection purposes: A quantitative review. *Journal of Cross-Cultural Psychology, 36*, 590–620.

Morris, M. A., & Robie, C. (2001). A meta-analysis of the effects of cross-cultural training on expatriate performance and adjustment. *International Journal of Training & Development, 5*, 112–125.

Murray, F. T., & Murray, A. (1986). SMR forum: Global managers for global businesses. *Sloan Management Review, 27*, 75–80.

Newman, J., Bhatt, B., & Gutteridge, T. (1978). Determinants of expatriate effectiveness: A theoretical and empirical vacuum. *Academy of Management Review, 3*, 655–661.

Ones, D. S., & Viswesvaran, C. (1999). Relative importance of personality dimensions for expatriate selection: A policy capturing study. *Human Performance, 12*, 275–294.

Perlmutter, H. V. (1969). The tortuous evolution of the multinational corporation. *Columbia Journal of World Business, 4*, 9–18.

Punnett, B., Crocker, O., & Stevens, M. (1992). The challenge for women expatriates and spouses: Some empirical evidence. *The International Journal of Human Resource Management, 3*, 585–592.

Romero, E. J. (2002). The effect of expatriate training on expatriate effectiveness. *Journal of Management Research, 2*, 73–78.

Şahin, F., Gurbuz, S., & Köksal, O. (2014). Cultural intelligence (CQ) in action: The effects of personality and international assignment on the development of CQ. *International Journal of Intercultural Relations, 39*, 152–163.

Scullion, H., & Collings, D. G. (2006). Alternative forms of international assignments. In H. Scullion & D. G. Collings (Eds.), *Global staffing* (pp. 159–173). New York: Routledge.

Selmer, J. (2001). Expatriate selection: Back to basics? *The International Journal of Human Resource Management, 12*, 1219–1233.

Selmer, J., Lauring, J., & Feng, Y. (2009). Age and expatriate job performance in greater China. *Cross Cultural Management: An International Journal, 16*, 131–148.

Shaffer, M. A., Harrison, D. A., Gregerson, H., Black, J. S., & Frezandi, L. A. (2006). You can take it with you: Individual differences and expatriate effectiveness. *Journal of Applied Psychology, 91*, 109–125.

Shankaran, G., Murray, R. A., & Miller, P. (2011). Short-term international assignments: Maximizing effectiveness, minimizing cost and risk. *International Tax Journal, 37*, 41–60.

Shen, J., & Edwards, V. (2004). Recruitment and selection in Chinese MNEs. *The International Journal of Human Resource Management, 15*, 814–835.

Sparrow, P., Brewster, C., & Harris, H. (2004). *Globalizing human resource management*. London: Routledge.

Stone, R. J. (1991). Expatriate selection and failure. *Human Resource Planning, 14*, 9–18.

Tahvanainen, M., Welch, D., & Worm, V. (2005). Implications of short-term international assignments. *European Management Journal, 23*, 663–673.

Takeuchi, R., Tesluk, P. E., Yun, S., & Lepak, D. P. (2005). An integrative view of international experience. *Academy of Management Journal, 48*, 85–100.

Tarique, I., & Schuler, R. S. (2010). Global talent management: Literature review, integrative framework, and suggestions for further research. *Journal of World Business, 45*, 122–133.

Tharenou, P. (2010). Women's self-initiated expatriation as a career option and its ethical issues. *International Journal of Management Reviews, 11*, 275–296.

Thomas, D. C., Elron, E., Stahl, G., Ekelund, B. Z., Ravlin, E. C., & Cerdin, J.-L., ... Lazarova, M. B. (2008). Cultural intelligence: Domain and assessment. *International Journal of Cross Cultural Management, 8*, 123–143.

Thomas, D. C., Liao, Y., Aycan, Z., Cerdin, J.-L., Pekerti, A. A., & Ravlin, E. C., ... van de Vijver, F. (2015). Cultural intelligence: A theory-based, short-form measure. *Journal of International Business Studies, 46*(9), 1099–1118. doi:10.1057/jibs.2014.67.

Tung, R. L. (1981). Selection and training of personnel for overseas assignments. *Columbia Journal of World Business, 16*, 68–78.

Tung, R. L. (1982). Selection and training procedures of U.S., European, and Japanese multi-nationals. *California Management Review, 25*, 57–71.

Tung, R. L. (1987). Expatriate assignments: Enhancing success and minimizing failure. *Academy of Management Executive, 1*, 117–125.

Tung, R. L. (1998). A contingency framework of selection and training of expatriates revis-ited. *Human Resource Management Planning, 15*, 27–35.

Webb, A., & Wright, C. (1996). The expatriate experience: Implications for career success. *Career Development Journal, 1*, 30–44.

Wechtler, H., Koveshnikov, A., & Dejoux, C. (2015). Just like a fine wine? Age, emotional intelligence, and cross cultural adjustment. *International Business Review, 24*, 409–418.

Wederspahn, G. M. (1992). Costing failures in expatriate human resource management. *Human Resource Planning, 15*, 27–35.

Welch, D., Worm, V., & Fenwick, M. (2003). Are virtual assignments feasible? *Management International Review, 43*, 95–114.

Wills, S., & Barham, K. (1994). Being an international manager. *European Management Journal, 12*, 49–58.

Zeira, Y., & Banai, M. (1985). Selection of expatriate managers in MNCs: The host environ-ment point of view. *International Studies of Management & Organization, 15*, 33–51.

Chapter 2

Global Talent Management: International Staffing Policies and Practices of South Korean Multinationals in China

Haiying Kang and Jie Shen

Abstract

Purpose – South Korean multinational enterprises (MNEs) have developed rapidly since the late 1950s. This chapter investigates South Korean MNEs' talent management, more specifically international recruitment and selection policies and practices in their Chinese operations.

Methodology/approach – Using the snowball method through Chinese and Korean networks we recruited ten Korean MNEs to participate in this research. We conducted semi-structured interviews with key individuals within the organisations.

Findings – It reveals that South Korean MNEs tend to adopt the polycentric approach or a mixed approach of being polycentric and ethnocentric to international staffing, with the number of expatriates reducing gradually over time. South Korean MNEs adopt 'one-way selection' in recruiting and selecting expatriates and localise recruitment procedures and selection criteria for host-country nationals.

Originality/value – South Korean MNEs have paid inadequate attention to: firstly, expatriates' career development; and secondly, personal and family

Global Talent Management and Staffing in MNEs
International Business & Management, Volume 32, 25–48
ISSN: 1876-066X/doi:10.1108/S1876-066X20160000032019

issues emerging from expatriation and repatriation. This study highlights these issues.

Keywords: Expatriate; international human resource management; international recruitment and selection; international staffing; multinational enterprise; South Korea

International staffing, one of the key initiatives in global talent management, includes recruitment and selection, which deals with 'critical issues faced by multinational corporations with regard to the employment of home, host and third country nationals to fill key positions in their headquarters and subsidiary operations' (Scullion & Collings, 2006, p. 3). Through staffing, MNEs coordinate and control global operations (Stroh & Caligiuri, 1998). Consequently, international staffing may influence how subsidiaries perform as well as the MNE as a whole (Colakoglu & Caligiuri, 2008; Colakoglu, Tarique, & Caligiuri, 2009). The international staffing literature has developed significantly during the last two decades (cf. Collings, Scullion, & Dowling, 2009; Dowling, Festing, & Engle, 2008; Shen & Edwards, 2004; Tharenou & Caulfield, 2010). However, despite a few exceptions, such as Kulkarni, Lengnick-Hall, and Valk (2010) and Shen and Edwards (2004), most research was conducted in Western contexts. Little is known about how MNEs originating in non-Western economies manage staffing policies and issues in their global operations. Hence, there is an urgent need to study how non-Western MNEs manage international recruitment and selection so that our knowledge base of international staffing literature can be enhanced.

South Korean (hereafter referred to as Korean) firms started operating overseas during the late 1950s and since then Korean MNEs have expanded significantly (SERI, 2008). In 2009, Korean MNEs had invested in more than 100 countries (Yang, Lim, Sakurai, & Seo, 2009) with fourteen Korean MNEs being on the Fortune 500 list (Fortune, 2010). However, a recent systematic literature review (Kang & Shen, 2010) found that only five studies examined staffing issues in Korean MNEs and they mostly concentrated on recruiting and selecting host-country nationals (HCNs). To fill this literature gap the current research investigates the major international staffing issues, namely: internal staffing approaches and the reasons for these approaches; recruitment procedures and selection criteria for both expatriates and HCNs; and repatriation management of Korean MNEs in China.

China is the largest outward FDI destination of these MNEs. The Chinese market is critical to Korea due to its size, location advantage, and favourable government policies regarding foreign investment. A large number of Korean MNEs have

Table 2.1: South korean direct investment in china (US $000).

Year	Number of Enterprises	Invested Amount
2001	1,805	660,910
2002	2,567	1,102,096
2003	3,163	1,833,067
2004	4,015	2,432,272
2005	4,672	2,866,773
2006	4,708	3,501,862
2007	4,614	5,444,819
2008	3,328	3,862,256
2009	2,127	2,476,927
2010	2,297	3,657,766
2011	2,211	3,541,844
2012	1,866	4,043,478
2013	1,881	5,145,567
2014	1,613	3,156,950
2015	1,647	2,853,662

Source: Export-Import Bank of Korea (2016).

invested in China and these investments increased rapidly once a diplomatic relationship began in 1992 (Lee, 2003). In 2007, South Korean investments reached their peak at $5.33 billion. China became Korea's number one FDI destination in 2012 (OECD, 2013). The global financial crisis meant that the amount of Korean investment in China decreased gradually from 2008. This investment in other countries also decreased accordingly. China, the United States, and Vietnam are the three biggest recipients of Korean investment. As shown in Table 2.1, Korean outward direct investment in China during the last decade increased substantially. Currently, all major Korean MNEs are operating in China, engaging in a wide range of industries, such as automobile, consumer electronics, internet service, marketing, finance, textile, footwear and toys (Lee, 2010; Kwon & Oh, 2001). Therefore, China is still an ideal laboratory for studying South Korean MNEs' IHRM policies and practices. An analysis of Korean MNEs' staffing practices in China is an important step towards understanding their global staffing practices, and therefore has the potential to contribute to the international staffing literature.

2.1. Literature Review and Research Questions

2.1.1. Global Talent Management: International Staffing

The definition of GTM is broad which generally embraces three key areas: (1) attracting (mainly include recruitment and selection) talents; (2) retaining key talents; (3) developing talents (Tarique & Schuler, 2010). Collings and Mellahi (2009) further emphasised that talent management are 'activities and processes that involve the systematic identification of key positions which differentially contribute to the organisation's sustainable competitive advantage ...' (p. 304). It is obvious that the staffing of key positions is critical in talent management. The research on talent management has increased dramatically, and they are not only focusing on staffing of key positions at top management level but also lower level positions (e.g. Collings & Mellahi, 2009). Talent identification and selection is essential for MNE performance, hence MNEs need to ensure they select the right people to the right positions (Myers & Woerkom, 2014). However identifying and selecting the right talents who have the right skills is considered one major challenge for contemporary MNEs (Tarique & Schuler, 2010). It is also suggested that GTM should not only focus on top-level, high performers, but also consider different levels of assignees, especially by witnessing a number of alternatives to traditional, long term expatriate assignments are increasing (Farndale, Scullion, & Sparrow, 2010).

2.1.2. International Staffing Approach

Staffing approaches are central to international recruitment and selection (Ando, 2011; Dörrenbächer & Geppert, 2010). There are four major international staffing approaches, these being ethnocentric, polycentric, geocentric and regiocentric in character (Perlmutter, 1969; Perlmutter & Heenan, 1974, 1979). The ethnocentric approach fills all the key positions in subsidiaries abroad with parent-country nationals (PCNs), while the polycentric approach does so with HCNs. The geocentric approach utilises the best people for senior positions regardless of their nationalities. Be consistent with this approach, it is suggested that MNEs should source key talents regardless of their locations so that the talent pools in different locations can be filled, thereby managing the global talents more effectively (Collings, 2014). Finally, the regiocentric approach selects the best people, but within a particular region.

Each approach has some advantages and disadvantages (e.g. Caligiuri & Colakoglu, 2007; Colakoglu et al., 2009; Dowling et al., 2008; Reiche & Harzing, 2009; Vo, 2009). The advantages of the ethnocentric approach are effective communication, ease of control and transfer of knowledge. However, this approach limits the development opportunities for HCNs which may impact on their morale, and in the long term cause repatriation problems. Moreover, expatriates may encounter difficulties in adapting to host working environments and the use of expatriates is normally more expensive than HCNs. In contrast, HCNs are familiar with local cultures and working environments and have local connections (Bruning, Bebenroth, & Pascha, 2011; Dörrenbächer & Geppert, 2010). However, the polycentric approach may result in coordination and control problems. The geocentric approach enables the MNE to develop effective international management teams, and it enhances a subsidiary's learning, innovation potential, and performance by facilitating the knowledge integration process (Gong, 2003). Yet, this approach involves high costs of training and relocation and increased difficulties in obtaining work permits in host countries. The regiocentric approach makes it easier for international managers to transfer, but limits their career paths within a given region and has the potential to lead to federalism on a regional basis (Dowling et al., 2008). MNEs may adopt different international staffing approaches that are determined by a range of host-contextual and firm-specific factors. For example, Australian and German MNEs tend to employ more HCN managers in their Chinese subsidiaries (Kühlmann & Hutchings, 2010) while Chinese MNEs tend to use more expatriates in overseas operations (Shen & Edwards, 2004). Given that little is known about international staffing approaches of Korean MNEs, we develop the following research question:

Research Question 1. What are the staffing approaches adopted by Korean MNEs?

2.1.3. Reasons for Using Expatriates

In the 1970s, Edström and Galbraith identified three common reasons why companies send expatriates on international assignments: filling skill gaps, management development, and organisational development (Edström & Galbraith, 1977). Four decades on, these three reasons are still relevant (Tungli & Peiperl, 2009). For instance, Japanese subsidiaries in Western countries are frequently managed by PCNs, particularly in the initial establishment phase because PCNs have low foreign language proficiency (Van den Born & Peltokorpi, 2010). It is, however, argued that the emphasis may have shifted somewhat from filling skill gaps to management development due to the growing importance of developing international managers and advances in technology, particularly since technology makes knowledge transfer so much easier and quicker (Kühlmann & Hutchings, 2010). In addition, maintaining control over the implementation of strategies, finance and marketing, enhancing communication between subsidiaries and the parent company, knowledge exchange (both to and from the subsidiary), socialisation with local managers, and company representations, make the use of expatriates important (Bruning et al., 2011; Dowling et al., 2008; Lasserre & Ching, 1997).

It is argued that different MNEs use expatriates for different reasons. Tungli and Peiperl (2009) indicated that the use of expatriates in Western MNEs (e.g. the US, the UK) is to fill skill gaps and to help establish new businesses. For emerging country MNEs, control and communication are the major reasons for using expatriates (Nigam & Su, 2010). For Japanese MNEs, in addition to filling skill gaps, coordinating and controlling local operations are also critical (Tungli & Peiperl, 2009).

We develop the following research question to explore the reasons for Korean MNEs using expatriates:

Research Question 2. What are the reasons for Korean MNEs using expatriates?

2.1.4. Recruitment Procedures and Selection Criteria

Effective recruitment and selection contributes significantly to expatriate performance (e.g. Cheng & Lin, 2009; Harrison & Shaffer, 2005; Mol, Born, & van der Molen, 2005). Research shows that most MNEs recruit talented expatriates internally (Shen & Lang, 2009) and consider the following selection criteria: job expertise, technical competence, personal traits/interpersonal abilities, cultural openness, ability to adjust to new environments, family issues (Anderson, 2005; Caligiuri, 2000; Reiche & Harzing, 2009; Templer, 2010; Tung, 1981), and previous international working experience (Culpan & Wright, 2002; Tsang, 2001). These criteria are regarded to be critical to expatriate performance in international assignments and their consideration may depend on reasons for using expatriates (Tungli & Peiperl, 2009).

Shen (2005) suggested that there are three general approaches to recruiting and selecting HCNs, these being the home-based, host-based and integrative approaches. According to Shen, MNEs that adopt the home-based approach export their home operation's recruitment procedures and selection criteria to overseas subsidiaries. Conversely, the host-based approach localises the recruitment and selection of HCNs. MNEs adopting the integrative approach seek recruitment and selection practices that best fit internal and external environments. In Korea, large companies adopt 'open recruitment' (*gongchae*); this refers to the tradition of hiring university graduates, especially from distinguished universities (Lee, 1998). The past decade has seen an increase in recruiting short-term contract workers from labour agencies due to the economic crises and changing workplace environment where Korean firms have to be more flexible in managing their workforce (Park & Yu, 2000). Small and medium-sized companies, on the other hand, rely on back-door recruitment or employee referral (Koch, Nam, & Steers, 1995). Back-door recruitment is carried out irregularly whenever companies have vacancies and this method relies on less formal hiring processes (Park & Yu, 2000).

Selection procedures in Korean domestic firms normally include written tests and interviews (Lee, 1998). Tests assess job-related or general knowledge (Kim, 1992). During the last decade, some *chaebols* (conglomerates, for example Samsung, Hyundai) dropped 'the knowledge test' and replaced it with an aptitude test (Kim, 1997; Kim & Briscoe, 1997). The major selection criteria are education, such as the prestige of a university (Yu & Rowley, 2009), specific subject knowledge and technical qualifications, and moral attitudes (Lee, 2004). Recently, large firms, such as Samsung have gradually put more emphasis on 'aptitude' to assess applicants' potentials (Pucik & Lim, 2001).

In China, the recruitment channels are diverse, including job fair, job centre, employment agency, head hunter, online recruitment, advertisements in the media and word of mouth (Chen, 2006; Cooke, 2005; Kim & Gao, 2010). Large firms and foreign invested enterprises (FIEs) tend to rely more on university job fairs and head hunters to recruit high-calibre employees (Chen, 2006). All employees sign labour contracts and these contracts' duration generally last between 1 and 5 years (Warner, 2010). Political attitude is considered important by state-owned enterprises (SOEs) (Hu & Leung, 2010), but no longer by privately owned enterprises (POEs), the latter emphasising the importance of education, skills, experience and performance (Shen, 2010). A review of the literature shows that Korean MNEs focus heavily on English fluency in selecting expatriates (Kang & Shen, 2010). Despite this, we still know little about the recruitment procedures and selection criteria in Korean MNEs. To fill this literature gap we develop the following research question:

Research Question 3. What are Korean MNEs' recruitment procedures and selection criteria for HCNs and expatriates?

2.1.5. Repatriation Management

Effective repatriation is important in retaining repatriates and enhancing global management transfer (Furuya, Stevens, Bird, Oddou, & Mendenhall, 2008; Scullion & Collings, 2006), hence it is crucial in GTM (Cerdin & Brewster, 2014). Without formal and systematic repatriation processes, talented expatriate managers are likely to leave the organisations and potential candidates will be reluctant to accept international assignments. All this could impact adversely on the supply of talents or key global managers (Farndale et al., 2010). Unsuccessful repatriation could be very expensive for both expatriates and organisations because employees may feel or fear career stagnation and displacement; organisations may face direct investment loss because employees are being underutilised (Riche & Harzing, 2009; Yan, Zhu, & Hall, 2002). Therefore, repatriation should receive equal attention as much as the process of expatriation does (Kulkarni et al., 2010; Lazarova & Cerdin, 2007). According to Dowling et al. (2008), repatriation can be divided into four phases: preparation, physical relocation, transition and readjustment. Preparation involves developing plans for repatriates' future and gathering information about new positions. Physical relocation refers to removing personal effects, breaking ties with colleagues and friends and travelling to the next posting. Transition is a period of finding a new position and re-establishing social and work networks. Readjustment involves coping with reverse culture shock and career demands that are followed by the re-entry. Scholars have argued that repatriation can be more complex and difficult than expatriation (Forster, 2000).

It has been found that MNEs usually provide assistance to relocation, but pay less attention to transition (Kulkarni et al., 2010; Newton, Hutchings, & Kabanoff,

2007), career planning (Pattie, White, & Tansky, 2010), and psychological adjustment (Pattie et al., 2010; Shen & Edwards, 2004). In specific, global career planning and development could help identify return on investment for both organisations and individuals (Cerdin & Brewster, 2014). To facilitate repatriation it is suggested that MNEs assign mentors to expatriates because mentors can help repatriates generate accurate work expectations and reduce stress (Sanchez Vidal, Sanz Valle, Barba Aragon, & Brewster, 2007). To understand repatriation management in Korean MNEs, we develop the following research question:

Research Question 4. How do Korean MNEs manage repatriation?

2.2. Methodology

2.2.1. Data Collection

Using the snowball method through Chinese and Korean networks we recruited ten Korean MNEs to participate in this research. The case study companies are involved in electronics, telecommunications (mobile phones), online services, automobiles, advertising and IT businesses; these activities are consistent with the industry pattern of Korean MNEs in China (Export-Import Bank of Korea, 2016). The company profiles are shown in Table 2.2. We conducted semi-structured interviews with one HR manager and a general manager in each subsidiary. We required that their nationalities to differ in order to obtain data that reflected different perspectives. Interviews were conducted in Chinese or English and interpretation was provided whenever needed. The interviews were tape-recorded and interview summaries were sent back to the interviewees for verification. Prior to the interviews, the researchers requested that they be provided with demographic information about the interviewees. Table 2.3 summarises the profiles of the interviewees. The interviews were conducted in 2011 from early March to the end of May. Data were also collected through company documents, reports and official websites. Some company documents especially regarding turnover rates of repatriates were also sought from company headquarters in Korea.

The data were content analysed. Coding examples and exemplary statements are shown in Table 2.4.

2.3. Results

2.3.1. Staffing Approach

The numbers of HCNs and expatriates in middle and senior managerial positions in the case companies are shown in Table 2.5. As shown in Table 2.5 five firms

Table 2.2: Company profiles.

Company	Year of Establishment in Korea/China	Industry	Location in China	No. of Overseas Subsidiaries/ Operating Countries	No. of Employees Globally/in China	Mode of Internationalisation
Telecom A	1997/2004	Online services	Beijing	4/4	400/76	FOE
Chemical A	1966/1992	Chemical	Beijing	15/6	10,000/2000	FOE
Telecom B	1984/1987	Mobile phone	Beijing	6/3	4,500/350	FOE
Advertising A	2005/2005	Advertising	Beijing	10/5	350/30	FOE
Telecom C	1984/2003	IT	Beijing	1/1	4,500/58	JV
Electronics A	1958/1993	Electronics	Yantai	100/44	100,000/36,000	FOE
Electronics B	1938/1992	Electronics	Tianjin	57/65	680,000/69,000	FOE
Auto A	1967/2002	Automobile	Beijing	18/8	68,000/7,400	JV
Finance A	1993/2005	Finance	Beijing	2/2	2,375/20	FOE
Telecom D	1999/2000	Mobile phone	Beijing	2/2	100/30	FOE

Note: FOE: Foreign-owned enterprise; JV: Joint-ventures.

Table 2.3: Interviewees' profiles.

Company	Position	Age	Gender	Working Years	Education	Nationality
Telecom A	Operation Manager	38	M	3	Bachelor	Korean
	General Manager	46	M	5	Master	Chinese
Chemical A	Marketing Manager	41	M	3	Master	Korean
	HR Manager	40	M	3	Bachelor	Chinese
Telecom B	Chief Operating officer	44	M	2	Bachelor	Korean
	General Manager	48	M	4	Bachelor	Chinese
Advertising A	Marketing Manager	33	F	3	Bachelor	Korean
	HR Manager	40	M	4	Bachelor	Chinese
Telecom C	Operation Manager	41	M	3	Bachelor	Korean
	General Manager	48	M	4	Diploma	Chinese
Electronics A	Marketing Manager	43	M	3	Master	Korean
	HR Manager	45	M	4	Bachelor	Chinese
Electronics B	Finance Manager	46	M	5	Bachelor	Korean
	General Manager	41	M	4	Bachelor	Chinese
Auto A	Marketing Manager	41	M	4	Bachelor	Korean
	HR Manager	46	M	3	Bachelor	Chinese
Finance A	Finance Director	39	F	4	Bachelor	Korean
	HR Manager	45	M	3	Bachelor	Chinese
Telecom D	Operation Manager	38	M	2	Bachelor	Korean
	HR Manager	46	F	2	Bachelor	Chinese

Table 2.4: Examples of coding and statements.

Category	Coding	Statement
Approach	PT (Polycentric tendency)	'Three expatriates will go back to Korea because Chinese employees have mastered the technology' (General Manager, Electronics B).
Reason	Control	'We need someone from headquarters to ensure everything to be aligned with headquarters' direction' (HR Manager, Chemical A).
Recruitment	Procedure	'We attend university job fairs' (HR Manager, Electronics A).
Criteria	Expatriate selection	'The first criterion for selecting an expatriate is his expertise' (Chief Operating Officer, Telecom B).
Repatriation	Support	'We normally consider expatriates' spouse careers and children's education as a personal responsibility' (Finance Director, Finance A).

Table 2.5: Nationalities of managers in the case study companies in 2011.

Company	Middle Managers Korean/Chinese	Senior Managers Korean/Chinese	Expatriate Managers (%)
Telecom A	2/20	1/3	11.5
Chemical A	10/28	4/6	29
Telecom B	3/32	1/5	9.5
Advertising A	2/4	1/2	33.3
Telecom C	1/7	1/9	10.5
Electronics A	13/29	4/10	37
Electronics B	1/9	1/3	14
Auto A	3/21	1/8	12
Finance A	4/3	2/0	66.7
Telecom D	5/13	1/1	30

including Telecom A, Telecom B, Telecom C, Electronics B and Auto A adopted the polycentric staffing approach. Five companies including Chemical A, Advertising A, Electronics A, Finance A and Telecom D adopted a mixture of the ethnocentric approach and the polycentric approach.

The staffing approaches in the majority of the case companies changed over time and the number of expatriates dropped significantly. For example, Telecom A had 10 expatriates (six senior managers/four middle managers) when the company firstly entered China in 2002. In 2006, six expatriates remained in the company. When the research was being conducted, this company had only three expatriate, but 23 HCN middle and senior managers. Similarly in Telecom C, the company had 10 (five expatriate senior and four middle managers) in 2003. Expatriate managers dropped to eight in 2007 and two in 2011. The number of PCN managers rose from 7 to 16 during the same period. The number of expatriates also dropped significantly in Telecom B, Electronics B, Auto A, Chemical A, Advertising A, Electronics A and Telecom D.

2.3.2. Reasons for Using Expatriates

Trust and control have been repeatedly mentioned in interviews. This was exemplified by the fact that all the case companies appointed expatriates to fill the positions of Director of Finance. General Manager (Chinese) at Telecom A commented, 'Anything to do with money, the Koreans want to put their hands on'. The following statement indicates that sending expatriates to China was to ensure everything to be aligned with corporate strategies:

> The headquarters sends lots of instructions over. Of course, they'd better have their own people here to see how things are done. Is it a trust issue? I am not saying that Koreans do not trust Chinese. However, as long as there is someone from Korea, the headquarters can have its mind set at ease? (HR Manager (Chinese) of Chemical A).

Communication was mentioned frequently as a reason. In the words of General Manager (Chinese) at Telecom B:

> Although some HCN managers speak little English and they can manage to communicate in English with Koreans, the headquarters feels more comfortable to speak Korean and think it is a way to avoid misunderstanding. So we leave expatriate managers to talk to the headquarters.

Marketing Managers (Korean) at Advertising A and Electronics A and Operation Manager (Korean) at Telecom D reported that expatriates possessed some technical skills that HCNs did not have. Most Chinese interviewees did not agree that all the technologies and knowledge their firms employed were 'cutting edge', but agreed that 'the way Koreans doing things is different from the Chinese'. Other commonly reported reasons for using expatriates included 'easy to expatriate due to short flight (about an hour)', 'representing the headquarters', and 'Koreans' willingness to work in China'. Cultural similarity and Koreans' willingness to work in China were also regarded as contributors to low premature return rates among Korean expatriates. Only Auto A reported two cases of expatriate premature return resulting from work conflicts with HCNs.

The major reason for the transition from the ethnocentric to the polycentric approach was that the need for expatriates diminished over time. The communication problems caused by language barriers were effectively sorted out by recruiting or promoting ethnic Korean Chinese. Ethnic Korean Chinese had a number of advantages compared to expatriates in that they speak Korean, are from a Korean cultural background and understand the Chinese culture. It was commonly asserted that Chinese operations are very close to Korea. Sending someone over on a short-term mission to solve problems was popular in the case companies. Expatriates' roles in control and knowledge transfer also decreased over time. The following remark typifies how these changes occurred and consequently how these changes impacted on international staffing approaches in Korean MNEs:

> Trust between the subsidiary and the headquarters has been developed over time. Once there is mutual understanding there is trust. When senior managers in the subsidiary understand and follow instructions control then will not become the headquarters' a major concern. Knowledge transfer was relatively intensive at the beginning and becomes intermittent once operations stabilise. In the late stage knowledge transfer can be achieved through training or sending short-term expatriates. This is my understanding why we have reduced the use of long-term expatriates. (Finance Manager of Electronics B)

2.3.3. Recruitment Procedures and Selection Criteria

The most common recruitment channels for HCNs included recruiting websites, company online recruitment, job centres, head-hunter agents and university job fairs. Using head hunters was regarded by managers from Telecom A, Telecom B and Auto A as the most effective way to recruit 'high-calibre' employees. A common statement that emerged was on the lines of: 'Once head-hunters know what kind of people we are looking for and they know where to find them. They make our recruitment job much easier' (Marketing Manager (Korean) at Auto A). All interviewees reported that they recruited HCNs, especially for lower positions through the internet extensively. Typically, General Manager (Chinese) in Electronics B said:

> We publish recruitment information mainly on public recruiting websites, for example, 51job. com, zhaopin.com. The main reasons we use these websites are that we want more applicants to access our recruiting information. The traditional recruitment channels, such as newspapers, are expensive. Nowadays, you cannot expect young graduates to read newspapers very often.

Korean MNEs were also generally interested in recruiting fresh Chinese university graduates. Typically, General Manager (Chinese) in Electronics A mentioned: 'We conduct presentations at prestigious universities to attract top graduates. I think these activities are really good opportunities for our company to be known to graduates. We have recruited a number of top graduates through this method'. Chief Operating Officer (Korean) at Telecom B commented: 'We believe that businesses have the social responsibility to recruit employees from universities. This would encourage students to go to university and study hard at university. We do so in Korea and we do the same here'.

All the case companies followed similar recruiting procedures in recruiting HCNs, as described by General Manager (Chinese) in Telecom B:

> After HR Team has screened CVs and supporting documents, qualified applicants will be required to take a language test (Korean/English for managerial positions), EQ/IQ test and

psychological test. Applicants who pass written tests will then go through interviews. In our company, we have two rounds of interviews. The first interview will be conducted by the Operation Director to assess applicants' professional knowledge and potentials. The second interview focuses on personality, which is conducted by the HR manager and relevant line managers. I would say procedures are rather rigorous.

All HCNs signed labour contracts with Korean MNEs and contract durations ranged from one to five years depending on positions. Expatriates are normally assigned rather than openly recruited. The following statement was generally supported by the interviewees:

> Generally, management will decide who will be chosen for expatriation. We don't openly advertise for expatriate positions because we think it unnecessary. We consider a number of factors to see whether the person is suitable or have the potential to work effectively in China. Employees can decline the appointment, but, in our company, most employees are willing to accept assignments in China. (Marketing Manager (Korean) in Electronics A)

Once an employee was chosen for an international assignment, the person was normally asked to get ready and leave fairly quickly. This is indicated in the statement, 'I got the expatriation notice only 2 weeks before I was asked to leave. It was very sudden to me. I wish I had more time to sort out family issues' (Operation Manager (Korean) in Telecom C). The period of working in an expatriate scenario generally lasted between three to five years. Korean MNEs also recruited Korean students who studied and Koreans who worked in China. Chemical A recruited two Koreans who were employed in China and Auto A, Chemical A, Finance A, Telecom A, B, and D all recruited a number of Korean students who studied in China. According to one statement, 'They are hired because they have lived in China for many years, speak Chinese fluently, understand the Chinese culture well, and have qualifications in particular areas'. Using this method, these Koreans were recruited normally to fill technical and low managerial positions.

All case companies had written selection criteria and job descriptions for recruiting HCNs. Criteria included education, technical certificate, age, and *hukou* (household registration status) for non-managerial employees. HR Manager in Electronics A, General Manager in Electronics B and HR Manager in Auto A explained that local governments required them to give priority to local residents in order to help solve local employment problems. For managerial positions, language (Korean or English) fluency, working experience and social network appeared to be more important, as indicated in the comments of HR Manager (Chinese) in Finance A: 'We prefer Chinese managers who have years of experience working in Western MNEs. These people normally have established good relationships with locals'.

Selection criteria for expatriates were similar across all case companies, and mainly included expertise, job performance, communication skill, age and personality. According to one comment:

> Expatriates are selected based on job performance. To be an expatriate, you must be an expert in your field, and have outstanding performance record. Working experience will help you

come up with new ideas to solve problems in a new environment. (Chief Operating Officer (Korean) at Telecom B)

Chief Operating Officer at Telecom B had worked in the company for ten years before being assigned to China. His department won 'the Best Sales and Operation' award for three consecutive years. Other Korean managers all had similar successful stories. With regard to communication, a typical statement was made by Marketing Manager (Korean) at Auto A:

> Communication is not only about the language ability, but also the way you communicate with HCNs, which is something to do with cultural empathy. In Korea, subordinates must follow whatever the orders managers give. Here in this country, if an expatriate manager does not build up *guanxi* with Chinese subordinates they will not cooperate. Consequently, there will be no harmony and the expatriate's performance as well as the whole department's performance would be affected.

It was popularly commented that personality and age were considered seriously in expatriate selection. For instance, Marketing Manager at Electronics A (Korean) said:

> Personality may be often ignored by some companies, but not the case in our company. The headquarters prefer someone who is extrovert and easy-going which is regarded as helpful in establishing interpersonal relationships. The age limit for expatriates in my company is 45.

Some other companies, such as Telecom A, B and Finance A set the age limit at 55. The interviewees generally agreed that their firms were effective in recruiting and selecting expatriates, as evidenced by low expatriate failure rates among expatriates assigned to China. Although there was no gender restriction on expatriation coincidently all expatriates in Chinese operations were males.

2.3.4. Repatriation

All the interviewees reported that their firms provided sufficient repatriation assistance in relation to relocation and organising farewell functions. Normally, the HR department coordinated all relocation issues. A typical remark was that the 'company wants to make sure that repatriation is as smooth as possible to expatriates'. When asked whether the company helped repatriates in handling reverse culture shock, almost all interviewees said that they did not realise there was a reverse culture shock problem given that the two national cultures are similar. However, expatriates were normally given a certain period of time off at the end of expatriation to deal with personal and family issues. Having time off ranged from two weeks to two months, for example, 'In the last month we do not expect them to come to work. They can either take their families for a tour or deal with family or job issues back in Korea'. Most expatriates did not bring spouses and children with them, and therefore did not need to worry about family issues upon repatriation. Korean MNEs helped expatriates with family issues in China, for instance paying tuition fees for children to study in international schools.

Career-wise, most interviewees thought that organisational policies were vague. Chinese managers were not aware of whether there was a career plan for expatriates. Expatriates revealed that there was in general no career planning for them and this concern is reflected in the following two statements:

> There is no career planning for me. My company did not make any promises about my future position. Even now I will complete this assignment in half a year and I have no idea what kind of position I will get back home. The only words I heard were like 'you should not have a problem to be promoted' or 'it really depends'. But, I am not worried about my future job. At least, I will get the same position as I had before. (Operation Manager (Korean) at Telecom C)

> In my opinion, the future promotion is not only dependent on the overseas experience. The promotion in my company normally takes four years from one position to a higher one. In addition, there are too many complicated factors, for example, position availability, relationship with the big boss. So, no one can guarantee promotion for me at this stage. (Operation Manager (Korean) at Telecom D).

However, all Korean managers agreed that although overseas performance was not the only factor for promotion, it is essential for future career development. A commonly held fear was the possibility of failure and what it implied: 'Basically speaking, if I did anything wrong here I am finished'. There was a strong sentiment among expatriates that they were open to joining another company or running their own businesses once their Chinese assignments were completed. Such a sentiment was indicated in the words of Finance Manager (Korean) in Electronics B: 'You will be extremely embarrassed if your colleagues who were your subordinators have become your boss when you are back in Korea.' According to Finance Manager (Korean) in Electronics B, four expatriates in his company went back to Korea between 2007 and 2011, and only two remained at headquarters. Most of them started their own businesses or joined another company. The turnover rates of repatriates who were assigned in China are shown in Table 2.6.

2.4. Discussion

The purpose of this study was to ascertain the characteristics of the international recruitment and selection policies and practices of Korean MNEs in China. Generally speaking, Korean MNEs in China tended to be polycentric in international staffing although some case companies adopted a mixed approach of being ethnocentric and polycentric. This finding is very contrary to the findings reported in previous studies, including Paik and Sohn (1998), Kang and Shen (2010), Taylor, Cho, and Hyun (2001) and Yang and Kelly (2009), where it was argued that Korean MNEs normally adopt the ethnocentric staffing approach.

The major reasons for using expatriates were control, communication and technology and knowledge transfer. These reasons are consistent with the prevailing international staffing literature (cf. Dowling et al., 2008; Edström & Galbraith, 1977;

Table 2.6: Expatriate turnover rate from 2007 to 2011.

Company	No. of Current Expatriates in China	No. of Repatriates	No. of Repatriates Who Left the Company	Turnover Rate
Telecom A	5	4	1	20%
Chemical A	37	5	2	5%
Telecom B	33	8	4	12%
Advertising A	4	2	0	0
Telecom C	6	4	1	17%
Electronics A	45	11	4	9%
Electronics B	6	4	2	33%
Auto A	5	3	1	20%
Finance A	3	1	0	0
Telecom D	3	2	1	33%

Source: Company documents from headquarters.

Shen, 2006). There are two critical reasons why Korean MNEs use HCNs in China. Firstly, there is a large Korean Chinese population in China and it is sensible and cost-effective to hire Korean Chinese who understand both Korean and Chinese cultures and languages. Second, China is geographically close to Korea, making it convenient to send assignees over on short-term contracts to solve problems or convey messages from the headquarters when such a need arises. This finding supports the literature, for example Schuler, Dowling, and De Cieri (1993), where it is argued that skills availability, labour costs and cultural similarity are major factors for using HCN managers. The current study also lends some support to Collings, Scullion, and Morley (2007), Mayerhofer, Hartmann, Michelitsch-Riedl, and Kollinger (2004), and Shen and Lang (2009) who contend that there is a trend for MNEs to use more short-term assignees — so-called 'flexpatriates' (Mayerhofer et al., 2004) because they are more cost-effective and experience no repatriation problems. Management development, which has been regarded as a common reason for using expatriates in Western MNEs (Adler & Bartholomew, 1992) is not considered very important by Korean MNEs. This is a significant limitation in Korean MNE's staffing practices and to a certain degree it may result in international assignments becoming a form of career hindrance for expatriates (Dickmann, Doherty, Mills, & Brewster, 2008; Suutari & Mäkelä, 2007).

Korean MNEs adopted the 'one-way' selection approach in recruiting expatriates with which potential expatriates were approached by managers and offered international assignments. This practice is different from the open recruitment method that has been widely practised in Western firms (Dowling et al., 2008). This practice has a range of disadvantages, the most important being that employees who are not suitable for international assignments may be reluctant to turn down an offer as they are worried that such a refusal may have a negative impact on their future careers. Plus, Korean MNEs normally did not allow sufficient time for employees to prepare for expatriation and did not consider family situations when recruiting and selecting expatriates. These limitations may have a significant impact on Korean expatriate performance in international assignments despite the overall expatriate premature return rates being low.

The major criteria for Korean MNEs selecting expatriates were job expertise, job performance, communication skills, cultural empathy and personality; which are commonly used by other Western and emerging MNEs (cf. Dowling et al., 2008; Kim & Slocum, 2008; Shen & Edwards, 2004). However, previous overseas experience is considered important in expatriate selection by MNEs in general (Dowling et al., 2008; Shen & Lang, 2009), but not by the case study Korean MNEs. The Korean criteria for selecting HCNs focused on education, age, and technical qualifications rather than political outlook and moral attitudes. It is in this context that the policies of Korean MNEs, other foreign MNEs in China and local Chinese enterprises converge (Braun & Warner, 2002; Li, 2003; Shen, 2010).

Korean MNEs focused on helping repatriates with relocation and transition but paid inadequate attention to repatriates' career development, readjustment and personal and family issues. This practice is similar to the approach of their Australian and Chinese counterparts when managing repatriation (Newton et al., 2007; Shen & Edwards, 2004), but different from that of European MNEs (Lazarova & Caligiuri, 2001). It is recognised that a lack of emphasis on career development, readjustment and personal and family issues in repatriation is more likely to contribute to high repatriate turnover (Lazarova & Caligiuri, 2001; Shen & Edwards, 2004). This study provides evidence that there are high turnover rates of Korean repatriates from MNEs operating in China.

2.4.1. Limitations and Future Study Directions

This study has a number of limitations which may undermine the generalisability of its research findings. First, the data were collected mainly from subsidiaries. Due to the possible incongruence regarding goals between subsidiaries and headquarters (Dowling et al., 2008), the perceived staffing practices of subsidiary managers may differ from that of their company's headquarters. Moreover, China is the only host country mentioned in this study. Due to the fact that IHRM policies and practices are greatly influenced by host-contextual factors (Schuler et al., 1993), the findings presented here may not represent Korean MNEs' staffing practices globally. For example, Kim and Slocum (2008) found that English fluency is a key criterion in selecting expatriates to work in the United States. However, this criterion may be not important for Chinese operations. Also, prior overseas experience is not considered important when selecting Korean expatriates in China due to cultural similarity and close geographical distance. Hence, we suggest that future studies collect data from both subsidiaries and headquarters and from multiple host countries in order to understand MNEs' global staffing practices. Moreover, the data were collected only from middle and senior managers whose perceptions of IHRM practices may differ substantially from non-managerial employees. We suggest that future studies should include non-managerial expatriates and HCNs.

2.4.2. Practical Implications

International staffing plays a key role in innovation, organisational learning, corporate integration and management development in MNEs, and therefore affects organisational performance and long-term sustainability (Collings et al., 2009). The findings of this study have significant implications for Korean as well as other MNEs. First, MNEs need to consider employees' willingness to take up international assignments and family issues in expatriate recruitment and selection. The 'two-way selection approach' would enable MNEs to recruit qualified and willing expatriates. Second, previous overseas experience should be considered as an important expatriate selection criterion as it is a key factor determining expatriate success (Dowling et al., 2008; Harvey & Buckley, 1998; Tung, 1984). Third, MNEs should pay more attention to repatriation management, especially with regard to career development. Korean MNEs should take the advice offered by Lazarova and Cerdin (2007), who argued that it is to everyone's benefit to sign a repatriate agreement with the expatriate candidate to guarantee a suitable position upon his/her return, and provide realistic job previews for expatriates before they come home (Feldman & Thomas, 1992). This practice will negate disappointment and unrealistic expectations. MNEs also need to develop a more strategic repatriation approach to retain the key talents while potential candidates could be also motivated to take international assignments (Farndale et al., 2010). They could improve repatriation adjustment by offering some developmental support, such as mentorship, coaching to assignees and their families during expatriation and repatriation (Shen & Hall, 2009).

2.5. Conclusions

A recent literature review (Kang & Shen, 2010) reveals that there is a lack of research on how Korean MNEs manage HR in their overseas operations. The current research fills this important literature gap and therefore contributes to the IHRM literature. The international recruitment and selection policies and practices that Korean MNEs employ in China can be characterised as polycentric in international staffing, 'one-way selection', localised HCN recruitment and selection, and a lack of emphasis on cultural adjustment and career development in expatriation and repatriation management. These characteristics can to a great extent be explained by existing IHRM models (e.g. Schuler et al., 1993), which argue that IHRM practices are influenced by host-contextual and firm-specific factors. Nevertheless, there are a number of limitations in Korean MNEs' international staffing practices and this study provides some advice for practical improvement.

References

Adler, N. J., & Bartholomew, S. (1992). Managing globally competent people. *The Executive*, *6*(3), 52–65.
Anderson, B. A. (2005). Expatriate selection: good management or good luck? *The International Journal of Human Resource Management*, *16*(4), 567–583.
Ando, N. (2011). Isomorphism and foreign subsidiary staffing policies. *Cross Cultural Management: An International Journal*, *18*(2), 131–143.
Braun, W., & Warner, M. (2002). Strategic human resource management in western multinationals in China. *Personnel Review*, *31*(5), 553–579.
Bruning, N. S., Bebenroth, R., & Pascha, W. (2011). Valuing Japan-based German expatriate and local manager's functions: Do subsidiary age and managerial perspectives matter? *The International Journal of Human Resource Management*, *22*(4), 778–806.
Caligiuri, P. M. (2000). Selecting expatriates for personality characteristics: A moderating effect of personality on the relationship between host national contact and cross-cultural adjustment. *Management International Review*, *40*(1), 61–80.
Caligiuri, P. M., & Colakoglu, S. (2007). A strategic contingency approach to expatriate assignment management. *Human Resource Management Journal*, *17*(4), 393–410.
Cerdin, J. L., & Brewster, C. (2014). Talent management and expatriation: Bridging two streams of research and practice. *Journal of World Business*, *49*(2), 245–252.
Chen, H. A. (2006). *Recruitment and selection in China: An application to the case of Lenovo*. Malaysia: School of Management, University of Nottingham.
Cheng, H. L., & Lin, C. Y. Y. (2009). Do as the large enterprises do? Expatriate selection and overseas performance in emerging markets: The case of Taiwan SMEs. *International Business Review*, *18*(1), 60–75.
Colakoglu, S., & Caligiuri, P. (2008). Cultural distance, expatriate staffing and subsidiary performance: The case of US subsidiaries of multinational corporations. *The International Journal of Human Resource Management*, *19*(2), 223–239.
Colakoglu, S., Tarique, I., & Caligiuri, P. (2009). Towards a conceptual framework for the relationship between subsidiary staffing strategy and subsidiary performance. *The International Journal of Human Resource Management*, *20*(6), 1291–1308.
Collings, D. G. (2014). Integrating global mobility and global talent management: Exploring the challenges and strategic opportunities. *Journal of World Business*, *49*(2), 253–261.
Collings, D. G., & Mellahi, K. (2009). Strategic talent management: A review and research agenda. *Human Resource Management Review*, *19*(4), 304–313.
Collings, D. G., Scullion, H., & Dowling, P. J. (2009). Global staffing: A review and thematic research agenda. *The International Journal of Human Resource Management*, *20*(6), 1253–1272.
Collings, D. G., Scullion, H., & Morley, M. J. (2007). Changing patterns of global staffing in the multinational enterprise: Challenges to the conventional expatriate assignment and emerging alternatives. *Journal of World Business*, *42*(2), 198–213.

Cooke, F. L. (2005). *HRM, work and employment in China*. Oxon: Routledge.

Culpan, O., & Wright, G. H. (2002). Women abroad: Getting the best results from women managers. *The International Journal of Human Resource Management*, *13*(5), 784–801.

Dickmann, M., Doherty, N., Mills, T., & Brewster, C. (2008). Why do they go? Individual and corporate perspectives on the factors influencing the decision to accept an international assignment. *The International Journal of Human Resource Management*, *19*(4), 731–751.

Dörrenbächer, C., & Geppert, M. (2010). Subsidiary staffing and initiative-taking in multinational corporations: A socio-political perspective. *Personnel Review*, *39*(5), 600–621.

Dowling, P. J., Festing, M., & Engle, A. (2008). *International human resource management*. (5th ed.). Hampshire, UK: Cengage Learning.

Edström, A., & Galbraith, J. R. (1977). Transfer of managers as a coordination and control strategy in multinational organizations. *Administrative Science Quarterly*, *22*(2), 248–263.

Export-Import Bank of Korea. (2016). *Foreign investment statistics by country*. Retrieved from http://211.171.208.92/odisas_eng.html. Accessed on February 25, 2016.

Farndale, E., Scullion, H., & Sparrow, P. (2010). The role of the corporate HR function in global talent management. *Journal of World Business*, *45*(2), 161–168.

Feldman, D. C., & Thomas, D. C. (1992). Career management issues facing expatriates. *Journal of International Business Studies*, *23*(2), 271–293.

Forster, N. (2000). Expatriates and the impact of cross cultural training. *Human Resource Management Journal*, *10*(3), 63–78.

Fortune. (2010). *Fortune 500*. Retrieved from http://money.cnn.com/magazines/fortune/fortune500/2010/full_list/. Accessed on June 15, 2010.

Furuya, N., Stevens, M. J., Bird, A., Oddou, G., & Mendenhall, M. (2008). Managing the learning and transfer of global management competence: Antecedents and outcomes of Japanese repatriation effectiveness. *Journal of International Business Studies*, *40*(2), 200–215.

Gong, Y. (2003). Toward a dynamic process model of staffing composition and subsidiary outcomes in multinational enterprises. *Journal of Management*, *29*(2), 259–280.

Harrison, D. A., & Shaffer, M. A. (2005). Mapping the criterion space for expatriate success: Task-and relationship-based performance, effort and adaptation. *The International Journal of Human Resource Management*, *16*(8), 1454–1474.

Harvey, M. G., & Buckley, M. R. (1998). The process for developing an international program for dual-career couples. *Human Resource Management Review*, *8*(1), 99–123.

Hu, F., & Leung, C. M. (2010). *Top management turnover, firm performance and government control: Evidence from China's listed state-owned enterprises*. Retrieved from http://www.business.illinois.edu/accountancy/research/vkzcenter/conferences/taiwan/papers/Hu_Leung.pdf

Kang, H. Y., & Shen, J. (2010). International human resource management policies and practices of South Korean MNEs: A review of the literature. *Asia Pacific Business Review*, *20*(1), 42–58.

Kim, C. S. (1992). *The culture of Korean industry: An ethnography of Poongsan corporation*. Tucson, AZ: The University of Arizona Press.

Kim, K. H., & Slocum, J. W. (2008). Individual differences and expatriate assignment effectiveness: The case of US-based Korean expatriates. *Journal of World Business*, *43*(1), 109–126.

Kim, L. (1997). The dynamics of Samsung's technological learning in semiconductors. *California Management Review*, *39*(3), 86–100.

Kim, S., & Briscoe, D. R. (1997). Globalization and a new human resource policy in Korea: Transformation to a performance-based HRM. *Employee Relations, 19*(4), 298–308.

Kim, Y., & Gao, F. Y. (2010). An empirical study of human resource management practices in family firms in China. *The International Journal of Human Resource Management, 21*(12), 2095–2119.

Koch, M., Nam, S. H., & Steers, R. M. (1995). Human resource management in South Korea. In L. F. Moore & P. D. Jennings (Eds.), *Human resource management on the Pacific Rim* (pp. 217–242). New York, NY: De Gmyter.

Kühlmann, T., & Hutchings, K. (2010). Expatriate assignments vs localization of management in China: Staffing choices of Australian and German companies. *Career Development International, 15*(1), 20–38.

Kulkarni, M., Lengnick-Hall, M. L., & Valk, R. (2010). Employee perceptions of repatriation in an emerging economy: The Indian experience. *Human Resource Management, 49*(3), 531–548.

Kwon, O. Y., & Oh, I. (2001). *Korean direct investment in Australia: Issues and prospects.* Brisbane: Australia Centre for Korean Studies, Griffith University.

Lasserre, P., & Ching, P. S. (1997). Human resources management in China and the localization challenge. *Journal of Asian Business, 13*(4), 85–99.

Lazarova, M. B., & Caligiuri, P. (2001). Retaining repatriates: The role of organizational support practices. *Journal of World Business, 36*(4), 389–401.

Lazarova, M. B., & Cerdin, J. L. (2007). Revisiting repatriation concerns: Organizational support versus career and contextual influences. *Journal of International Business Studies, 38*(3), 404–429.

Lee, H. C. (1998). Transformation of employment practices in Korean businesses. *International Studies of Management & Organization, 28*(4), 26–39.

Lee, C. W. (2003). Changing labor relations and human resources management of Korean Businesses in China and future challenges. *e-labor News,* No. 21 (July).

Lee, H. (2010). The destination of outward FDI and the performance of South Korean multinationals. *Emerging Markets Finance and Trade, 46*(3), 59–66.

Lee, S. H. (1998). Organizational flexibility in Korean companies: Rules and procedures on managerial discretion and employee behaviour. *The International Journal of Human Resource Management, 9*(3), 478–493.

Lee, Y. I. (2004). South Korean companies in transition: An evolving strategic management style. *Strategic Change, 13*(1), 29–35.

Li, J. (2003). Strategic human resource management and MNEs' performance in China. *International Journal of Human Resource Management, 14*(2), 157–173.

Mayerhofer, H., Hartmann, L. C., Michelitsch-Riedl, G., & Kollinger, I. (2004). Flexpatriate assignments: a neglected issue in global staffing. *The International Journal of Human Resource Management, 15*(8), 1371–1389.

Mol, S. T., Born, M. P., & van der Molen, H. T. (2005). Developing criteria for expatriate effectiveness: Time to jump off the adjustment bandwagon. *International Journal of Intercultural Relations, 29*(3), 339–353.

Myers, M. C., & Woerkom, M. V. (2014). The influence of underlying philosophies on talent management: Theory, implications for practice, and research agenda. *Journal of World Business, 49,* 192–203.

Newton, S., Hutchings, K., & Kabanoff, B. (2007). Repatriation in Australian organisations: Effects of function and value of international assignment on program scope. *Asia Pacific Journal of Human Resources, 45*(3), 295–313.

Nigam, R., & Su, Z. (2010). Climbing up the performance ladder: A conceptual framework for emerging country multinationals. *International Journal of Business and Management, 5*(4), 13–25.

OECD. (2013). *FDI in figures*. Retrieved from www.oecd.org/investment/statistics.htm. Accessed on July 21, 2013.

Paik, Y. S., & Sohn, J. H. D. (1998). Confucius in Mexico: Korean MNEs and the maquiladoras. *Business Horizons, 41*(6), 25–33.

Park, W. S., & Yu, G. C. (2000). *Transformation and new patterns of HRM in Korea*. Michigan: Citeseer.

Pattie, M., White, M. M., & Tansky, J. (2010). The homecoming: A review of support practices for repatriates. *Career Development International, 15*(4), 359–377.

Perlmutter, H. V. (1969). The tortuous evolution of the multinational corporation. *Columbia Journal of World Business, 4*(1), 9–18.

Perlmutter, H. V., & Heenan, D. A. (1974). How multinational should your top managers be? *Harvard Business Review, 52*(6), 121–132.

Perlmutter, H. V., & Heenan, D. A. (1979). *Multinational organizational development*. Reading, MA: Addison-Wesley.

Pucik, V., & Lim, J. C. (2001). Transforming human resource management in a Korean Chaebol: A case study of Samsung. *Asia Pacific Business Review, 7*(4), 137–160.

Reiche, S., & Harzing, A. W. (2009). International assignments. In A. W. K. Harzing & A. Pinnington (Eds.), *International human resource management*. London: Sage.

Sanchez Vidal, E. M., Sanz Valle, R., Barba Aragon, I. M., & Brewster, C. (2007). Repatriation adjustment process of business employees: Evidence from Spanish workers. *International Journal of Intercultural Relations, 31*(3), 317–337.

Schuler, R. S., Dowling, P. J., & De Cieri, H. (1993). An integrative framework of strategic international human resource management. *Journal of Management, 19*(2), 419–459.

Scullion, H., & Collings, D. G. (2006). *Global staffing*. London: Routledge.

SERI. (2008). *Study on Korean and Taiwanese investment patterns in China*. Retrieved from http://www.seriworld.org/04/wldBookV.html?mn=E&natcd=&mncd=0301&key=2008080 8000001&pPage=1&listopt=FL. Accessed on May 05, 2010.

Shen, J. (2005). Effective international performance appraisals: Easily said, hard to do. *Compensation & Benefits Review, 37*(4), 70–79.

Shen, J. (2006). Factors affecting international staffing in Chinese MNEs'. *International Journal of Human Resource Management, 17*(2), 295–315.

Shen, J. (2010). 'Employees' satisfaction with HRM in Chinese privately-owned enterprises. *Asia Pacific Business Review, 16*(3), 339–354.

Shen, J., & Edwards, V. (2004). Recruitment and selection in Chinese MNEs. *The International Journal of Human Resource Management, 15*(4), 814–835.

Shen, J., & Lang, B. (2009). Cross-cultural training and its impact on expatriate performance in Australian MNEs. *Human Resource Development International, 12*(4), 371–386.

Shen, Y., & Hall, D. T. T. (2009). When expatriates explore other options: Retaining talent through greater job embeddedness and repatriation adjustment. *Human Resource Management, 48*(5), 793–816.

Stroh, L. K., & Caligiuri, P. M. (1998). Increasing global competitiveness through effective people management. *Journal of World Business, 33*(1), 1–16.

Suutari, V., & Mäkelä, K. (2007). The career capital of managers with global careers. *Journal of Managerial Psychology, 22*(7), 628–648.

Tarique, I., & Schuler, R. S. (2010). Global talent management: Literature review, integrative framework, and suggestions for future research. *Journal of World Business, 45*(2), 122–133.

Taylor, R., Cho, D. Y., & Hyun, J. H. (2001). Korean companies in China: Strategies in the localisation of management. In C. Rowley, T. W. Sohn, & J. Bae (Eds.), *Managing Korean business: Organisation, culture, human resources and change* (pp. 161–181). London: Frank Cass.

Templer, K. J. (2010). Personal attributes of expatriate managers, subordinate ethnocentrism, and expatriate success: A host-country perspective. *The International Journal of Human Resource Management, 21*(10), 1754–1768.

Tharenou, P., & Caulfield, N. (2010). Will I stay or will I go? Explaining repatriation by self-initiated expatriates. *The Academy of Management Journal, 53*(5), 1009–1028.

Tsang, E. W. K. (2001). Adjustment of mainland Chinese academics and students to Singapore. *International Journal of Intercultural Relations, 25*(4), 347–372.

Tung, R. L. (1981). Selecting and training of personnel for overseas assignments. *Colombia Journal of World Business, 16*(2), 67–78.

Tung, R. L. (1984). Strategic management of human resources in the multinational enterprise. *Human Resource Management, 23*(2), 120–143.

Tungli, Z., & Peiperl, M. (2009). Expatriate practices in German, Japanese, UK, and US multi-national companies: A comparative survey of changes. *Human Resource Management, 48*(1), 153–171.

Van den Born, F., & Peltokorpi, V. (2010). Language policies and communication in multinational companies. *Journal of Business Communication, 47*(2), 97–118.

Vo, A. N. (2009). Career development for host country nationals: A case of American and Japanese multinational companies in Vietnam. *The International Journal of Human Resource Management, 20*(6), 1402–1420.

Warner, M. (2010). In search of Confucian HRM: Theory and practice in Greater China and beyond. *The International Journal of Human Resource Management, 21*(12), 2053–2078.

Yan, A., Zhu, G., & Hall, D. T. (2002). International assignments for career building: A model of agency relationships and psychological contracts. *Academy of Management Review, 27*(3), 373–391.

Yang, I., & Kelly, A. (2009). Assumptions in Korean organizations and their implications in a cross-cultural setting. *Advances in Global Leadership, 5*, 297–320.

Yang, X., Lim, Y., Sakurai, Y., & Seo, S. (2009). Internationalization of Chinese and Korean firms. *Thunderbird International Business Review, 51*(1), 37–51.

Yu, G. C., & Rowley, C. (2009). The changing face of Korean human resource management. In C. Rowley & Y. S. Paik (Eds.), *The changing face of Korean management* (pp. 29–51). London: Routledge.

Chapter 3

How do Assigned and Self-Initiated Expatriate CEOs Differ? An Empirical Investigation on CEO Demography, Personality, and Performance in China

Jan Selmer, Jakob Lauring, Ling Eleanor Zhang and Charlotte Jonasson

Abstract

Purpose — In this chapter, we focus on expatriate CEOs who are assigned by the parent company to work in a subsidiary and compare them to those who themselves have initiated to work abroad as CEOs. Since we do not know much about these individuals, we direct our attention to: (1) who they are (demographics), (2) what they are like (personality), and (3) how they perform (job performance).

Methodology/approach — Data was sought from 93 assigned expatriate CEOs and 94 self-initiated expatriate CEOs in China.

Findings — Our findings demonstrate that in terms of demography, self-initiated CEOs were more experienced than assigned CEOs. With regard to personality, we found difference in self-control and dispositional anger: Assigned expatriate CEOs had more self-control and less angry temperament than their self-initiated counterparts. Finally, we found assigned expatriate CEOs to rate their job performance higher than self-initiated CEOs.

Originality/value — Although there may not always be immediate benefits, career consideration often plays a role when individuals choose whether to

Global Talent Management and Staffing in Mnes
International Business & Management, Volume 32, 49–79
Copyright © 2016 by Emerald Group Publishing Limited
All rights of reproduction in any form reserved
ISSN: 1876-066X/doi:10.1108/S1876-066X20160000032002

become an expatriate. For many years, organizations have used expatriation to develop talented managers for high-level positions in the home country. Recently, however, a new trend has emerged. Talented top managers are no longer expatriated only from within parent companies to subsidiaries. Self-initiated expatriates with no prior affiliation in the parent company are increasingly used to fill top management positions in subsidiaries.

Keywords: Expatriates; self-initiated; personality; CEOs; top managers; adjustment

3.1. Introduction

The fast internationalization of the business environment has resulted in a need to manage global operations as well as expatriate staff worldwide in an effective way. This has contributed to an increased focus in academic research on expatriates and their international assignments. One area, however, that has received less attention is the expatriate top managers (Sekiguchi, Bebenroth, & Li, 2011). This is an important research gap because the management of foreign subsidiaries is a prime concern for multinational corporations (MNCs) operating in an increasingly globalized world (Birkinshaw & Hood, 1998). As CEOs are central actors in managing the subsidiary, they must be able to overcome cultural and linguistic barriers for leading the top management team (Tseng & Liao, 2009), identifying local opportunities (Almeida & Phene, 2004), sensing changes (Stanek, 2000), and aligning the subsidiary's activities with those of the parent company (Gong, 2003; Luo, 2002). Developing and selecting talented CEOs is also an important element of global talent management. Talents, especially talented top managers, can serve as a source of competitive advantage for MNCs. Top managers of MNC subsidiaries have, for example, the power and obligation to some extent to influence important decision-making at headquarters and its implementation at subsidiaries (Mellahi & Collings, 2010). Hence, expatriate CEOs are important actors in MNCs thus worth further research attention.

In domestic research, a number of studies have argued that since CEOs can be perceived as an organization's principle strategic decision maker (Calori, Johnson, & Sarnin, 1994; Carpenter, Geletkanycz, & Sanders, 2004), the personal characteristics of that person are particularly important for the whole organization (Nadkarni & Herrmann, 2010; Peterson, Smith, Martorana, & Owens, 2003). Individual attributes, such as personality and cognitive abilities, have been found to determine how intensely CEOs search for information, how much information they scan, how they learn about external environmental and internal organizational events or trends, and which sources they rely on to obtain and disseminate information (Hambrick, 1982; Miller & Toulouse, 1986; Nadkarni & Herrmann, 2010). Hence, the specific individual character of an expatriate CEO is likely to vary, and thus their ability to influence their surroundings may vary with them. In this paper, we are particularly interested in the differences between assigned expatriate CEOs and self-initiated expatriate CEOs.

International assignments serve as a crucial tool to develop managers in terms of global awareness and well-honed international skills, and prepare them as future global leaders for MNCs (Kobrin, 1988; Shay & Baack, 2004; Takeuchi, Marinova, Lepak, & Liu, 2005). Studies suggest that CEOs who have expatriation experience tend to be more effective at managing and leading MNCs than CEOs who do not have international experience (Carpenter & Fredrickson, 2001; Daily, Certo, & Dalton, 2000; Roth, 1995). Extended expatriation experience is found to be essential for managers who want to make it to the very top of a MNC (Martin, 2004). Some recent studies have also proposed a complex link between expatriation experience and career success (for a review see Bolino, 2007). Expatriate CEOs who excel during expatriation, successfully learn about critical oversea markets, and who develop strong cross-cultural leadership skills are likely to improve their career prospects by their expatriation experience (Suutari, 2003). However, surveys with human resource professionals sometimes yield different results. For example, in a study conducted by Stroh, Black, Mendenhall, and Gregersen (2005), the majority of managers with expatriation experience did not believe that their international assignments had helped their career development while most human resource executives believed that expatriation experience had a positive career impact. Therefore, we still need more focused studies exploring how expatriation experience may have an impact on managers' careers (Stahl, Miller, & Tung, 2002). Furthermore, there is a shortage of CEOs who have had expatriation experience. Although many firms often prefer to hire CEOs with international assignment experience, relatively few US MNCs are led by CEOs with an international background (Carpenter, Sanders, & Gregersen, 2001). Hence, it is important to provide more in-depth understanding of expatriate CEOs and uncover why these CEOs have chosen expatriation and how their international experience have helped them in entering into the upper echelon.

3.2. Assigned and Self-Initiated Expatriates

For several years, the expatriate adjustment literature has focused on expatriates as a homogenous group sent from a parent company. These individuals assigned by their parent companies to the foreign location have often been labeled assigned expatriates (AE) (Peltokorpi & Froese, 2009). However, recently, scholars have started to look also at different types of expatriates such as expatriate academics

(Lauring & Selmer, 2015; Selmer & Lauring, 2013b), expatriate NGOs, (Fee & Gray, 2012), foreign executives in local organizations (Arp, Hutchings, & Smith, 2013), public expatriates (Selmer & Fenner, 2009), inpatriates (Moeller, Harvey, & Williams, 2010; Reiche, 2006) and flexpatriates (Mayerhofer, Müller, & Schmidt, 2010). The greatest interest, however, has been directed toward the growing group of self-initiated expatriates (SIEs) who relocate on their own initiative without the support of a parent organization (Selmer & Lauring, 2010; Tharenou, 2013).

Although it is challenging to propose one definition capturing all SIE types, SIEs are clearly neither short-term travelers (sojourners) nor immigrants (Richardson, 2006). Their intensions are to stay and work in a foreign country for a number of years and then return to the homeland or move on to another country. As long as a foreign national worker has the intension to return or move on, they can be defined as SIEs and not immigrants (Selmer & Lauring, 2014b). Moreover, a SIE has been defined as any individual who is hired directly on contractual basis to work in a foreign country and not transferred overseas by parent organizations (Andresen, Bergdolt, & Margenfeld, 2012b; Lee, 2005). Also, SIEs take jobs in a foreign country, often with no planned time period, and with the legal employment decision made by a new work contract partner (Inkson & Myers, 2003; Tharenou, 2010). To summarize, what seems to distinguish SIEs in relation to AEs is the agency involved in taking the job (Al Ariss, 2013), the lack of connections to a foreign parent company (Tharenou, 2013), and the reduced organizational support (Carr, Inkson, & Thorn, 2005; Jokinen, Brewster, & Suutari, 2008).

More specifically, Selmer and Lauring (2010) define SIEs with regard to three specific characteristics, namely that they had acquired their current job independently (self-initiated), that their current job was a steady position (regular job) and that their nationality was different than that of the host country (expatriate). This is further developed by Cerdin and Selmer (2014) who use four defining characteristics for SIEs: (1) self-initiated international relocation, (2) regular employment, (3) intentions of a temporary stay, and (4) skilled/professional qualifications.

Generally, due to clear differences between AEs and SIEs (Peltokorpi & Froese, 2009), more research has been called for to better understand issues associated with SIEs and their expatriation (Suutari & Brewster, 2000; Vance & Paik, 2005). The interest in SIEs has led to a rapidly growing number of academic publications on this group and how they can be distinguished from AEs (Cerdin & Selmer, 2014; Tharenou, 2013).

A number of differences between SIEs and traditional AEs have been proposed by extant studies. In terms of demographic differences, a number of variations between SIEs and AEs have been identified. First, women tend to seek for expatriation more frequently than men. In a number of studies, SIE samples even had slightly more women than men (Jokinen et al., 2008; Peltokorpi & Froese, 2009; Selmer & Lauring, 2012; Suutari & Brewster, 2000). This suggests that self-initiated expatriation tends to be less gendered than traditional expatriate assignments where males are clearly dominating (Andresen, Biemann, & Pattiec, forthcoming;

Tharenou, 2010). This difference in gender between SIEs and AEs is important: Although women's relative participation in international assignments has been increasing, they nevertheless remain underrepresented (Altman & Shortland, 2008). There are several theoretical as well as empirical reasons explaining this lack of female expatriate presence from different angles, including that of the organization, the individual and the society, such as the lack of women mentors and role models (Linehan, Scullion, & Walsh, 2001), and the lack of social support (Caligiuri & Lazarova, 2002). In a similar vein, although women are no less interested than men in international assignments subject to location constraints (e.g., Lowe, Downes, & Kroeck, 1999), yet the barriers for undertaking international assignments such as work-family conflicts (e.g., Linehan & Walsh, 2000) and the competitive advantages that female expatriates can potentially bring (Guthrie, Ash, & Stevens, 2003; Tung, 2004) are yet to be established in expatriation research (Altman & Shortland, 2008).

SIE and AEs have been found to be relatively similar with regard to education level (Cerdin & Le Pargneux, 2010; Doherty, Dickmann, & Mills, 2011; Froese & Peltokorpi, 2012). They are also similar in terms of age (Andresen, Al Ariss, & Walther, 2012a; Andresen, Bergdolt, & Margenfeld, 2012b). However, SIEs have more often been found to have a spouse who was born in the host country (Peltokorpi & Froese, 2009; Suutari & Brewster, 2000).

There are also differences between SIEs and AEs in relation to their mobility orientation (cf. Lauring & Selmer, 2014). For example, SIEs have often been found to stay longer in the host country compared to AEs, as they choose to embark on an international career on their own initiative (Doherty et al., 2011; Peltokorpi & Froese, 2009). Jokinen et al. (2008) found that SIEs in general have a higher global mobility than AEs. This may be related to Suutari and Brewster's (2000) finding that SIEs generally see the personal interest in developing international experience as more important than AEs do. Accordingly, SIEs are more globally mobile and see this mobility as important to their personal development and career opportunities (Andresen et al., forthcoming). Hence, while AEs tend to focus on career and economic reasons to expatriate, SIEs typically have additional motives for their expatriation, including cultural and travel opportunities, family, and life change/escape (Selmer & Lauring, 2010; Thorn, 2009).

In relation to intercultural issues, some studies have found SIEs to be better at adjusting to the new cultures and better at coping with cultural friction than AEs (Peltokorpi & Froese, 2009; Shaffer, Kraimer, Chen, & Bolino, 2012; Tharenou, 2013). SIEs have also been found to develop larger social networks (Näsholm, 2012; Von Borell de Araujo, Teixeira, Da Cruz, & Malini, forthcoming). AEs, on the other hand, find it more difficult to learn the local language (Kühlmann & Hutchings, 2010). SIEs are thus more likely to have stronger cross-cultural abilities and larger social networks including networks consisting of host country nationals. However, although SIEs are often better equipped to adjust to the local culture, there could also be many problems because they do not receive the same preparations or support from a home organization (Carr et al., 2005; Jokinen et al., 2008).

The academic focus on SIEs is driven not only by the fact that international assignments are expected to continue increasing in the coming years (GRTS, 2013; van Erp, van der Zee, Giebels, & van Duijn, 2014), but also that SIEs now have assumed a prominent role in this growth being more numerous than AEs (65% vs. 35%) (Doherty, 2013; Doherty et al., 2011).

There is also increasing attention on the growing group of SIEs from the industry. A corporate interest is driven by SIEs being accessible from the host country and relatively inexpensive not requiring an expatriate compensation package as often the case with AEs (Andresen et al., 2012b; Banai & Harry, 2004; McKenna & Richardson, 2007; Tharenou & Harvey, 2006). Moreover, the pool of headquarter nationals willing to expatriate has been argued to be shrinking mostly due to dual career issues (Tharenou, 2013). Yet, for some types of job roles, SIEs are still less useful than AEs. For example, AEs tend to be superior in implementing firm strategy by transferring HQ corporate culture or information (Tan & Mahoney, 2003; Tharenou, 2013; Tharenou & Caulfield, 2010). Hence, organizations may not be able to substitute all AEs with SIE.

Another reason that SIEs may not always be as effective expatriates as AEs could be related to the selection process. Most organizations apply measures of systematic, formal and informal assessment of AEs relocating to foreign subsidiaries (Anderson, 2005; Mendenhall & Macomber, 1997; Welch, 1994), because an expatriation has been argued to be the single largest investment that a multinational corporation can attach to any individual employee (Selmer, 2001). In comparison, the selection of SIEs may not be as rigorous.

As one of the most important types of subsidiary managers, subsidiary's CEO position can also be filled either by the assignment of an expatriate (i.e., AE CEO) or by the appointment of a local expatriate candidate (i.e., SIE CEO). Choosing between AE CEOs and SIE CEOs has important strategic impacts on a subsidiary's operations, given that AEs and SIEs differ significantly from each other in terms of demographics and skill sets (Kessapidou & Varsakelis, 2003). However, little research has been conducted on expatriate top managers, and so far comparisons between AEs and SIEs are based on the whole population instead of solely on expatriate CEOs (Selmer & Leon, 1997). It is surprising that CEOs have been ignored with the stream of research on expatriate assignment within the international human resource literature.

Hence, the purpose of this study is to investigate systematically the differences between AE CEOs and SIE CEOs. In this regard, we seek to find out how the two groups differ in terms of (1) who they are (demographics), (2) what they are like (personality), and (3) what results they produce (performance). More specifically, we compare AE CEOs and SIE CEOs in relation to demographic characteristics, personality traits, and performance outcome. This is important because expatriates have too often been perceived as a homogeneous group (Selmer & Lauring, 2010). Revealing potential differences could make the study of expatriate managers, in this case CEOs, more detailed and contextualized.

In the coming three sections, we review literature on central variables that may differ between AE Ceos and SIE Ceos. At the end of each section, we induce a research question based on research gaps identified as basis for empirical analysis.

3.3. Demographics: Who Are They?

Since the groups of AEs and SIEs differ on central demographic variables, this may also well be the case for the Ceos of these two groups (cf. Froese & Peltokorpi, 2013; Peltokorpi & Froese, 2009). Here we focus on age, gender, marital status, and experience.

3.3.1. Age

Age groups vary in physical features and attitudes related to life span. As age increases, individuals go through various biological (Greller & Simpson, 1999; Kliegel, McDaniel, & Einstein, 2000; Sterns & Miklos, 1995) and psychological changes (Gecas, 1982; Leonard, Beauvais, & Scholl, 1999; Maurer, 2001). These alterations may be reflected in the health, cognitive abilities, performance, and experience of the individual (Kooij, Lange, Jansen, & Dikkers, 2008). This may also affect the role that an expatriate CEO takes in a foreign company.

Warr (2001) summarized the limited empirical evidence on the motivational effects of key job features at different ages and found that the importance attached to high job demands and job variety decreased with aging, while the importance attached to job security and physical security increased when individuals aged. In a similar vein, Mehrabian and Blum (1996) found that achievement motivation declined with age. This may be related to the notion that younger employees have more favorable attitudes toward risk-taking (Vroom & Pahl, 1971). Since being a SIE could be more risky without organizational support, there could be more younger SIEs willing to take the risk and becoming SIE Ceos. Previous empirical studies have proposed that AEs are slightly older than SIEs (Peltokorpi & Froese, 2009). On the other hand, AE Ceos may generally have higher human, social and economic capital (visibility, contacts and salary level) than their younger colleagues. For example, older people were found to be less concerned with financial gain from their work compared to younger people possibly due to already being secure (Greller & Simpson, 1999). This gives them more opportunities to decide where to take a job on their own initiative. Hence, age may well distinguish whether an individual becomes a SIE CEO or an AE CEO although it is not entirely clear how age may cause such distinction.

3.3.2. Gender

Gender differences are generally related to alternative sex roles (Krach et al., 2009) and to differences in biological (physical and psychological) characteristics

(Gove, 1994) that can be related to men and women respectively. In this regard, Balkan (1966) originally argued that males are guided predominantly by controlling tendencies referred to as agentic goals. This includes self-assertion, self-efficacy, and mastering (Carlson, 1971). Concurrently, males tend to forcefully pursue goals having personal consequences (Beutel & Marini, 1995). In contrast, females are believed to be guided by communal concerns emphasizing interpersonal affiliation and a desire to be in harmonious relations with others and themselves (Eagly & Crowley, 1986; Hall & Mast, 2008). In general it is argued that psychological literature consistently presents men as more assertive, goal directed and instrumental, whereas women are more affiliative, sensitive and emotional (Gove, 1994).

In relation to more specific issues, studies have consistently reported that men are more interested in their career (Bartol & Manhardt, 1979). In addition, with regard to financial concerns, Mahmoud (1996) found that pay affected work satisfaction of men but not of women. Elizur (2001) similarly found that men ranked pay higher than women. Conversely, women valued interaction with people, convenient working hours and job security higher than men. Sexton and Bowman-Upton (1990) found that women scored lower on risk-taking than men. Based on this, it could be speculated that more male expatriates than female would choose to expatriate on their own initiative. On the other hand, studies have consistently found a more equal gender distribution among SIEs than OEs (Jokinen et al., 2008; Peltokorpi & Froese, 2009; Selmer & Lauring, 2012; Suutari & Brewster, 2000). Hence, again there may be gender differences between AE and SIE CEOs although current literature has not presented us with a clear pattern in this respect.

3.3.3. Marital Status

Marital status has been consistently reported to be relevant to expatriate outcomes (Selmer & Lauring, 2011a). In general, research has found that employees who are not married put more focus on opportunities for career advancement compared to their married counterparts. Married couples, on the other hand, seemed to be more inclined to strike a balance between work life and family life (Wong, Siu, & Tsang, 1999). In relation to this, the marital status of expatriates is particularly important because international assignments affect the family as a whole (Brown, 2008). The influence of family status and whether there is a trailing spouse are researched to impact on expatriation success (De Cieri, Dowling, & Taylor, 1991; Stone, 1991). For example, the inability of the trailing spouse to adjust to the host country has been reported as an important reason for expatriate failure (Dowling & Welch, 2004; Tung, 1987). Marital status is also relevant for the assignment success of SIEs as personal and social life in the host country plays an important part in their adaptation to that country (Crowley-Henry, 2007). Drawing upon interviews with 38 female US expatriates (20 of them married), Caligiuri, Joshi, and Lazarova (1999) proposed that spousal support was a key element in female expatriates' adjustment to the oversea assignment. Crowley-Henry (2007) further proposed that married couples with children were less motivated to be mobile unless circumstances rendered no alternative. Married CEOs may not choose to expatriate on their own initiative as marriage may lead to risk-averse behaviors among CEOs. For example, executive marriage has been found to affect acquisition activity, the level of capital investment and stock return volatility (Roussanov & Savor, 2014). Hence, although there could be differences between AE and SIE CEOs in terms of marriage, it is not clear how significantly marital status may differentiate AEs and SIEs.

3.3.4. Experience

A number of studies have demonstrated that past experience significantly affect future decision-making (Tesluk & Jacobs, 1998). Experience will facilitate learning that aids employees to cope with events that are beyond one's control and recognize personal limits (Morrison & Brantner, 1992). Reiger and Rees (1993), for example, found that years of work experience significantly affected motivation to a number of work-related actions. This could also be the case for expatriates. Past expatriation experience is an important source of information which can assist in reducing uncertainty for the next international assignment (Black, Mendenhall, & Oddou, 1991). In a survey study with 124 SIEs in Japan, Peltokorpi and Froese (2012) found out that longer working experience in the host country had a positive impact on SIEs interaction adjustment. Long duration of expatriation, together with command of the local language (cf. Lauring & Klitmøller, 2015; Selmer & Lauring, 2015) and a few other factors, were found to contribute to expatriate spouses' adjustment (Ali, Van der Zee, & Sanders, 2003; Lauring & Selmer, 2010). In addition to the duration of expatriation experience, the type of expatriation experience may also matter in predicting expatriation success or failure. In an empirical study with Western expatriates in Hong Kong, Selmer (2002) found out that previous expatriation experience to non-Asian countries was helpful for work-related adjustment only, that is, not on general and interaction adjustment. In general, AE CEOs are on a shorter contract (Andresen et al., 2012a, 2012b) and thus SIEs may gain more experience. Based on the research gaps identified in the literature review above, we present the first research question of our study:

Research Question 1. How do assigned expatriate CEOs differ from their self-initiated counterparts in terms of demographics?

3.4. Personality: What Are They Like?

Personality traits are relatively stable, enduring, and measurable patterns of how individuals feel, think, and behave. Personality traits could have implications for adjustment and performance in a foreign context (Selmer & Lauring, 2013a, 2014a, 2014c). Downes, Varner, and Musinski (2007) further pointed out that since no road maps exist to cover every circumstance, stable traits such as personality are critical for expatriate CEOs. In contrast, dynamic traits, such as functional capabilities, technical expertise, skills, language proficiency, and market knowledge are more important for functional or technical expatriate managers (Resick, Whitman, Weingarden, & Hiller, 2009).

In domestic research, a large number of studies have focused on how the personality of CEOs affects organizational outcomes (Miller & Toulouse, 1986; Resick et al., 2009; Simsek, Heavey, & Veiga, 2010). Personality traits such as overconfidence (Simon & Houghton, 2003) and hubris (Hayward & Hambrick, 1997) have been explored and generally found to negatively affect firm performance. CEO masculinity, conservatism (Lord, De Vader, & Alliger, 1986), and extroversion (Judge, Bono, Ilies, & Gerhardt, 2002), however, were shown to have positive implications for organizations. In an international context, Spreitzer, McCall, and Mahoney (1997) found traits such as being culturally adventurous, open to criticism, and flexible to be useful for predicting the future success of international executives.

In relation to AEs and SIEs, it may be speculated that SIEs possess different personality traits that encourage them to self-assign themselves internationally. These traits of SIEs are not necessarily shared with AEs, and yet they equip the SIEs with additional resistance to cope with cross-cultural shock and its associated stress. In this study, we explore a number of personality traits in relation to variance between AE CEOs and SIE CEOs, namely proactive personality, self-control, and dispositional anger. These traits could be particularly important for expatriate CEOs — especially in countries such as China. In a meta-analysis, Fuller and Marler (2009) show that a proactive personality's relationship with job performance is particularly noteworthy because it is stronger than that reported for any of the Big Five factors or the Big Five collectively. Also, self-control has been found to be one of the most prominent predictors of performance and success across different samples (Tangney, Baumeister, & Boone, 2004; Wang, Karns, & Meredith, 2003). As a collectivist country, China is known for the emphasis on conformity to societal rules (Bodycott & Lai, 2012). This is a reason for emotional self-regulation being perceived as essential for the individual's functioning in the group (Chen et al., 2015). Lacking self-control and display of strong emotions can be at odds with the maintenance of interdependent social interaction (Markus & Kitayama, 1991). In this regard, Zhou, Eisenberg, Wang, and Reiser (2004) maintain that self-focused emotions such as anger motivate individuals to eliminate the threat to the sense of self and to assert the self's independence. This is, however, seen as harmful to the collectivity of the social unit. Similarly, Kitayama, Mesquita, and Karasawa (2006) argue that anger as a socially disengaging emotion is particularly problematic because it can be destructive for the social harmony of the group.

3.4.1. Proactive Personality

One personal attribute that has attracted scholarly attention in the last couple of decades is proactive personality. As a result of heightened global competition and the need for continuous innovation, organizations rely increasingly upon the initiatives of their leaders (Frese, Garst, & Fay, 2007; Zhang, Wang, & Shi, 2012). The proactive personality concept was originally developed by Bateman and Crant (1993) who defined it as a tendency to affect one's environment. Such individuals, according to Crant (2000), "identify opportunities and act on them, show initiative, take action, and persevere until meaningful change occurs" (p. 439). Hence, proactive personality can be argued to be a relatively stable disposition in which to take personal initiative in a broad range of activities and situations (Fuller & Marler, 2009).

Seibert, Kraimer, and Crant (2001) argue that proactive individuals "select, create, and influence work situations that increase the likelihood of career success" (p. 847). As such, proactive behavior, expressed as taking charge, being creative, and voice behavior, has been found to signal leadership potential (Fuller & Marler, 2009). Moreover, research results show that individuals rated high on proactive personality engage more in networking because it enables them to successfully achieve positive outcomes in their organization or for their career development in general (Thompson, 2005). Thus, there could be a difference between AE CEOs and SIE CEOs since the latter group shows more self-reliant initiative when choosing their career path.

3.4.2. Self-Control

Self-control has been argued to be one of the most historically efficient means of ensuring that social and moral order are sustained (Harter, 1983). However, individuals are not equally competent at managing their lives, holding their tempers, keeping their diets, persevering at work, fulfilling their promises, saving money, controlling their alcohol consumption, or keeping secrets (Tangney et al., 2004). Self-control is generally viewed as a personality trait defined by the individual's willpower to alter or override dominant response tendencies and to regulate behavior, thoughts, and emotions (Bandura, 1989; Metcalfe & Mischel, 1999; Wang et al., 2003). As such, self-control emphasizes the importance of controlling immediate impulses and responses, interrupting undesired behavioral tendencies and refrain from acting on them (Logue, 1988). Self-control can also be perceived as a capacity to change and adapt the self so as to produce a better, more optimal fit between the self and the external world (Rothbaum, Weisz, & Snyder, 1982). Finally, it has been argued that self-control requires one to make decisions and to act in accordance with long-term rather than short-term orientations (de Ridder, Lensvelt-Mulders, Finkenauer, Stok, & Baumeister, 2012). This is because self-control enables a person to make decisions and to act in accordance with continuing rather than short-term outcomes (de Ridder et al., 2012). This can be in the form of temptation resistance, impulse overcoming, task persistence, and emotion regulation. Hence, self-control helps to promote desirable behavior and inhibit undesirable behavior. Some researchers have also compared self-control with the functionality of a muscle (e.g., Muraven & Baumeister, 2000). In this line of thinking, self-control is argued to tap into a limited resource. Depletion of this resource will thus make subsequent self-control failure more likely (de Ridder et al., 2012). Some individuals, however, will have a larger pool to draw from than others. In this, the role of willpower and an active self in the exertion of self-control has often been highlighted (Baumeister, Bratslavsky, Muraven, & Tice, 1998). This type of self-control as self-management has also been found to have positive consequences on one's career (Raabe, Frese, & Beehr, 2007). Since AE CEOs have already experienced the process of accommodating and adjusting to work in the same organization, it could be speculated that they differ from SIE CEOs in that respect.

3.4.3. Trait Anger

Anger can be defined as a negatively toned emotion subjectively experienced as an aroused state of antagonism towards someone or something perceived to be the source of an aversive event (Owen, 2011). Anger is commonly experienced and therefore regarded as one of the basic human emotions and vary in intensity, from mild annoyance or aggravation to fury and rage (Averill, 1982; Plutchik, 2002). Approximately one in ten people have been found to experience difficulties with controlling their anger (Owen, 2011). Spielberger, Jacobs, Russell, and Crane (1983) state-trait theory of anger suggests that the state of feeling angry varies in intensity and duration and produces physiological reactivity that increases along with the intensity of subjective anger feelings.

Trait anger, on the other hand, has been shown to be firmly established in one's personality in adulthood (Deffenbacher, Richards, Filetti, & Lynch, 2005). As such, it is argued to be an enduring disposition that predisposes individuals to experience the same environmental anger triggers but with a more intense, enduring, and aroused state anger than individuals low in trait anger (Dear, Watt, & Dockerill, 2003; Quinn, Rollock, & Vrana, 2014). Compared with low trait anger individuals, those high in trait anger may show maladaptive anger expressions (Quinn et al., 2014) and poor judgment of stimuli in social situations (Reio & Callahan, 2004). In other words, high trait anger may reduce the expatriate's ability to act according to the context. Secondly, trait anger has in general been associated with a range of reasoning biases including external attribution bias, selective attention expectancy bias, and interpretation bias that are known to be disruptive to intercultural interaction (cf. Wingrove & Bond, 2005). This could lead to reduced contact to local individuals decreasing the social feedback necessary to make behavioral adjustment to fit the new work situation. With respect to workplace socialization and learning associated with workplace socialization, high levels of anger have been shown to impede learning, decision-making, interpersonal relations, and performance, especially in stressful environments such as those faced by expatriates (Reio & Callahan, 2004). Since individuals high in trait anger could have difficulties in maintaining good relations to colleagues others over a long time span, they may more readily leave their organization. Hence, trait anger could potentially be higher for SIE Ceos than AE Ceos. Hence, we present the second research question.

Research Question 2. How do assigned expatriate Ceos differ from their self-initiated counterparts in terms of personality traits?

3.5. Performance: How Do They Contribute?

There is little consensus as to what constitutes performance in general terms. However, performance at work often refers to the core technical duties of the job, also known as task performance or in-role performance (Fisher, 2003). The evaluation of individual performance is often related to motivation, prior experience and confidence in oneself and other organization members (Lewin, Dembo, Festinger, & Sears, 1944). Differential motivations such as structural constraints and opportunities as well as subjective states may influence the abilities of individuals to achieve their intended objectives (Mizruchi, 1991).

In relation to expatriation, research studies have highlighted the importance of international experience of the top management team to the performance of international small and medium-sized enterprises (Monks, Scullion, & Creaner, 2001). Due to the complex nature of international assignments, it is challenging to directly measure expatriates' performance. For example, Briscoe and Schuler argued that the key to successfully manage the performance of expatriates is acknowledging the need to adapt the appraisal system to take into consideration the host context, as standardized systems may not provide the most accurate measures for expatriate performance. Extant anecdotal studies have informed us that AEs and SIEs need to be treated separately regarding with what they can contribute to the organization and the factors influencing their respective performances. Quick, Gavin, Cooper, and Quick (2000) found out that health issues could potentially have significant implications for executive AEs' performance, especially that of short-term executive AEs, as their families may not accompany them, and therefore they can work excessive hours and lose their work-life balance leading to stress, burn-out, and eventually poor performance. Contrasting AEs with SIEs, Biemann and Andresen (2010) found that SIEs start their expatriation at a younger age, have a higher organizational mobility, and also expect higher benefits from expatriation experiences for their future careers. Drawing upon a survey with more than 200 Finnish expatriates, Jokinen et al. (2008) found significant similarities and some differences in AEs' and SIEs' career capital (i.e., career knowing-how, knowing-why, and knowing-whom). The importance of social capital to job performance has been noted in the literature (e.g., Boxman, De Graaf, & Flap, 1991; Granovetter, 1974; Kim, 2002). As one type of social capital, the differences and similarities of AEs' and SIEs' career capital uncovered by Jokinen et al. inform us that AE CEOs and SIE CEOs may have different performance levels. Accordingly, we present the last research question:

Research Question 3. How do assigned expatriate CEOs differ from their self-initiated counterparts in terms of performance?

3.6. Method

This study was part of a larger investigation. In the current research project, expatriate CEOs residing in China were targeted. China was originally chosen for this study because the cultural and linguistic contexts have been argued to differ extraordinarily from most other countries to the extent of making them very challenging destinations for expatriates to adjust to (Selmer, 2006; Selmer, Lauring, & Feng, 2009; Shi & Franklin, 2013). Moreover, the personality traits, self-control and dispositional anger, have been found to be particularly influential in China (Wang et al., 2003). Hence, as a challenging country to be expatriated to and with specific preferences for personality traits, the Chinese context is well-suited to explore differences between different types of expatriate top managers.

Three screening questions were applied to only retain members of the targeted group. We asked whether the respondents were currently living in China and whether their nationality was different from that of the host country (indicating expatriate status). Their status of being CEOs was gauged by the direct question: "What is your current position?" The fixed response alternatives included: (1) CEO/ General Manager (GM), (2) Top manager, (3) Middle manager, (4) Team leader, and (5) Non-managerial staff. Since only CEOs were targeted in the current study, only respondents selecting the first category were retained.

A web-based survey software package was used to administer the questionnaire. The invitation e-mail was sent to individuals based on information from various commercially available lists of foreign businesses in China. All in all, the online questionnaire was sent to 1,702 business expatriates in China. Eventually, and after three reminders, 351 responses were received amounting to a response rate of 20.6%. Of these, 187 respondents passed the screening questions as well as indicating that they were a CEO/GM. To distinguish between SIEs and AEs we asked: Was you job (1) Assigned to you by your parent country firm or a similar organization? Or (2) Acquired independently (self-initiated) or recruited directly by the host company?

For the purpose of this study, the total sample of expatriate CEOs in China was divided into two groups based on whether they were AE CEOs ($n = 93$) or SIE CEOs ($n = 94$). AE CEOs had an average age of 46.58 years (SD = 8.47). On average, they had spent 5.82 years in their host location in China (SD = 4.02), 5.11 years in their current job (SD = 3.26) and had worked abroad as an expatriate for 9.87 years (SD = 6.79), including their current job. Table 3.1 reveals that a clear majority of the AE CEOs was male (95.7%) and married (88.2%) and most of them had a higher education degree (61.5%). An overwhelming majority of the AE CEOs was of non-Asian nationality (95.7%). The largest nationality groups were from Germany (41), Denmark (17), and Italy (9). The rest of the assigned expatriates came from 16 different countries.

Some of the demographics of the SIE CEOs were different. Although their average age was similar to AE CEOs, 46.29 years (SD = 8.92), on average, they had spent a much longer time, 10.22 years, in their host location in China (SD = 5.22). They had also spent a longer average time in their current job, 6.48 years (SD = 4.13) and had worked longer abroad as an expatriate, 14.33 years (SD = 5.50), including their current employment. As displayed in Table 3.1, even for the SIE CEOs, most were male (90.4%) and married (83.0%) and a majority also had a higher education degree (55.9). Similar to AE CEOs, an overwhelming majority of the SIE CEOs had non-Asian nationalities (97.9%). The same nationality groups also dominated the sample of SIE CEOs; Germany (33), Denmark (20), and Italy (13). The remaining respondents came from 13 different countries.

One-way ANOVAs confirmed that there were intergroup differences among the above background variables for the AE CEOs and the SIE CEOs regarding *time in host location, time in current job in host location*, and *time as an expatriate*. Where appropriate, these three background variables are used as covariates in the MANCOVA analyses.

Table 3.1: Background of the sub-samples (*N* = 187).[a]

Background Variables	Assigned Expatriate CEOs *n* = 93		Self-Initiated Expatriate CEOs *n* = 94	
	Frequency	%	Frequency	%
Gender				
Male	89	95.7	85	90.4
Female	4	4.3	9	9.6
Married				
Yes	82	88.2	78	83.0
No	11	11.8	16	17.0
Educational level				
Doctorate	6	6.6	8	8.6
Master	50	54.9	44	47.3
Bachelor	19	20.9	28	30.1
Professional qualifications	16	17.6	13	14.0
Nationality group				
Other Asia	4	4.3	2	2.1
Non-Asia	89	95.7	92	97.9

[a]Frequency totals could be less than the stated *n* due to missing values.

Background variables were measured by single direct questions to the respondents. For example, *age* was measured by the question: "How old were you on your last birthday?" *time as an expatriate* was assessed by: "How long have you worked abroad as an expatriate, including the current job?" *time in current job in host location* was measured by "How long have you had your current job in the host location?" and *time in host location* was assessed by "How long have you lived in the host location?" The personality trait variables as well as the performance variable were assessed by established multi-item scales. *Proactive personality* was gauged by a six-item, seven-point scale (Parker, 1998). Response categories were 1 = "strongly disagree" to 7 = "strongly agree," sample item: "If I see something I don't like, I fix it" (alpha = .74). *Self-control* was assessed by a thirteen-item, four-point scale (Tangney et al., 2004). The scale was anchored at 1 = "not at all" and 4 = "very much," sample item: "People would say that I have iron self-discipline" (alpha = .84). *Angry temperament* was assessed by a four-item, four-point scale (Spielberger et al., 1983). Response categories ranged from 1 = "almost never" to 4 = "almost always," sample item: "I am a hot-headed person" (alpha = .87). *Job Performance* was measured by a four-item, seven-point scale by Early (1987). Response categories ranged from (1) = "Poor" to (4) = "Neutral" to (7) = "Excellent," sample item: "How would you rate the quality of your performance?" (*alpha = .76*).

3.7. Results

Sample means, standard deviations, and zero-order Pearson correlations of all variables are provided in Table 3.2.

The research questions were examined through MANCOVAs and ANCOVAs. Regarding demographics, Table 3.3 indicates a significant multivariate intergroup effect for the AE CEOs and the SIE CEOs ($F = 9.03$; $p < .001$). The SIE CEOs had a higher mean score on *time as an expatriate* ($F = 18.90$; $p < .001$), for *time in current job in host location* ($F = 6.63$; $p < .05$) and on *time in host location* ($F = 43.39$; $p < .001$) than their assigned counterparts. These results provide an affirmative answer to Research Question 1.

Table 3.2: Means, standard deviations, and correlations among the variables.[a]

Variables	Mean	SD	1	2	3	4
1. Job performance	5.88	.62	1.00			
2. Self-control	3.78	.59	.28***	1.00		
3. Angry temperament	2.86	1.31	−.15	−.31***	1.00	
4. Proactive personality	5.57	.69	.42***	.30***	.02	1.00

[a]$166 \leq n \leq 178$ due to missing values. *$p < .05$; **$p < .01$; ***$p < .001$ (2-tailed).

Table 3.3: MANCOVA and ANCOVA for demographics by assigned expatriate CEOs and self-initiated expatriate CEOs.[a]

	Assigned Expatriate CEOs Mean (SD) $n = 93$	Self-initiated Expatriate CEOs Mean (SD) $n = 92$	Multivariate Effect	Uni-Variate F-Ratios
			9.03***	
Age	46.58 (8.47)	46.51 (8.89)		.00
Gender	1.04 (.20)	1.09 (.28)		1.47
Marital status	1.12 (.33)	1.16 (.37)		.76
Time as an expatriate	9.87 (6.79)	14.33 (7.17)		18.90***
Time in current job in host location	5.11 (3.26)	6.51 (4.09)		6.63*
Time in host location	5.82 (4.02)	10.32 (5.21)		43.39***

[a]$N = 185$. *$p < .05$; ***$p < .001$.

Table 3.4: MANCOVA and ANCOVA for personality traits by assigned expatriate CEOs and self-initiated expatriate CEOs.[a,b]

	Assigned Expatriate CEOs Mean (SD) $n = 83$	Self-initiated Expatriate CEOs Mean (SD) $n = 83$	Multivariate Effect	Uni-Variate F-Ratios
			6.48***	
Self-control	3.93 (.54)	3.63 (.60)		12.95***
Angry temperament	2.63 (1.19)	3.08 (1.39)		11.80***
Proactive personality	5.59 (.73)	5.55 (.65)		.03

[a]$N = 166$.
[b]Covariates: Time as an expatriate, time in current job in host location, time in host location.
***$p < .001$.

Table 3.4 displays a significant multivariate intergroup effect for the AE CEOs and the SIE CEOs ($F = 6.48$; $p < .001$) in terms of the studied personality traits. The AE CEOs had a higher mean score on *self-control* ($F = 12.95$; $p < .001$) than their self-initiated counterparts but for *angry temperament* ($F = 11.80$; $p < .001$), it was the other way around. These results provide an affirmative answer to Research Question 2.

Table 3.5: ANCOVA for job performance by assigned expatriate CEOs and self-initiated expatriate CEOs.[a,b]

	Assigned Expatriate CEOs Mean (SD) $n = 90$	Self-initiated Expatriate CEOs Mean (SD) $n = 88$	Uni-Variate F-Ratio
Job performance	5.97 (.60)	5.78 (.63)	6.11*

[a]$N = 178$.
[b]Covariates: time as an expatriate, time in current job in host location, time in host location. *$p < .05$.

Examining group differences in terms of performance, an ANCOVA showed that the AE CEOs had a higher mean score on *job performance* ($F = 6.11$; $p < .05$) than the SIE CEOs. This result answers Research Question 3 affirmatively (Table 3.5).

3.8. Discussion

3.8.1. Main Findings

The answer to all of the three research questions was affirmative, although the extent to which the two groups of expatriate CEOs were different varied. The first research question, exploring the intergroup differences in demographics between AE and SIE CEOs, showed interesting, but perhaps expected results. Experience-related demographics were higher in score for the SIE CEOs than AE CEOs. To the best of our knowledge, this is novel personal information about SIE CEOs. It is consistent with previous studies indicating that SIEs tend to stay longer in host locations than their assigned colleagues. Although SIEs tend to be described as adventurous young people who only seek for temporary experience abroad (Inkson, Arthur, Pringle, & Barry, 1997), a number of studies have found that a significant number of SIEs are localized professionals who prefer to stay in the host country for an extensive amount of time rather than return home (Suutari & Brewster, 2000; Vance & Paik, 2005). AEs are usually restricted regarding their duration of stay in the host country by their contract ranging from six months to five years (Peltokorpi & Froese, 2009). In a survey study with 179 expatriates in Japan, Peltokorpi and Froese (2009) found out that the average length of stay in the host country by SIEs was significantly higher than that of AEs. Relating our research finding to the specific empirical context of our study, SIE CEOs have overall longer stays in China than AE CEOs, probably because network is slow to build, and a good amount of social network is essential for expatriates to qualify for high-level positions such as CEO. We did not find any differences between the two groups in terms of age, gender, and marital status. While no other studies seem to have compared AEs and SIEs in relation to marital status, some studies have pointed out that these two groups are similar with regard to age (Andresen et al., 2012a, 2012b). It was, however, surprising to find that the two groups were similar in terms of gender as earlier studies have found substantially more women among SIEs than AE. However, this tendency seems to even out as individuals move to higher positions.

For the differences in the examined personality traits, explored by the second research question, we found that the AE CEOs had better self-control than their self-initiated colleagues. On the other hand, SIE CEOs had more angry temperament than their assigned counterparts. This may appear to be surprising given that SIE CEOs tend to have longer duration of stay in the host country and may thus acquire more local cultural and social knowledge. Our findings seem to demonstrate little connection between the learned knowledge and personality traits such as self-control and angry temperament among SIE CEOs. This difference between SIE CEOs and AE CEOs is important since having good self-control and not displaying an angry temperament are essential in countries like China. Being able to control one's emotions publicly is related to one of the most fundamental concepts in the Chinese culture: face (Buckley, Clegg, & Tan, 2006). Leung and Yee-kwong Chan (2003) defined face as the pride, respect and dignity of individuals as a result of their social achievement and the practice of it. Ho (1976) explained that the amount of face a person has is context and situation dependent: one's face could be further enhanced or diminished during social interactions based on the appropriateness of his or her behaviors. Being able to control one's angry temperament in front of one's subordinates is important for preventing losing face in advance, retrieving face after the event and gaining face (Chu, 2006). For a leader, such as a company's CEO in China, not to demonstrate his or her anger publicly is also reflected in the concept of "giving face" or "making face" for others in order to establish a harmonious atmosphere (Chiao, 1981). Showing no concern for face saving in social interactions often leads to conflict, and consequentially Chinese individuals are inclined to use all kinds of means to not only save one's own face, but also consider others' faces (Huang, Davison, & Gu, 2008).

For the third research question, exploring differences in job performance, we found that the AE CEOs had a better self-rated job performance than their SIE counterparts. Although the difference was not substantial, it could nevertheless be important. To what extent this difference was caused by the different personality traits of the two studied groups cannot be determined though. It is not unlikely that personality traits have a significant impact on expatriates' job performance since AEs have a double advantage over their self-initiated colleagues with more beneficial personality traits and less detrimental ones. Another reason for AE CEOs to have better performance than SIE CEOs could be that AE CEOs have been in the same MNC for a longer period and are thus familiar with the company development and strategy, and also possess special skills which are needed in the foreign subsidiary (Edström & Galbraith

1977; Selmer, 1998). AE CEOs usually have detailed objectives and job descriptions defined before they start working in the host country. In comparison, SIE CEOs would need to invest more time and efforts learning about the organization and their new job role as a CEO in the organization. In a similar vein, extant studies have proposed that AEs tend to have better work adjustment than SIEs (e.g., Peltokorpi & Froese, 2009). Better work adjustment of AEs may consequentially lead to better job performance, as the degree of cross-cultural adjustment has been commonly used as a proxy to indicate expatriates' performance due to the complexity of directly measuring expatriate performance (Collings, Scullion, & Morley, 2007).

3.8.2. Implications

The findings of our study further contribute to the recent yet burgeoning literature on diversity within the expatriate population (e.g., Dowling, Festing, & Engle, 2008; Selmer & Lauring, 2011b; Tung, 2008). Globalization and internationalization of business has resulted in international assignments being increasingly frequent and increasingly complicated (Mayerhofer, Hartmann, Michelitsch-Riedl, & Kollinger, 2004). Consequently, there is a new range of roles and career paths for expatriates (Collings et al., 2007).

The findings of our study further emphasize that it is important to separate AEs and SIEs since they differ significantly from each other in several work-related dimensions (Froese & Peltokorpi, 2012; Inkson et al., 1997; Suutari & Brewster, 2000). Firstly, SIEs decide themselves that they would like to move and work abroad. There is usually no fixed period of stay in the foreign country. AEs, on the other hand, are dispatched by multinational companies to achieve a specific job or organization related goals with a pre-decided period ranging from six months to five years. In the case of expatriate CEOs, SIE CEOs seem to stay longer in the host country than AE CEOs. Secondly, SIEs do not usually have a structured career path in the manner of AEs. They often perceive their overseas working experience to be part of their self-development or part of another personal agenda. AEs are usually motivated to work abroad because of the financial benefits or increased opportunities for career progression (Miller & Cheng, 1978). Our findings demonstrate that career development, especially regarding the possibility to secure senior positions such as CEO and GM, is important to both SIEs and AEs. Our findings have thus expanded the stream of literature on AEs and SIEs to leadership positions.

There are several practical implications of our research. The findings can assist core decisions of MNC global talent management; to "make" or "buy" (develop and assign internally, or recruit externally). In terms of CEOs for foreign operations, and especially in China, these are crucial decisions for MNCs. Given the more suitable match of AE CEOs than their self-initiated counterparts, at least in terms of personality traits of the investigated expatriate CEOs, it is more beneficial for MNCs to assign instead of recruiting them. Additionally, AE CEOs seem to be better performers at work as they have known the MNC for a longer time and are more aware of the tacit knowledge within the organization as well as the organizational culture and histories of strategy development. They are more suitable as candidates for subsidiary CEOs, maybe also because they have closer ties with the MNC, and are therefore more committed to working hard for the MNC. Since personality traits are relatively stable personal characteristics, the personality traits of expatriate CEO candidates are not likely to change due to cross-cultural training or more expatriation experience. Besides, SIE CEOs already had more expatriation experience than their assigned colleagues. Hence, selection and testing for suitable personality traits would be the preferred human resource measures of the selection process of expatriate CEOs for assignments in China. Furthermore, MNCs are recommended to emphasize the importance of international experiences for expatriates' career development. MNCs are also recommended to take into consideration that SIE CEOs tend to stay longer in the host country. Therefore, SIE CEOs might be more suitable candidates if MNCs have made long-term development plan in the host country.

Our study is one of the first studies to explore the differences between AE CEOs and SIE CEOs. Future studies could examine the career path of these two types of CEOs longitudinally in relation to their personality traits and work-related outcomes. It would be also important for future studies to explore whether there is a trend for more AE CEOs to become SIE CEOs and vice versa, and under what conditions. Furthermore, future studies could examine differences such as region, gender and professional background in detail.

3.9. Conclusions

In this book chapter, we draw upon results from a survey with 93 AE CEOs and 94 SIE CEOs in China. We found that these two groups are significantly different from each other in terms of demographics, personality and job performance. Although we found that self-initiated CEOs have longer duration of stay than assigned CEOs, assigned CEOs nevertheless have better self-control and tend to self-rate as better performers than self-initiated CEOs. The findings of our study calls for more focused research on these two types of expatriates in leadership positions.

References

Al Ariss, A. (2013). Self-Initiated expatriation and migration in the management literature: Present theorizations and future research directions. *Career Development International,* *18*(1), 78−96.

Ali, A., Van der Zee, K., & Sanders, G. (2003). Determinants of intercultural adjustment among expatriate spouses. *International Journal of Intercultural Relations, 27*(5), 563−580.

Almeida, P., & Phene, A. (2004). Subsidiaries and knowledge creation: The influence of the MNC and host country on innovation. *Strategic Management Journal, 25*, 847−864.

Altman, Y., & Shortland, S. (2008). Women and international assignments: Taking stock − a 25-year review. *Human Resource Management, 47*(2), 199−216.

Anderson, B. A. (2005). Expatriate selection: Good management or good luck? *International Journal of Human Resource Management, 16*(4), 567−583.

Andresen, M., Al Ariss, A., & Walther, M. E. (2012a). *Self-initiated expatriation: Individual, organizational, and national perspectives.* London: Routledge.

Andresen, M., Bergdolt, F., & Margenfeld, J. (2012b). What distinguishes self-initiated expatriates from assigned expatriates and migrants? In M. Andresen, A. Al Arises, & M. Walther (Eds.), *Self-initiated expatriation* (pp. 166−194). London: Routledge.

Andresen, M., Biemann, T., & Pattiec, M. W. (forthcoming). What makes them move abroad? Reviewing and exploring differences between self-initiated and assigned expatriation. *International Journal of Human Resource Management.*

Arp, F., Hutchings, K., & Smith, W. A. (2013). Foreign executives in local organisations: An exploration of differences to other types of expatriates. *Journal of Global Mobility, 1*(3), 312−335.

Averill, J. R. (1982). *Anger and aggression: An essay on emotion.* New York, NY: Springer.

Balkan, K. (1966). Inandik'ta 1966 yilinda bulunan eski Hitit çağina ait bir bagiş belgesi [türk u. dt.] Eine Schenkungsurkunde aus der althethitischen Zeit, gefunden in Inandik 1966.

Banai, M., & Harry, W. (2004). Boundaryless global careers: The international itinerants. *International Studies of Management and Organization, 34*(3), 96−120.

Bandura, A. (1989). Human agency in social cognitive theory. *American Psychologist, 44*, 1175−1184.

Bartol, K. M., & Manhardt, P. J. (1979). Sex differences in job outcome preferences: Trends among newly hired college graduates. *Journal of Applied Psychology, 64*, 477–482.

Bateman, T. S., & Crant, J. M. (1993). The proactive component of organizational behavior. *Journal of Organizational Behavior, 14*, 103−118.

Baumeister, R. F., Bratslavsky, E., Muraven, M., & Tice, D. M. (1998). Ego-depletion: Is the active self a limited resource? *Journal of Personality and Social Psychology, 74*, 1252−1265.

Beutel, A., & Marini, M. (1995). Gender and values. *American Sociological Review, 60*, 436–448.

Biemann, T., & Andresen, M. (2010). Self-initiated foreign expatriates versus assigned expatriates. *Journal of Managerial Psychology, 25*(4), 430−448.

Birkinshaw, J., & Hood, N. (1998). Multinational subsidiary evolution: Capability and charter change in foreign-owned subsidiary companies. *Academy of Management Review, 23*(4), 773−795.

Black, J. S., Mendenhall, M. E., & Oddou, G. R. (1991). Toward a comprehensive model of international adjustment: An integration of multiple theoretical perspectives. *Academy of Management Review, 1*(6), 291–317.

Bodycott, P., & Lai, A. (2012). The influence and implications of Chinese culture in the decision to undertake cross-border higher education. *Journal of Studies in International Education, 16*(3), 252−270.

Bolino, M. C. (2007). Expatriate assignments and intra-organizational career success: Implications for individuals and organizations. *Journal of International Business Studies, 38*(5), 819−835.

Boxman, E. A., De Graaf, P. M., & Flap, H. D. (1991). The impact of social and human capital on the income attainment of Dutch managers. *Social Networks, 13*(1), 51–73.

Brown, R. J. (2008). Dominant stressors on expatriate couples during international assignments. *International Journal of Human Resource Management, 19*(6), 1018–1034.

Buckley, P. J., Clegg, J., & Tan, H. (2006). Cultural awareness in knowledge transfer to China – The role of Guanxi and Mianzi. *Journal of World Business, 41*(3), 275–288.

Caligiuri, P. M., Joshi, A., & Lazarova, M. (1999). Factors influencing the adjustment of women on global assignments. *International Journal of Human Resource Management, 10*(2), 163–179.

Caligiuri, P., & Lazarova, M. (2002). A model for the influence of social interaction and social support on female expatriates' cross-cultural adjustment. *International Journal of Human Resource Management, 13*(5), 761–772.

Calori, R., Johnson, G., & Sarnin, P. (1994). CEO's cognitive maps and the scope of the organization. *Strategic Management Journal, 15*, 437–457.

Carlson, R. (1971). Sex differences in ego functioning: Exploratory studies of agency and communion. *Journal of Consulting and Clinical Psychology, 37*, 267–277.

Carpenter, M. A., & Fredrickson, J. W. (2001). Top management teams, global strategic posture, and the moderating role of uncertainty. *Academy of Management Journal, 44*(3), 533–545.

Carpenter, M. A., Geletkanycz, M. A., & Sanders, W. G. (2004). The upper echelons revisited: Antecedents, elements, and consequences of top management team composition. *Journal of Management, 30*, 749–778.

Carpenter, M. A., Sanders, W. G., & Gregersen, H. B. (2001). Bundling human capital with organizational context: The impact of international assignment experience on multinational firm performance and CEO pay. *Academy of Management Journal, 44*(3), 493–511.

Carr, S. C., Inkson, K., & Thorn, K. (2005). From global careers to talent flow: Reinterpreting 'brain drain'. *Journal of World Business, 40*(4), 386–398.

Cerdin, J.-L., & Le Pargneux, M. L. (2010). Career anchors: organization-assigned and self-initiated expatriates. *Thunderbird International Business Review, 52*(4), 287–299.

Cerdin, J.-L., & Selmer, J. (2014). Who is a self-initiated expatriate? Towards conceptual clarity of a common notion. *International Journal of Human Resource Management, 25*(9), 1281–1301.

Chen, S. H., Main, A., Zhou, Q., Bunge, S. A., Lau, N., & Chu, K. (2015). Effortful control and early academic achievement of Chinese American children in immigrant families. *Early Childhood Research Quarterly, 30*, 45–56.

Chiao, C. (1981). Chinese strategic behavior: Some general principles. Paper presented at the a conference in honor of Professor John M. Roberts, November–December, in Claremont, CA.

Chu, R. (2006). Social interactions among the Chinese: On the issue of face. *Chinese Social Psychological Review, 2*, 79–106.

Collings, D. G., Scullion, H., & Morley, M. J. (2007). Changing patterns of global staffing in the multinational enterprise: Challenges to the conventional expatriate assignment and emerging alternatives. *Journal of World Business, 42*, 198–213.

Crant, J. M. (2000). Proactive behavior in organizations. *Journal of Management, 26*, 435–462.

Crowley-Henry, M. (2007). The protean career: Exemplified by first world foreign residents in Western Europe? *International Studies of Management & Organization, 37*(3), 44–64.

Daily, C. M., Certo, S. T., & Dalton, D. R. (2000). International experience in the executive suite: The path to prosperity? *Strategic Management Journal, 21*(4), 515–523.

De Cieri, H., Dowling, P., & Taylor, K. (1991). The psychological impact of expatriate relocation on partners. *The International Journal of Human Resource Management, 2*(3), 377–414.

de Ridder, D. T. D., Lensvelt-Mulders, G., Finkenauer, C., Stok, F. M., & Baumeister, R. F. (2012). Taking stock of self-control: A meta-analysis of how trait self-control relates to a wide range of behaviors. *Personality and Social Psychology Review, 16*(1), 76–99.

Dear, G. E., Watt, B. D., & Dockerill, J. (2003). Factor structure of the Spielberger Anger Expression scales when used with Australian prisoners. *Psychological Reports, 92*(2), 617–620.

Deffenbacher, J. L., Richards, T. L., Filetti, L. B., & Lynch, R. S. (2005). Angry drivers: A test of state-trait theory. *Violence and Victims, 20*, 455–469.

Doherty, N. (2013). Understanding the self-initiated expatriate: A review and directions for future research. *International Journal of Management Reviews, 15*(4), 447–469.

Doherty, N., Dickmann, M., & Mills, T. (2011). Exploring the motives of company-backed and self-initiated expatriates. *International Journal of Human Resource Management, 22*(3), 595–611.

Dowling, P., & Welch, D. (2004). *International human resource management: Managing people in a global context* (4th ed.). London: Thomson Learning.

Dowling, P. J., Festing, M., & Engle, A. D. (2008). *International human resource management: Managing people in a multinational context* (5th ed.). London: Cengage Learning EMEA.

Downes, M., Varner, I., & Musinski, L. (2007). Personality traits as predictors of expatriate effectiveness: A synthesis and reconceptualization. *Review of Business, 27*(3), 16–23.

Eagly, A. H., & Crowley, M. (1986). Gender and helping behavior: A meta-analytic review of the social psychological literature. *Psychological Bulletin, 100*(3), 283.

Early, P. C. (1987). Intercultural training for managers: A comparison of documentary and interpersonal methods. *Academy of Management Journal, 30*, 685–698.

Edström, A., & Galbraith, J. (1977). Transfer of managers as a coordinating and control strategy in multi-national organizations. *Administrative Science Quarterly, 22*, 248–263.

Elizur, D. (2001). Gender and work values: A comparative analysis. *The Journal of Social Psychology, 134*(2), 201–212.

Fee, A., & Gray, S. J. (2012). The expatriate-creativity hypothesis: A longitudinal field test. *Human Relations, 65*, 1515–1538.

Fisher, C. D. (2003). Why do lay people believe that satisfaction and performance are correlated? Possible sources of a commonsense theory. *Journal of Organizational Behavior, 24*, 753–777.

Frese, M., Garst, H., & Fay, D. (2007). Making things happen: Reciprocal relationships between work characteristics and personal initiative (PI) in a four-wave longitudinal structural equation model. *Journal of Applied Psychology, 92*(4), 1084–1102.

Froese, F. J., & Peltokorpi, V. (2012). The impact of expatriate personality traits on cross-cultural adjustment: A study with expatriates in Japan. *International Business Review, 21*(4), 734–746.

Froese, F. J., & Peltokorpi, V. (2013). Organizational expatriates and self-initiated expatriates: differences in cross-cultural adjustment and job satisfaction. *International Journal of Human Resource Management, 24*(10), 1953–1967.

Fuller, B., & Marler, L. E. (2009). Change driven by nature: A meta-analytic review of the proactive personality literature. *Journal of Vocational Behavior, 75*(3), 329–345.

Gecas, V. (1982). The self concept. *Annual Review of Sociology, 8*, 1–33.

Gong, Y. (2003). Staffing in multinational enterprises: Agency, resources, and performance. *Academy of Management Journal, 46*(6), 728–739.

Gove, W. R. (1994). Why we do what we do: A biopsychosocial theory of human motivation. *Social Forces, 73*(2), 363–394.

Granovetter, M. (1974). *A study of contacts and careers.* Cambridge, MA: Harvard University Press.

Greller, M. M., & Simpson, P. (1999). In search of late career: Review of contemporary social science research applicable to the understanding of late career. *Human Resource Management Review, 9*(3), 309–347.

GRTS (2013). *Global relocation trends survey.* Woodridge: Brookfield Relocation Services.

Guthrie, J. P., Ash, R. A., & Stevens, C. D. (2003). Are women "better" than men?: Personality differences and expatriate selection. *Journal of Managerial Psychology, 18*(3), 229–243.

Hambrick, D. C. (1982). Environmental scanning and organizational strategy. *Strategic Management Journal, 3*, 159–174.

Harter, S. (1983). Developmental perspectives on the self-system. In P. H. Mussen & E. M. Hetherington (Eds.), *Handbook of child psychology: Socialization, personality, and social development* (pp. 275–385). New York, NY: Wiley.

Hall, J. A., & Mast, M. S. (2008). Are women always more interpersonally sensitive than men? Impact of goals and content domain. *Personality and Social Psychology Bulletin, 34*, 144–155.

Hayward, M. L., & Hambrick, D. C. (1997). Explaining the premiums paid for large acquisitions: Evidence of CEO hubris. *Administrative Science Quarterly, 42*(1), 103–127.

Ho, D. Y.-f. (1976). On the concept of face. *American Journal of Sociology, 81*(4), 867–884.

Huang, Q., Davison, R. M., & Gu, J. (2008). Impact of personal and cultural factors on knowledge sharing in China. *Asia Pacific Journal of Management, 25*(3), 451–471.

Inkson, K., Arthur, M. B., Pringle, J., & Barry, S. (1997). Expatriate assignment versus overseas experience: International human resource development. *Journal of World Business, 2*, 351–368.

Inkson, K., & Myers, B. A. (2003). "The big OE": self-directed travel and career development. *Career Development International, 8*(4), 170–181.

Jokinen, T., Brewster, C., & Suutari, V. (2008). Career capital during international work experiences: contrasting self-initiated expatriate experiences and assigned expatriation. *International Journal of Human Resource Management, 19*(6), 979–998.

Judge, T. A., Bono, J. E., Ilies, R., & Gerhardt, M. W. (2002). Personality and leadership: A qualitative and quantitative review. *Journal of Applied Psychology, 87*, 765–780.

Kessapidou, S., & Varsakelis, N. (2003). National culture and its impact on the choice of managing director in international production: the case of foreign firms in Greece. *International Journal of Human Resource Management, 14*(2), 285–295.

Kim, Y. (2002). Executive social capital and its impacts on job promotion. *Academy of Management Proceedings: J1–J6.*

Kitayama, S., Mesquita, B., & Karasawa, M. (2006). Cultural affordances and emotional experience: Socially engaging and disengaging emotions in Japan and the United States. *Journal of Personality and Social Psychology, 91*, 890–903.

Kliegel, M., McDaniel, M. A., & Einstein, G. O. (2000). Plan formation, retention, and execution in prospective memory: A new approach and age-related effects. *Memory & cognition, 28*(6), 1041–1049.

Kobrin, S. J. (1988). Expatriate reduction and strategic control in American multinational corporations. *Human Resource Management, 27*(1), 63–75.

Kooij, D., Lange, A., Jansen, P., & Dikkers, J. (2008). 'Older Workers' motivation to continue to work: Five meanings of age: A conceptual review. *Journal of Managerial Psychology, 23*(4), 364–394.

Krach, S., Blümel, I., Marjoram, D., Lataster, T., Krabbendam, L., Weber, J., ... Kircher, T. (2009). Are women better mindreaders? Sex differences in neural correlates of mentalizing detected with functional MRI. *BMC Neuroscience, 10*(1), 1.

Kühlmann, T., & Hutchings, K. (2010). Expatriate assignments vs localization of management in China. *Career Development International, 15*(1), 20–38.

Lauring, J., & Klitmøller, A. (2015). Corporate language-based communication avoidance in MNCs: A multi-sited ethnography approach. *Journal of World Business, 50*, 46–55.

Lauring, J., & Selmer, J. (2010). The supportive expatriate spouse: An ethnographic study of spouse involvement in expatriate careers. *International Business Review, 19*(1), 59–69.

Lauring, J., & Selmer, J. (2014). Global mobility orientation and the success of self-initiated expatriates in greater China. *Asia Pacific Business Review, 20*(4), 523–540.

Lauring, J., & Selmer, J. (2015). Job engagement and work outcomes in a cognitively demanding context: The case of expatriate academics. *Personnel Review, 44*(4), 629–647.

Lee, C. H. (2005). A study of underemployment among self-initiated expatriates. *Journal of World Business, 40*, 172–187.

Leonard, N. H., Beauvais, L. L., & Scholl, R. W. (1999). Work motivation: The incorporation of self-concept-based pro cesses. *Human Relations, 52*, 969–998.

Leung, T. K., & Yee-kwong Chan, R. (2003). Face, favour and positioning – a Chinese power game. *European Journal of Marketing, 37*(11/12), 1575–1598.

Lewin, K., Dembo, T., Festinger, L., & Sears, P. (1944). Level of aspiration. In J. Hunt (Ed.), *Personality and behavior disorders* (pp. 333–378). New York, NY: Ronald.

Linehan, M., Scullion, H., & Walsh, J. S. (2001). Barriers to women's participation in international management. *European Business Review, 13*(1), 10–19.

Linehan, M., & Walsh, J. S. (2000). Beyond the traditional linear view of international managerial careers: a new model of the senior female career in an international context. *Journal of European Industrial Training, 24*(2/3/4), 178–189.

Logue, A. W. (1988). Research on self-control: An integrating framework. *Behavioral and Brain Sciences, 11*, 665–709.

Lord, R. G., De Vader, C. L., & Alliger, M. (1986). A meta-analysis of the relation between personality traits and leadership perceptions: An application of validity generalization procedures. *Journal of Applied Psychology, 71*, 402–410.

Lowe, K. B., Downes, M., & Kroeck, K. G. (1999). The impact of gender and location on the willingness to accept overseas assignments. *International Journal of Human Resource Management, 10*(2), 223–234.

Luo, Y. (2002). Organizational dynamics and global integration: a perspective from subsidiary managers. *Journal of International Management, 8*, 189–215.

Mahmoud, M. (1996). Work satisfaction and gender. *International Review of Modern Sociology, 26*, 67–79.

Markus, H. R., & Kitayama, S. (1991). Culture and the self: Implications for cognition, emotion, and motivation. *Psychological Review, 98*(2), 224–253.

Martin, J. (2004). The global CEO. *CHIEF EXECUTIVE-NEW YORK-*: 24–31.

Maurer, T. J. (2001). Career-relevant learning and development, worker age, and beliefs about self-efficacy for development. *Journal of Management, 27*, 123–140.

Mayerhofer, H., Hartmann, L. C., Michelitsch-Riedl, G., & Kollinger, I. (2004). Flexpatriate assignments: A neglected issue in global staffing. *The International Journal of Human Resource Management, 15*(8), 1371–1389.

Mayerhofer, H., Müller, B., & Schmidt, A. (2010). Implications of flexpatriates' lifestyles on HRM practices. *Management Revue: The International Review of Management Studies, 21*(2), 155–173.

McKenna, S., & Richardson, J. (2007). The increasing complexity of the internationally mobile professional. *Cross Cultural Management, 14*(4), 307–320.

Mehrabian, A., & Blum, J. S. (1996). Temperament and personality as functions of age. *International Journal of Aging and Human Development, 42*(4), 251–269.

Mellahi, K., & Collings, D. G. (2010). The barriers to effective global talent management: The example of corporate elites in MNEs. *Journal of World Business, 45*(2), 143–149.

Mendenhall, M., & Macomber, J. (1997). Rethinking the strategic management of expatriates from a nonlinear dynamics perspective. In Z. Aycan (Ed.), *Expatriate management: Theory and research* (pp. 41–46). Greenwich: JAI Press.

Metcalfe, J., & Mischel, W. (1999). A hot/cool system analysis of delay of gratification: Dynamics of willpower. *Psychological Review, 106*, 3–19.

Miller, E. L., & Cheng, J. L. (1978). A closer look at the decision to accept an overseas position. *Management International Review, 3*, 25–33.

Miller, D., & Toulouse, J. (1986). Chief executive personality and corporate strategy and structure in small firms. *Management Science, 32*(11), 1389–1409.

Mizruchi, M. S. (1991). Urgency, motivation, and group performance: The effect of prior success on current success among professional basketball teams. *Social Psychology Quarterly, 54*(2), 181–189.

Moeller, M., Harvey, M., & Williams, W. (2010). Socialization of inpatriate managers to the headquarters of global organizations: A social learning perspective. *Human Resource Development Review, 9*(2), 169–193.

Monks, K., Scullion, H., & Creaner, J. (2001). An empirical study of international HRM in Irish international firms. *Personnel Review, 30*(5), 536–553.

Morrison, R. F., & Brantner, T. M. (1992). What enhances or inhibits learning a new job? A basic career issue. *Journal of Applied Psychology, 77*(6), 926–941.

Muraven, M., & Baumeister, R. F. (2000). Self-regulation and depletion of limited resources: Does self-control resemble a muscle? *Psychological Bulletin, 126*(2), 247–259.

Nadkarni, S., & Herrmann, P. (2010). CEO personality, strategic flexibility, and firm performance: The case of the Indian business process outsourcing industry. *Academy of Management Journal, 53*(5), 1050–1073.

Näsholm, M. H. (2012). Global careerists' identity construction. *International Journal of Managing Projects in Business, 5*(4), 804–812.

Owen, J. M. (2011). Transdiagnostic cognitive processes in high trait anger. *Clinical Psychology Review, 31*(2), 193–202.

Parker, S. K. (1998). Enhancing role breadth self-efficacy: The roles of job enrichment and other organizational interventions. *Journal of Applied Psychology, 83*, 835–852.

Peltokorpi, V., & Froese, F. J. (2009). Organizational expatriates and self-initiated expatriates: Who adjusts better to work and life in Japan? *The International Journal of Human Resource Management, 20*(5), 1096–1112.

Peltokorpi, V., & Froese, F. (2012). The impact of expatriate personality traits on crosscultural adjustment: A study with expatriates in Japan. *International Business Review, 21,* 734–746.

Peterson, R. S., Smith, D. B., Martorana, P. V., & Owens, P. D. (2003). The impact of chief executive officer personality on top management team dynamics: One mechanism by which leadership affects organizational performance. *Journal of Applied Psychology, 88*(5), 795–808.

Plutchik, R. (2002). *Emotions and life, perspectives from psychology, biology and evolution.* Washington, DC: American Psychological Association.

Quick, J. C., Gavin, J. H., Cooper, C. L., & Quick, J. D. (2000). Executive health: Building strength, managing risks. *The Academy of Management Executive, 14*(2), 34–44.

Quinn, C. A., Rollock, D., & Vrana, S. R. (2014). A test of Spielberger's state-trait theory of anger with adolescents: Five hypotheses. *Emotion, 14*(1), 74–84.

Raabe, B., Frese, M., & Beehr, T. A. (2007). Action regulation theory and career self-management. *Journal of Vocational Behavior, 70*(2), 297–311.

Reiche, B. S. (2006). The inpatriate experience in multinational corporations: An exploratory case study in Germany. *International Journal of Human Resource Management, 17,* 1572–1590.

Reiger, R. C., & Rees, R. T. (1993). Teachers and motivation: A demographic study. *Education, 113*(3), 482–484.

Reio, T. G., & Callahan, J. L. (2004). Affect, curiosity, and socialization-related learning: A path analysis of antecedents to job performance. *Journal of Business and Psychology, 19*(1), 3–22.

Resick, C. J., Whitman, D. S., Weingarden, S. M., & Hiller, N. J. (2009). The bright-side and the dark-side of CEO personality: Examining core self-evaluations, narcissism, transformational leadership, and strategic influence. *Journal of Applied Psychology, 94*(6), 1365–1381.

Richardson, J. (2006). Self-directed expatriation: Family matters. *Personnel Review, 35*(4), 469–486.

Roth, K. (1995). Managing international interdependence: CEO characteristics in a resource-based framework. *Academy of Management Journal, 38*(1), 200–231.

Rothbaum, F., Weisz, J., & Snyder, S. (1982). Changing the world and changing the self: A two-process model of perceived control. *Journal of Personality and Social Psychology, 42*(1), 5–37.

Roussanov, N., & Savor, P. (2014). Marriage and managers' attitudes to risk. *Management Science, 60*(10), 2496–2508.

Seibert, S. E., Kraimer, M. L., & Crant, J. M. (2001). What do proactive people do? A longitudinal model linking proactive personality and career success. *Personnel Psychology, 54,* 845–874.

Sekiguchi, T., Bebenroth, R., & Li, D. (2011). Nationality background of MNC affiliates' top management and affiliate performance in Japan: knowledge-based and upper echelons perspectives. *International Journal of Human Resource Management, 22*(5), 999–1016.

Selmer, J. (1998). Expatriation: Corporate policy, personal intentions and international adjustment. *International Journal of Human Resource Management, 9,* 996–1007.

Selmer, J. (2001). Expatriate selection: Back to basics? *The International Journal of Human Resource Management, 12*(8), 1219–1233.

Selmer, J. (2002). Practice makes perfect? International experience and expatriate adjustment. *Management International Review, 42*(1), 71–87.

Selmer, J. (2006). Language ability and adjustment: Western expatriates in China. *Thunderbird International Business Review, 48*(3), 347–368.

Selmer, J., & Fenner, C. R. (2009). Job factors and work outcomes of public sector expatriates. *Human Resource Management Journal, 19*(1), 75–90.

Selmer, J., & Lauring, J. (2010). Self-initiated academic expatriates: Inherent demographics and reasons to expatriate. *European Management Review, 7*(3), 169–179.

Selmer, J., & Lauring, J. (2011a). Marital status and work outcomes of self-initiated expatriates: Is there a moderating effect of gender? *Cross Cultural Management, 18*(2), 198–213.

Selmer, J., & Lauring, J. (2011b). Self-initiated academic expatriates: Inherent demographics and reasons to expatriate. *European Management Review, 7*(3), 169–179.

Selmer, J., & Lauring, J. (2012). Reasons to expatriate and work outcomes of self-initiated expatriates. *Personnel Review, 41*(5), 665–684.

Selmer, J., & Lauring, J. (2013a). Dispositional affectivity and work outcomes of expatriates. *International Business Review, 22*(3), 568–577.

Selmer, J., & Lauring, J. (2013b). Self-initiated expatriate academics: Personal characteristics and work outcomes. In A. Haslberger & V. Vaiman (Eds.), *Managing talent of self-initiated expatriates: A neglected source of the global talent flow* (pp. 181–201). Houndmills, U.K.: Palgrave Macmillan.

Selmer, J., & Lauring, J. (2014a). Mobility and emotions: Dispositional affectivity and adjustment of self-initiated expatriates. *International Studies of Management and Organization, 44*(3), 25–43.

Selmer, J., & Lauring, J. (2014b). Self-initiated expatriates: An exploratory study of adjustment of adult third-culture kids vs. adult mono-culture kids. *Cross Cultural Management, 21*(4), 422–436.

Selmer, J., & Lauring, J. (2014c). Unhappy expatriates at work: Subjective ill-being and work outcomes. *European Journal of International Management, 8*(6), 579–599.

Selmer, J., & Lauring, J. (2015). Host country language ability and expatriate adjustment: The moderating effect of language difficulty. *International Journal of Human Resource Management, 26*(3), 401–420.

Selmer, J., Lauring, J., & Feng, Y. (2009). Age and expatriate job performance in Greater China. *Cross Cultural Management: An International Journal, 16*, 131–148.

Selmer, J., & Leon, C. (1997). Succession procedures for expatriate chief executives. *Human Resource Management Journal, 7*(3), 80–88.

Sexton, D., & Bowman-Upton, N. (1990). Eetnale and male entrepreneurs: Psychological gharacteristics and their role in genderrelated discrimination. *Journal of Business Venturing, 5*, 29–36.

Shaffer, M. A., Kraimer, M. L., Chen, Y.-P., & Bolino, M. C. (2012). Choices, challenges, and career consequences of global work experiences: A review and future agenda. *Journal of Management, 38*, 1282–1327.

Shay, J. P., & Baack, S. A. (2004). Expatriate assignment, adjustment and effectiveness: An empirical examination of the big picture. *Journal of International Business Studies, 35*(3), 216–232.

Shi, X., & Franklin, P. (2013). Business expatriates' cross-cultural adaptation and their job performance. *Asia Pacific Journal of Human Resources, 52*(2), 193–214.

Simon, M., & Houghton, S. M. (2003). The relationship between overconfidence and the introduction of risky products: Evidence from a field study. *Academy of Management Journal, 46*(2), 139–149.

Simsek, Z., Heavey, C., & Veiga, J. F. (2010). The impact of CEO self-evaluation on the firms entrepreneurial orientation. *Strategic Management Journal, 31,* 110−119.

Spielberger, C. D., Jacobs, G., Russell, S., & Crane, R. S. (1983). Assessment of anger: The state-trait anger scale. *Advances in Personality Assessment, 2,* 159−187.

Spreitzer, G. M., McCall, M. W., & Mahoney, J. D. (1997). Early identification of international executive potential. *Journal of Applied Psychology, 82*(1), 6−29.

Stahl, G. K., Miller, E., & Tung, R. (2002). Toward the boundaryless career: A closer look at the expatriate career concept and the perceived implications of an international assignment. *Journal of World Business, 37*(3), 216−227.

Stanek, M. B. (2000). The need for global managers: A business necessity. *Management Decision, 38*(4), 232−242.

Sterns, H. L., & Miklos, S. M. (1995). The aging worker in a changing environment: Organizational and individual issues. *Journal of Vocational Behavior, 47,* 248–268.

Stone, R. J. (1991). Expatriate selection and failure. *Human Resource Planning, 14*(1), 9–18.

Stroh, L., Black, J., Mendenhall, M., & Gregersen, H. (2005). *Global leaders, global assignments: An integration of research and practice.* London: Lawrence Erlbaum.

Suutari, V. (2003). Global managers: Career orientation, career tracks, life-style implications and career commitment. *Journal of Managerial Psychology, 18*(3), 185−207.

Suutari, V., & Brewster, C. (2000). Making their own way: International experience through self-initiated foreign assignments. *Journal of World Business, 35*(4), 417−436.

Takeuchi, R., Marinova, S., Lepak, D., & Liu, W. (2005). A model of expatriate withdrawal-related outcomes: Decision making from a dualistic adjustment perspective. *Human Resource Management Review, 15,* 119−138.

Tan, D., & Mahoney, J. T. (2003). Explaining the utilization of managerial expatriates from the perspectives of resource-based, agency, and transaction-costs theories. *Advances in International Management, 15,* 179−205.

Tangney, J. P., Baumeister, R. F., & Boone, A. L. (2004). High self-control predicts good adjustment, less pathology, better grades, and interpersonal success. *Journal of Personality, 72,* 271−324.

Tesluk, P. E., & Jacobs, R. R. (1998). Toward an integrated model of work experience. *Personnel Psychology, 51*(2), 321−355.

Tharenou, P. (2010). Women's self-initiated expatriation as a career option and its ethical issues. *Journal of Business Ethics, 95*(1), 73−88.

Tharenou, P. (2013). Self-initiated expatriates: An alternative to company-assigned expatriates? *Journal of Global Mobility, 1*(3), 336−356.

Tharenou, P., & Caulfield, N. (2010). Will I stay or will I go? Explaining repatriation by self-initiated expatriates. *Academy of Management Journal, 53*(5), 1009−1028.

Tharenou, P., & Harvey, M. (2006). Examining the overseas staffing options utilized by Australian headquartered multinational corporations. *International Journal of Human Resource Management, 17*(6), 1095−1114.

Thompson, J. A. (2005). Proactive personality and job performance: A social capital perspective on mediating behaviors. *Journal of Applied Psychology, 90,* 1011−1017.

Thorn, K. (2009). The relative importance of motives for international self-initiated mobility. *Career Development International, 14,* 441–464.

Tseng, C.-H., & Liao, Y.-S. (2009). Expatriate CEO assignment: A study of multinational corporations' subsidiaries in Taiwan. *International Journal of Manpower, 30*(8), 853−870.

Tung, R. L. (1987). Expatriate assignments: Enhancing success and minimizing failure. *Academy of Management Executive, 1*(2), 117–126.

Tung, R. L. (2004). Female expatriates: The model global manager? *Organizational Dynamics, 33*(3), 243–253.

Tung, R. L. (2008). The cross-cultural research imperative: the need to balance cross-national and intra-national diversity. *Journal of International Business Studies, 39*, 41–46.

van Erp, K. J. P. M., van der Zee, K. I., Giebels, E., & van Duijn, M. A. J. (2014). Lean on me: The importance of own and partner intercultural personality dimensions for the success of an international assignment. *European Journal of Work and Organizational Psychology, 23*(5), 706–728.

Vance, C. M., & Paik, Y. (2005). Forms of host-country national learning for enhanced MNC absorptive capacity. *Journal of Managerial Psychology, 20*(7), 590–606.

Von Borell de Araujo, B. F., Teixeira, M. L. M., Da Cruz, P. B., & Malini, E. (forthcoming). Understanding adaptation of organisational and self-initiated expatriates in Brazilian culture. *International Journal of Human Resource Management, 25*(18), 2489–2509.

Vroom, V. R., & Pahl, B. (1971). Relationship between age and risk taking among managers. *Journal of Applied Psychology, 55*, 399–405.

Wang, A., Karns, J., & Meredith, W. (2003). Motivation, stress, self-control ability, and self-control behavior of preschool children in China. *Journal of Research in Childhood Education, 17*(2), 175–187.

Warr, P. (2001). Age and work behaviour: Physical attributes, cognitive abilities, knowledge, personality traits, and motives. *International Review of Industrial and Organizational Psychology, 16*, 1–36.

Welch, D. (1994). Determinants of international human resource management approaches and activities: A suggested framework. *Journal of Management Studies, 31*(2), 139–164.

Wingrove, J., & Bond, A. J. (2005). Correlation between trait hostility and faster reading times for sentences describing angry reactions to ambiguous situations. *Cognition and Emotion, 19*(3), 463–472.

Wong, S., Siu, V., & Tsang, N. (1999). The impact of demographic factors on Hong Kong hotel employees' choice of job-related motivators. *International Journal of Contemporary Hospitality Management, 11*(5), 230–241.

Zhang, Z., Wang, M., & Shi, J. (2012). Leader-follower congruence in proactive personality and work outcomes: The mediating role of leader-member exchange. *Academy of Management Journal, 55*(1), 111–130.

Zhou, Q., Eisenberg, N., Wang, Y., & Reiser, M. (2004). Chinese children's effortful control and dispositional anger/frustration: Relations to parenting styles and children's social functioning. *Developmental Psychology, 40*(3), 352–366.

Chapter 4

Career Capital Development of Self-Initiated Expatriates in China

Ying Guo, Hussain G. Rammal and Peter J. Dowling

Abstract

Purpose − The purpose of this chapter is to provide an overview of SIEs' career development through international assignment. In particular, the research focus is on career capital acquirement and development of SIEs through their international assignment in China.

Methodology/approach − We review studies on SIEs and comparative studies between SIEs and OEs. We apply the career capital theory to discuss SIEs' career capital development in terms of knowing-how, knowing-why and knowing-whom through expatriation assignment in China.

Findings − This chapter focuses on SIEs' career capital accumulation through international assignments in China, and we develop three propositions that will guide future studies: the knowing-whom career capital development of SIEs through expatriation is increased more in network quantity than network quality in China; the knowing-why career capital development of SIEs through expatriation is influenced by the age and career stage of SIEs; and the knowing-how career capital development of SIEs through expatriation — task-related skills and local engagement skills — is influenced by the SIE's intercultural ability and organization support respectively.

Practical implications − In practice, a better understanding of SIEs' career capital development in terms of knowing-how, knowing-why and knowing-whom help companies make the decision to select the relevant staffing pattern. This study also has practical implications in relation to the design and

Global Talent Management and Staffing in MNEs
International Business & Management, Volume 32, 81−100
Copyright © 2016 by Emerald Group Publishing Limited
All rights of reproduction in any form reserved
ISSN: 1876-066X/doi:10.1108/S1876-066X20160000032003

selection of the training, learning and development activities provided to the employees.

Originality/value – The chapter contributes to the expatriate management literature by focusing on SIEs' career development through their international assignment in China. SIEs' career development is related to their cross-cultural adjustment and has impacts on the completion and success of the expatriation assignment.

Keywords: Self-initiated expatriates; Career capital; China; organization assigned expatriates

4.1. Introduction

The increasing levels of foreign direct investment (FDI) in developing countries have made expatriate management an important field of research in International Business. The use of expatriates can help companies establish a diverse workforce, which has significant impacts on organization innovation and performance. On the other hand, employing expatriates can become a burden for some companies due to the costs associated with it. In a globalized economy, more individuals have the opportunities and desire to work abroad, and as a result an increasing number of self-initiate expatriates (SIEs) are joining the global labor market. However, extant studies on the understanding the behaviors and perspectives of SIEs is limited and insufficient (Suutari & Brewster, 2000; Vance, 2005). Most expatriate studies conducted in this area during the last decade tend to focus on organization/company assigned expatriates (OEs), and have emphasis on three issues: global leadership, expatriate adjustment and repatriation adjustment (Tseng, Chou, & Yu, 2010). Although SIEs and OEs share some similarities in relation to international assignments, the more important and urgent research call is to understand the distinct characteristics of SIEs as they differ from OEs in the aspects of motivators, relocation cost, job role, and job level for conducting an international assignment.

Considering international assignments in a distinct cultural and institutional environment such as expatriates from developed countries conducting work in a developing country, it would seem that there exists more challenges for SIEs than OEs. These challenges exist because SIEs generally do not receive sufficient support from the organization such as relocation allowance and housing assistance as they are self-directed to the host country. Although there are a few studies discussed SIEs (see for example, Inkson & Myers, 2003; Lee, 2005; Myers & Pringle, 2005; Richardson, 2006; Richardson & Mallon, 2005; Richardson & McKenna, 2006;

Vance, 2005), the body of knowledge exploring SIEs' development in China remains limited, and more research is required to enrich our understanding of the relevant issues in this unique socio-economic context.

China was the top destination for inward FDI in 2014 (UNCTAD, 2015), and is host to a large number of expatriates. However, expatriates continue to rate China as a challenging destination for international assignments considering its cultural and institutional conditions (Brookfield Global Relocation Services, 2016). Without sufficient support from the organization, SIEs working in China can face a number of challenges. In this chapter, we highlight these issues through a systematic review of the literature on SIEs. We use China as an example to illustrate how SIEs develop their career capital through their international assignment in the country. The next section reviews and discusses the current studies on SIEs and the comparative studies on SIEs and OEs. We then apply the career capital perspective to discuss SIEs' career capital development in China. This chapter concludes by establishing an agenda for future research.

4.2. Overview of SIEs

Historically, the term expatriates were used to describe individuals who were assigned by an organization to work in one of their overseas subsidiaries (Edström & Galbraith, 1977). The focus of these expatriates is to develop their career within the company and they do not commit to the subsidiary in the host country beyond expatriation period. However, there are increasing overseas job opportunities provided to the individuals who are skilled and desire to work abroad in the globalized economy (Froese, 2012). Inkson, Arthur, Pringle, and Barry (1997) conducted the in-depth interviews with 75 young people from New Zealand and the interviewees described SIEs as young people who are eager to seek international experience. Although understanding the way in which SIEs operate in and adjust to foreign countries is an important research area in International Human Resource Management, due to the infancy of the research in this area, it needs further investigation (Howe-Walsh & Schyns, 2010; Suutari & Brewster, 2000). In this section, we first review studies on SIEs and then summarize the extant studies comparing SIEs and OEs.

Depending on the research perspective taken, SIEs have been described in a number of different ways. Scholars give the definition of SIEs from different perspectives to serve their research purpose. For example, Collings, Scullion, and Morley (2007, p. 204) describe SIEs as those individuals "whose international experience is not initiated by an international transfer within an organization but rather those who relocate abroad without organizational assistance and of their own accord." Cerdin and Pargneux (2010, p. 288) consider SIEs to be those "who choose to go abroad on their own to find work there, without being sent by an organization from their home country." Cerdin and Selmer's (2014) study reviews the definitions of SIEs in extant studies and provides four characteristics that should be considered together to identify SIEs: self-initiated international relocation, regular employment, intentions of a temporary stay, and professional qualifications. The motivation to SIEs varies in different contexts, which includes seeking adventure, experiencing different culture, obtaining international experience, and improving self and career development (Doherty, Dickmann, & Mills, 2011; Howe-Walsh & Schyns, 2010; Peltokorpi & Froese, 2009). Unlike OEs sponsored by the company, there is no expatriate package such as relocation service, housing, schooling, and health cover provided by the company to SIEs (Howe-Walsh & Schyns, 2010). As SIEs choose to work overseas, the duration of their stay in the host country and in the company is not clearly defined and they generally do not have a definite repatriation plan (Al Ariss, 2010; Froese, 2012; Howe-Walsh & Schyns, 2010; Peltokorpi & Froese, 2009; Tharenou & Caulfield, 2010).

For the purpose of this study, we consider SIEs to be those individuals who choose to work in another country and are responsible for organizing their own employment and managing their living conditions (Inkson et al., 1997; Jokinen, Brewster, & Suutari, 2008; Lee, 2005; Tharenou & Caulfield, 2010). These individuals tend to reside temporarily in a country for the duration of their work before perhaps moving to another country (Haslberger & Vaiman, 2013). This distinguishes them from skilled-migrants, who permanently move and reside in another country (Cerdin, Diné, & Brewster, 2013).

4.2.1. Research on SIEs

Although SIEs are one of the most important group in global market, research in this field lags practice (Myers & Pringle, 2005; Suutari & Brewster, 2000). Our review of studies related to SIEs identified three key research themes: motivation for SIE assignments, SIEs' cross-cultural adjustment and influencing factors of SIEs' job performance and career development.

4.2.1.1. Motivation for SIE Assignments
Different from OEs, SIEs are possible to work in both domestic and international firms. The motivations for individuals to undertake a SIE role include things like: family, career, financial incentives, adventure, and culture. Extant study examines the significance of family in choosing to work abroad for some group of SIEs such as married SIEs and academic SIEs (Richardson, 2006; Richardson & Mallon, 2005; Thorn, 2009). Another motivator to SIEs is to seek job opportunities and career development through international work experience (Doherty et al., 2011; Howe-Walsh & Schyns, 2010). Some studies also highlight seeking adventure, experiencing different culture and obtaining more travel opportunities as being relevant for some SIEs as they are willing to have a different lifestyle (Inkson et al., 1997; Richardson & Mallon, 2005; Selmer & Lauring, 2010). Thorn (2009)

conducted a large sample internet survey with the New Zealanders who work and live overseas and found culture, travel and career are the most important motivators. Additionally, Doherty et al. (2011) examined the impacts of the country's characteristics, the individual's perception of and their desire to stay in that country on choosing the destination for expatriation. The nationality of the SIEs also influences their relocation options as their movement across territories and duration of the assignment is linked to their country's travel documents and the exemption they can receive to live and work in various countries (Harvey, 2011).

4.2.1.2. SIEs' Cross-cultural Adjustment
Expatriate adjustment is a multi-faceted phenomenon that includes issues such as work adjustment, interaction adjustment, and general adjustment dimension (Black, 1988; Black, Mendenhall, & Oddou, 1991). Work adjustment can be explained as the degree to which people feel comfortable working abroad regarding task completion and job performance; interaction adjustment can be explained as the degree to which people feel comfortable working abroad regarding the interaction with host country nationals (HCNs) within or outside of workplace; and general adjustment can be explained as the degree to which people feel comfortable working abroad regarding the host country environment such as food, utilities, health care, transport, leisure, and living conditions (Black, 1988; Black et al., 1991). Black et al. (1991) proposed a comprehensive model of expatriate cross-cultural adjustment which includes pre-departure and post-arrival factors of expatriate anticipatory and in-country adjustment. The model is considered to be the most influential theoretical foundation of expatriate management studies (Bhaskar-Shrinivas, Harrison, Shaffer, & Luk, 2005). For example, some scholars examine the associations between the influencing factors such as previous working experience and expatriates' cross-cultural adjustment by using Black et al.'s (1991) model (see for example, Froese, Peltokorpi, & Ko, 2012; Kim & Slocum, 2008). Although lots of expatriate management studies have examined expatriate cross-cultural adjustment, these researches are more focusing on OEs than SIEs. We find few studies have examined SIEs' cross-cultural adjustment in the host country and these studies can be categorized into two groups. The first group is focusing on the influencing factors of SIEs' cross-cultural adjustment. The potential longer commitment to the host country and the individual's desire to work and live in the host country have positive impacts on SIEs' engagement with HCNs and adjustment to the local environment (Peltokorpi, 2008; Peltokorpi & Froese, 2009). Froese et al. (2012) found host country language proficiency and social interaction with HCNs help with foreign workers' general and interaction adjustment when they conduct international assignments in Korea; this study also examined the positive impacts of using English at work, communication and conflicts styles on SIEs' work adjustment in Korea. The other group is focusing on the comparison of cross-cultural adjustment between SIEs and OEs in the host country. For example, Peltokorpi and Froese (2009) conducted a survey with

179 expatriates in Japan and found SIEs have better performance in relation to their general and interaction adjustment compared to OEs.

4.2.1.3. Influencing Factors of SIEs' Job Performance and Career Development
Another research stream in this research area primarily focuses on the factors influencing SIEs' job performance and career development. For example, Selmer and Lauring (2011) find that married academic SIEs perform better compared to non-married SIEs through an online questionnaire survey. Career orientations are important to the SIEs in different age groups; however, it becomes less important to OEs (Biemann & Andresen, 2010). Some studies argue that SIEs' international assignment provides a future career direction and definite focus for SIEs' self-development (Inkson & Myers, 2003). For example, Cao, Hirschi, and Deller (2012) proposed a conceptual framework which identifies the relationships between three patterns of career capital (namely protean career attitude, career networks and cultural intelligence) and SIEs' career success. Through a survey with 132 SIEs in Germany, Cao, Hirschi, and Deller's (2013) study confirmed the positive impacts of protean career attitude on SIEs' career satisfaction. However, Rodriguez and Scurry's (2014) research challenges the argument that SIEs' assignment is positively related to their career advancement and highlights the importance of contextual impacts on SIEs' career development in the host country.

4.2.2. Empirical Studies on SIEs Versus OEs

To capture the research on SIEs', we conducted a search for empirical studies compared OEs and SIEs' career development. We searched the relevant empirical-based articles published between 1997 and 2016, with the keywords "international experience," "company assigned expatriate," "organizational assigned expatriate," "self-initiated expatriate" and "self-directed expatriates" in Google Scholar, EBSCOhost, and Emerald Management Plus. The selection of the publication years was followed the comparative studies between SIEs and OEs, which was first mentioned in the literature in 1997 (Inkson et al., 1997). The articles only conducted empirical research on one group of expatriates (OEs or SIEs) were excluded. Eleven articles were identified that matched these criteria and summarized in Table 4.1.

The articles present in Table 4.1 compared SIEs and OEs from three facets: expatriate individual characteristics, motivations for expatriate assignment and expatriate work outcomes. Considering the SIEs sample employed in these empirical studies, we found the survey participants and interviewees of SIEs have distinct characteristics in terms of age, gender, duration of the expatriation, job positions and previous oversea work experience in the organization compared to OEs (Andresen, Biemann, & Pattie, 2015; Cerdin & Pargneux, 2010; Jokinen et al., 2008; Richardson, 2006; Suutari & Brewster, 2000). Suutari and Brewster's (2000) study found SIEs make the decision to work abroad as they desire to have international experience and the poor job market in their home country is another reason.

Table 4.1: Review of OE and SIE literature (1997–2016) by perspective, findings and country setting.

Authors	Comparison Perspectives	Key Findings	Country Setting
Inkson et al. (1997)	Initiatives, goals, funding, career type	SIEs experience more individual development than OE.	New Zealand
Suutari and Brewster (2000)	Age, gender, spouse-related factors, international experience, marital status, employer & task-related factors	SIEs are more motivated by obtaining international experience and expect to stay longer in host country compared to OEs.	Finland
Jokinen et al. (2008)	Career capital	OEs obtain more knowing-whom capital than SIEs.	Finland
Peltokorpi (2008)	Cross-cultural adjustment	SIEs adjust better regarding interaction with host environment than OEs.	Japan
Peltokorpi and Froese (2009)	Cross-cultural adjustment	SIEs experience better interactions with HCNs than OE.	Japan
Biemann and Andresen (2010)	Career orientation, motivation, development	SIEs expect higher level of organizational mobility and internationalism than OE.	Germany
Cerdin and Pargneux (2010)	Motivation	Internationalism is a more important motivation to OEs than SIE.	France
Doherty et al. (2011)	Motivation	SIEs more emphasize on host country location and reputation, whereas career motivations are more important to OE.	Multiple countries
von Borell de Araujo et al. (2014)	Cross-cultural adaptation	SIEs are better adapted to the host country than OEs.	Brazil

Table 4.1: Continued.

Authors	Comparison Perspectives	Key Findings	Country Setting
Rodriguez and Scurry (2014)	Career capital	Expatriation is not positively related to career capital development and the study highlights the importance of contextual impacts.	Qatar
Andresen et al. (2015)	Career path, gender, human capital	More SIEs hold lower job position and prefer organization mobility than OEs. No difference found between SIEs and OEs in terms of boundaryless and protean career orientation	Multiple countries

Source: Adapted from Guo and Rammal (2014).

However, recent studies highlight adventure and lifestyle as the career anchors of SIEs (Cerdin & Pargneux, 2010; Doherty et al., 2011). Five articles empirically investigate work outcomes in terms of cross-cultural adjustment, work attitude and career capital by comparing SIEs and OEs (Jokinen et al., 2008; Peltokorpi, 2008; Peltokorpi & Froese, 2009; Rodriguez & Scurry, 2014; von Borell de Araujo, Teixeira, da Cruz, & Malini, 2014). Peltokorpi and Froese (2009) find SIEs to be better at general and interaction adjustment than OEs in Japan. Similarly, von Borell de Araujo et al. (2014) observe that SIEs are more engaged with the host country compared to OEs when they conduct international assignment in Brazil. Nevertheless, Biemann and Andresen (2010) in their study of organizations in Germany found that SIEs were not as well adjusted to their organization when compared to OEs. Only two extant studies compare SIEs and OEs from the perspective of career capital. Jokinen et al. (2008) did not find any differences in terms of knowing-why and knowing-how between SIEs and OEs; however, they observed that OEs obtain more knowing-whom capital than SIEs. Rodriguez and Scurry's (2014) study challenges the positive relations between SIEs expatriation and career capital development, and highlights the importance of contextual factors in influencing SIEs' career development in Qatar. As this chapter focuses on the career capital development of SIEs in China, we review the career capital studies in expatriate management area in the next section and discuss the issue of SIEs' career capital development in the country.

4.3. Career Capital Development of SIEs in China

Although expatriation is considered the important method of international management development, our understanding on the influence of expatriate assignments on expatriate career development in the host country is still limited (Bonache, Brewster, & Suutari, 2001). Career capital is one of the useful measure of expatriate career development, which is accumulated through their expatriation. Considering the context of Chinese society, the focus of this chapter is to understand SIEs' career capital development in this country.

4.3.1. Career Capital Perspective in Expatriate Studies

Based on the resource-based view (RBV), Defillippi and Arthur (1994) identified three patterns of career capital, namely knowing-whom, knowing-how, and knowing-why. The key value of the career capital perspective is central to the individual's potential career development and opportunities through the employment (Arthur & Bennett, 1995; Defillippi & Arthur, 1994). The three types of career capital are interrelated and the investing activities in one aspect influence the development of the other two components (Inkson & Arthur, 2001; Parker, Khapova, & Arthur, 2009).

Knowing-why career capital refers to the employees' motivation and personal meaning of work in their career path (Arthur, DeFillippi, & Jones, 2001; Dickmann & Harris, 2005). It is discussed in the literature in the forms of individual's identity, awareness of interests and values, confidence and self-evaluation of the career path (see for examples, Cappellen & Janssens, 2008; Inkson & Arthur, 2001; Parker et al., 2009). Knowing-how career capital refers to the explicit and tacit career knowledge and set of skills and abilities held by the individual employee, and used in conducting their work tasks in their career lives (Inkson & Arthur, 2001; Nonaka & Takeuchi, 1995). As it is difficult to transfer the tacit knowledge, companies tend to gain access to the tacit knowledge through hiring the employees with the required skills (Defillippi & Arthur, 1994). Knowing-how career capital incorporates human capital as the result of investment in formal and informal training and learning activities (Arthur et al., 2001). Knowing-whom career capital refers to an individual's professional networks, social relations and interactions, which also relates to the intra- and inter-organizational level networks the individuals initiate and develop independently (Adler & Kwon, 2002; Dickmann & Harris, 2005; Nahapiet & Ghoshal, 1998). The knowing-whom component of career capital also includes the contents of the ties in the individuals' career network such as obligation, affection, and the information access through the networks (Parker et al., 2009). Singh, Ragins, and Tharenou (2009) summarize the knowing-why and knowing-how components as motives and knowledge respectively, and consider knowing-whom career capital as individuals' relationship building and development in the workplace.

The application of career capital in expatriate management research primarily focuses on the development of career capital through expatriate international assignments. Expatriation could be considered as a mutual benefit practice for both organization and expatriates. The use of expatriates help organization achieve a diverse workforce and also access the knowledge especially the tacit knowledge carried by the expatriates, normally this kind of knowledge is limited in the local labor market. In addition, expatriates are able to develop and accumulate career capital through international assignments (Dickmann & Doherty, 2008; Dickmann & Harris, 2005; Inkson & Arthur, 2001). In different research settings, scholars define and measure the three components of career capital in various forms: knowing-why is explained as protean career attitude, protean ideas, identity perspective, and cultural capital; knowing-whom is defined as career network and social capital; knowing-how is viewed as cultural intelligence, competence, internal, and external capital (see for examples, Mäkelä & Brewster, 2009; Mäkelä, Suutari, Brewster, Dickmann, & Tornikoski, 2016; Parker et al., 2009).

Extant study has examined that international assignment has significant impacts on expatriate career capital development in terms of knowing-why component (Jokinen et al., 2008). Expatiates become more confident in their work through international assignments, and also have clear perception and understanding of their advantages and disadvantages in their future career development (Suutari &

Mäkelä, 2007). For example, Mäkelä et al. (2016) apply career capital perspective to discuss the impacts of expatriate assignments on expatriate perceived marketability. We found most study in extant literature considering career capital development only related to OEs, the studies on SIEs' career capital accumulation is still limited (see for exceptions: Jokinen et al., 2008; Rodriguez & Scurry, 2014). Rodriguez and Scurry (2014), studied SIEs' career capital acquisition in Qatar and found expatriation is not related to the development of career capital in this research setting, which is inconsistent research finding with the previous studies. The authors highlight the importance of contextual considerations in this research stream. This is similar to the research call provided by Favell, Feldblum, and Smith (2007) which highlights the importance of considering cultural, political, institutional, and economic influence when studying individual movement in international assignment studies. The career capital development of SIEs in the Chinese context is discussed in the next section.

4.3.2. Career Capital Development of SIEs in China

China is host to a large number of expatriates from across the globe. In 2011, around 600,000 foreigners stayed in China for at least six months (Cao & Zhao, 2012). However, the survey conducted by Brookfield Global Relocation Services (2016) found Western expatriates ranked China as one of the most challenging destination for expatriation because of its distinct cultural and institutional systems.

Considering the cultural perspective, Chinese traditional culture and social values are influenced by various thoughts such as Taoism, Buddhism, and Confucianism (Fan, 2000; Kirkbride, Tang, & Westwood, 1991). China remains a collectivist and relationship oriented society with a unique institutional and cultural environment, and thus the indigenous form of relationship (referred to as *guanxi*) is used in the society. Regarding the institutional aspect, China is transitioning from a planned to a market-oriented economy, and the institutional system is not well-established which related to the concerns about enforceability of commercial contracts (Dunfee & Warren, 2001; Lovett, Simmons, & Kali, 1999). Hence, it is important to explore SIEs' career development in such a unique country.

4.3.2.1. Knowing-Whom Career Capital

The studies on knowing-whom tend to view the networks established by expatriates in the host country. Through international assignments, expatriates gain access to task-related and career-related information and other resource by initiating and maintaining networks within and outside their organization in the host country (Farh, Bartol, Shapiro, & Shin, 2010; Seibert, Kraimer, & Liden, 2001). Previous studies show that SIEs are in the disadvantage position to establish such relationships compared to OEs (Jokinen et al., 2008). We argue that in the Chinese context, the situation is more complicated when the cultural and institutional environment is considered.

In China, the term *guanxi* is used to express social networks and it refers to relations, exchanges, process, connections and exchanges (Fan, 2002). The earliest discussions of *guanxi* can be traced back to more than 2000 years ago in Confucian texts such as the *Lunyu* (Confucian Analects) and it refers to *lun* in the Confucian classics (King, 1991). Distinct from the task-oriented nature of people in Western society, Chinese people tend to place emphasis on interpersonal relations as a way of accessing the required resources (Chan & Suen, 2005). *Guanxi* is embedded in every facet of Chinese society; it helps solve problems and gets things done when doing business in China (Bian, 1997; Fan, 2002; Park & Luo, 2001; Smart, 1993). As a traditional agriculture society, people in China are bounded by blood, kinship, and a geographic basis. The whole society consists of people linked by various relationship bases, and *guanxi* is used to describe the relationship between different individuals or groups. Stemming from Confucian theory, five kinds of *guanxi* (called *wu lun* in Chinese) are employed to depict interpersonal relationships rooted in the hierarchical Chinese society. These include the relationships between emperor and subject, father and son, husband and wife, brother and brother, and friend and friend (Farh, Earley, & Lin, 1997).

Chinese society is depicted as a differential mode of association, the distance between the individual and other group depends on the closeness of their relations which is called *guanxi* base (Fei, 2004). There are clear boundaries between different groups in the Chinese society and the identified role of being insider or outsider of the groups depends on the *guanxi* base. For example, the insiders of the individual's *guanxi* network include the relatives and familiar people. Individuals tend to change the role from outsider to insider should make efforts on initiating and establishing *guanxi* at the individual level. To become the insider of a group is considered one of the most important approach to conduct business in China as the role of insider is able to provide the access to relevant information and knowledge and help build trust among group members. Some scholars highlights the importance of individuals' networks in providing resource, which has positive impacts on their career success (Yao, 2013; Zhang, Liu, Loi, Lau, & Ngo, 2010). However, it is difficult for expatriate to access *guanxi* network as they are lack of *guanxi* base in China. The initiating, developing, and maintaining *guanxi* requires long-term orientation and the key feature of *guanxi* network is reciprocity which is distinct from social network (Tsang, 1998; Yao, 2013). In addition, *guanxi* is built at the individual level and the organization might lose the existing *guanxi* network with current business partners if some employees who initiated the *guanxi* network decide to leave the company (Fan, 2002; Leung & Wong, 2001; Tsang, 1998).

Considered as the outsiders of the host country, expatriates are lack of the established *guanxi*. However, it is important for them to initiate, develop, and maintain their *guanxi* network in the host country, which has positive impacts on their international assignment completion and future career development. Compared to SIEs, OEs receive sufficient support from their organization. To develop their *guanxi* network, OEs are able to seek assistance from their colleagues in the subsidiary as well as the colleagues who lived and worked in China before. In doing so, OEs should have better understanding of the local business environment and better adjustment to the host country. However, some study examined that SIEs adjust better to the local environment than OEs (Peltokorpi, 2008; Peltokorpi & Froese, 2009). SIEs have more opportunities to interact with a large number of HCNs as they have to arrange their work and life in the host country by themselves. However, the assistance and support from the connections and interactions with the HCNs might not be sufficient for SIEs' career development. Considering the network developed with the HCNs, we argue that the OEs' network in the host country is more effective than SIEs in terms of career capital accumulation. OEs general hold higher management positions in the organization and they have more opportunities to work with decision-makers and government official, whereas it is difficult for SIEs to access *guanxi* network at that level as they generally are not involved in the higher level management structure within the organization. We therefore propose that:

Proposition 1. The knowing-whom career capital development of SIEs through expatriation is increased more in network quantity than network quality in China.

4.3.2.2. Knowing-Why Career Capital

Career capital development is significant to expatriate career success and help to achieve high level of job performance (Suutari & Mäkelä, 2007). Previous studies on OEs and SIEs found that the knowing-why aspect of career capital is fundamentally different for these two patterns of expatriates. The completion of the task or the goal assigned by their organization is the major motivation for OEs, because the achievement of the goal is related to their promotion opportunities and future career advancement within the company. In contrast, SIEs consider the international experience as a way of self-development, and thus the completion of organization goals is not the primary motivator (Inkson et al., 1997). Some scholars highlight the importance of developing knowing-why career capital for SIEs in helping achieve career objectives and advancement in their working lives (Doherty et al., 2011; Suutari & Brewster, 2000). The knowledge of local market, cross-cultural management skills, and experience is the key focus of SIEs' knowing-why career capital development (Richardson & Mallon, 2005). Some studies use protean career attitude to represent knowing-why career capital of SIEs. Individuals with protean career attitudes intend to be more proactive and independent in their career development path (Briscoe & Hall, 2006). For example, Cao et al. (2013) argue that protean career attitude, as an important facet of knowing-why career capital, has impacts on SIEs' career advancement through international assignment.

SIEs working in China with a protean career attitude tend to adjust to local environment and engage with local people by learning from, communicating, and interacting with local people through expatriate assignment (Cerdin & Pargneux, 2010; Doherty et al., 2011; Inkson et al., 1997). However, as a dynamic process, knowing-why is influenced by the context and individual experiences (Ibarra, 2003). Experienced expatriates are more confident with their work and have stronger belief in their own career development (Kohonen, 2005). We argue that the development of SIEs' knowing-why career capital is influence by the expatriate's age and the stage of their career. International assignments in China can help expatriates identify their career path and make sense of their work. We observe that the younger and early career SIEs acquire more knowing-why career capital, as compared to experienced SIEs who tend to already have knowledge about why they choose to work in China. These reasons can include career benefits or family issues or relocation to China from another country. Hence, they acquire less knowing-why career capital than the SIEs at their early career stage when they commence international assignments in China. Hence, our next proposition is:

Proposition 2. The knowing-why career capital development of SIEs through expatriation is influenced by the age and career stage of SIEs. The younger and early career SIEs acquire more knowing-why capital through expatriation in China.

4.3.2.3. Knowing-How Career Capital

Expatriate knowing-how career capital focuses on knowledge, skills, and ability acquisition through international assignment (Dickmann & Harris, 2005). Some studies use cultural intelligence, intercultural competency to represent knowing-how career capital, which help understand international business operation and improve management skills. These skills are held by the individual and can be transferred to other organizations through individual mobility (Carpenter, Li, & Jiang, 2012; Jokinen et al., 2008; Suutari & Mäkelä, 2007).

Considering SIEs' work in the Chinese context, we discuss their knowing-how career capital under two skills: task-related skills and local engagement skills. Task-related skills refer to the professional knowledge and work-related competencies that help SIEs conduct international assignments in China. Local engagement skills relate to the intercultural ability in adjustment to the local environment and engagement with the HCNs. Although previous studies have observed that SIEs perform better in interaction adjustment to the local society (Peltokorpi, 2008; Peltokorpi & Froese, 2009), we argue that the development of SIEs' knowing-how career capital varies in considering task-related skills and local engagement skills in China.

SIEs' interactions with HCNs can help them understand traditional values and social norms in China, which increase their knowing-how career capital accumulation. Hence, we argue that SIEs' knowing-how career capital development in terms of local engagement skills is dependent on their intercultural ability. Considering the task-related skills of expatriates, organizations primarily send those individuals overseas who possess skills and knowledge that are not necessarily available in the host country. However, SIEs may not have specific skills or knowledge that the host country be lacking in as they are self-directed to take on an international assignment

(Andresen et al., 2015). In general, SIEs tend to be given lower level jobs in the host country, due to their perceived lack of long-term commitment to the company objectives and the lack of familiarity with the organization's culture. Jokinen et al.'s (2008) study finds that SIEs tend to experience a lower level of knowing-how career capital in terms of the knowledge of the organization. Al-Horr and Salih (2011) explain that this situation is due to the temporary contract of SIEs, who might not commit to the company and it may result in waste if company invest time and training in the development of SIEs. Hence, we argue that SIEs' knowing-how career capital development in terms of their task-related skills is dependent on the attitude and the support from their organization.

Proposition 3. The knowing-how career capital development of SIEs through expatriation — task-related skills and local engagement skills — is influenced by organizational support and individual's intercultural ability respectively.

4.4. Conclusion and Limitation

This chapter contributes to the global talent management literature by discussing the career capital development of SIEs when conducting international assignments in China. Although there have been an increasing number of studies focusing on SIEs, it is still limited when compared to the traditional international assignment pattern such as OEs. Our review of the extant literature on SIEs, and the comparison between SIEs and OEs has helped us develop three propositions in relation to SIEs' knowing-whom, knowing-why and knowing-how career capital within the Chinese context. The level of liability of foreignness experienced by expatriates can be higher in China than in other countries as Chinese society highly emphasizes on *guanxi*. OEs receive sufficient local support from their organization's *guanxi* network and thus their interactions with HCNs might be limited, whereas SIEs have more opportunities to interact and communicate with HCNs as they have to arrange their work and life in the host country. From the career perspective, the effectiveness of SIEs' knowing-whom career capital development in China might be lower than OEs as their network building tend to involve people of influence at a lower level. OEs' connections have higher management positions in the organizations, whereas SIEs' *guanxi* network building is more focusing on the middle and lower levels. We believe it is also possible for SIEs to initiate and develop their network and connections with the people at higher management positions; however the process might be slow due to the lack of organizational support. Hence, SIEs' knowing-whom career capital development in China is increased more in network quantity than network quality compared to OEs. This is also related to knowing-how component of SIEs' career capital development. OEs generally have a higher level of knowledge and skills in relation to the job in the organization than SIEs. The company's attitude on SIEs and the support provided to SIEs are important for them to acquire relevant task-related skills through their assignment. In addition to the task-related skills, we argue that local engagement skills of knowing-how career capital are related to SIEs' intercultural ability. Regarding the knowing-why career capital, the motivation for being an expatriate in China varies for SIEs at different ages and the stages of their career path. We argue that SIEs at their early career stage acquire more knowing-why career capital through international assignment in China compared to the senior and experienced SIEs.

Our chapter has practical implications for SIEs and the organizations that employ them in China. SIEs can benefit from the discussion of this chapter to get a better perception and understanding of their work in China as well as potential career development in their work lives. Through this study, SIEs make sense of their self-directed job in China, the benefits of this job in their career path, the way to improve their career development in China and the knowledge on their potential career development in other contexts. The company should take into consideration the age, experience, career path stage of the SIEs and invest in time and training which help to retain SIEs. For example, some HR practices in relation to knowledge or expatriation experience sharing within the organization will help SIEs to manage their career effectively, this also has positive impacts on SIEs' commitment to the organization and helps the company decrease the employee turnover rate. As this study is conceptual, future studies could attempt to design and examine the propositions empirically in China and other similar contexts in terms of culture and institutional environments.

References

Adler, P. S., & Kwon, S. W. (2002). Social capital: Prospects for a new concept. *Academy of Management Review, 27*(1), 17−40.
Al Ariss, A. (2010). Modes of engagement: Migration, self-initiated expatriation, and career development. *Career Development International, 15*(4), 338−358.
Al-Horr, K., & Salih, A. H. (2011). Convergence or diversity in national recruitment and selection practices: A case study of the state of Qatar. *Journal of Business Diversity, 11*, 47−55.
Andresen, M., Biemann, T., & Pattie, M. W. (2015). What makes them move abroad? Reviewing and exploring differences between self-initiated and assigned expatriation. *International Journal of Human Resource Management, 26*(7), 932−947.
Arthur, M. B., DeFillippi, R. J., & Jones, C. (2001). Project-based learning as the interplay of career and company non-financial capital. *Management Learning, 32*(1), 99−117.
Arthur, W., Jr., & Bennett, W., Jr. (1995). The international assignee: The relative importance of factors perceived to contribute to success. *Personnel Psychology, 48*(1), 99−114.
Bhaskar-Shrinivas, P., Harrison, D. A., Shaffer, M. A., & Luk, D. M. (2005). Input-based and time-based models of international adjustment: meta-analytic evidence and theoretical extensions. *Academy of Management Journal, 48*(2), 257−281.

Bian, Y. (1997). Bringing strong ties back in: Indirect ties, network bridges, and job searches in China. *American Sociological Review, 62*(3), 366–385.

Biemann, T., & Andresen, M. (2010). Self-initiated foreign expatriates versus assigned expatriates: Two distinct types of international careers? *Journal of Managerial Psychology, 25*(4), 430–448.

Black, J. S. (1988). Work role transitions: A study of American expatriate managers in Japan. *Journal of International Business Studies, 19*(2), 277–294.

Black, J. S., Mendenhall, M., & Oddou, G. (1991). Toward a comprehensive model of international adjustment: An integration of multiple theoretical perspectives. *The Academy of Management Review, 16*(2), 291–317.

Bonache, J., Brewster, C., & Suutari, V. (2001). Expatriation: A developing research agenda. *Thunderbird International Business Review, 43*(1), 3–20.

Briscoe, J. P., & Hall, D. T. (2006). The interplay of boundaryless and protean careers: Combinations and implications. *Journal of Vocational Behaviour, 69,* 4–18.

Brookfield Global Relocation Services. (2016). *Breakthrough to the future of global talent mobility: 2016 global mobility trends survey.* Retrieved from http://globalmobilitytrends.brookfieldgrs.com/assets2016/downloads/Full-Report-Brookfield-GRS-2016-Global-Mobility-Trends-Survey.pdf

Cao, L., Hirschi, A., & Deller, J. (2012). Self-initiated expatriates and their career success. *Journal of Management Development, 31*(2), 159–172.

Cao, L., Hirschi, A., & Deller, J. (2013). The positive effects of a protean career attitude for self-initiated expatriates: Cultural adjustment as a mediator. *Career Development International, 18*(1), 56–77.

Cao, Y., & Zhao, Y. (2012). *Foreigners face visa scrutiny in Beijing.* Retrieved from http://usa.chinadaily.com.cn/china/2012-05/15/content_15290763.htm. Accessed on May 10, 2013.

Cappellen, T., & Janssens, M. (2008). Global managers' career competencies. *Career Development International, 13*(6), 514–537.

Carpenter, M. A., Li, M., & Jiang, H. (2012). Social Network Research in Organizational Contexts: A Systematic Review of Methodological Issues and Choices. *Journal of Management, 38*(4), 1328–1361.

Cerdin, J.-L., Diné, M. A., & Brewster, C. (2013). Qualified immigrants' success: Exploring the motivation to migrate and to integrate. *Journal of International Business Studies, 45*(2), 151–168.

Cerdin, J.-L., & Selmer, J. (2014). Who is a self-initiated expatriate? Towards conceptual clarity of a common notion. *International Journal of Human Resource Management, 25*(9), 1281–1301.

Cerdin, J. L., & Pargneux, M. L. (2010). Career anchors: A comparison between organization-assigned and self-initiated expatriates. *Thunderbird International Business Review, 52*(4), 287–299.

Chan, E. H. W., & Suen, H. C. H. (2005). Dispute resolution management for international construction projects in China. *Management Decision, 43*(4), 589–602.

Collings, D. G., Scullion, H., & Morley, M. J. (2007). Changing patterns of global staffing in the multinational enterprise: Challenges to the conventional expatriate assignment and emerging alternatives. *Journal of World Business, 42*(2), 198–213.

Defillippi, R. J., & Arthur, M. B. (1994). The boundaryless career: A competency-based perspective. *Journal of Organizational Behavior, 15*(4), 307–324.

Dickmann, M., & Doherty, N. (2008). Exploring the career capital impact of international assignments within distinct organizational contexts. *British Journal of Management, 19*(2), 145–161.

Dickmann, M., & Harris, H. (2005). Developing career capital for global careers: The role of international assignments. *Journal of World Business, 40*(4), 399–408.

Doherty, N., Dickmann, M., & Mills, T. (2011). Exploring the motives of company-backed and self-initiated expatriates. *The International Journal of Human Resource Management, 22*(3), 595–611.

Dunfee, T. W., & Warren, D. E. (2001). Is guanxi ethical? A normative analysis of doing business in China. *Journal of Business Ethics, 32*(3), 191–204.

Edström, A., & Galbraith, J. R. (1977). Transfer of managers as a coordination and control strategy in multinational organizations. *Administrative Science Quarterly, 22*(2), 248–263.

Fan, Y. (2000). A classification of Chinese culture. *Cross Cultural Management: An International Journal, 7*(2), 3–10.

Fan, Y. (2002). Questioning guanxi: Definition, classification and implications. *International Business Review, 11*(5), 543–561.

Farh, C. I. C., Bartol, K. M., Shapiro, D. L., & Shin, J. (2010). Networking abroad: A process model of how expatriates form support ties to facilitate adjustment. *The Academy of Management Review (AMR), 35*(3), 434–454.

Farh, J. L., Earley, P. C., & Lin, S. C. (1997). Impetus for action: A cultural analysis of justice and organizational citizenship behavior in Chinese society. *Administrative Science Quarterly, 42*(3), 421–444.

Favell, A., Feldblum, M., & Smith, M. P. (2007). The human face of globality: A research agenda. *Society, 44*, 15–25.

Fei, S. T. (2004). *Rural China (in Chinese)*. Beijing: Beijing Publication.

Froese, F. J. (2012). Motivation and adjustment of self-initiated expatriates: The case of expatriate academics in South Korea. *The International Journal of Human Resource Management, 23*(6), 1095–1112.

Froese, F. J., Peltokorpi, V., & Ko, K. A. (2012). The influence of intercultural communication on cross-cultural adjustment and work attitudes: Foreign workers in South Korea. *International Journal of Intercultural Relations, 36*(3), 331–342.

Guo, Y., & Rammal, H. G. (2014). *The development of expatriate career capital in China: A review of organization assigned and self-initiated expatriate literature*. Paper presented at the Australia and New Zealand International Business Academy Conference, Auckland.

Harvey, W. S. (2011). British and Indian scientists moving to the United States. *Work and Occupations, 38*(1), 68–100.

Haslberger, A., & Vaiman, V. (2013). Self-initiated expatriates: A neglected source of the global talent flow. In V. Vaiman & A. Haslberger (Eds.), *Talent management of self-initiated expatriates: A neglected source of global talent* (pp. 1–18). Hampshire: Palgrave Macmillan.

Howe-Walsh, L., & Schyns, B. (2010). Self-initiated expatriation: Implications for HRM. *The International Journal of Human Resource Management, 21*(2), 260–273.

Ibarra, H. (2003). *Working identity*. Boston, MA: Harvard Business School Press.

Inkson, K., & Arthur, M. B. (2001). How to be a successful career capitalist. *Organizational Dynamics, 30*(1), 48–61.

Inkson, K., Arthur, M. B., Pringle, J., & Barry, S. (1997). Expatriate assignment versus overseas experience: Contrasting models of international human resource development. *Journal of World Business, 32*(4), 351–368.

Inkson, K., & Myers, B. A. (2003). "The big OE": Self-directed travel and career development. *Career Development International, 8*(4), 170–181.

Jokinen, T., Brewster, C., & Suutari, V. (2008). Career capital during international work experiences: Contrasting self-initiated expatriate experiences and assigned expatriation. *The International Journal of Human Resource Management, 19*(6), 979–998.

Kim, K., & Slocum, J. W., Jr. (2008). Individual differences and expatriate assignment effectiveness: The case of US-based Korean expatriates. *Journal of World Business, 43*(1), 109–126.

King, A. Y. C. (1991). Kuan-hsi and network building: A sociological interpretation. *Daedalus, 120*(2), 63–84.

Kirkbride, P. S., Tang, S. F., & Westwood, R. I. (1991). Chinese conflict preferences and negotiating behaviour: Cultural and psychological influences. *Organization Studies, 12*(3), 365–386.

Kohonen, E. (2005). Developing global leaders through international assignments: An identity construction perspective. *Personnel Review, 34*(1), 22–36.

Lee, C. H. (2005). A study of underemployment among self-initiated expatriates. *Journal of World Business, 40*(2), 172–187.

Leung, T., & Wong, Y. (2001). The ethics and positioning of guanxi in China. *Marketing Intelligence & Planning, 19*(1), 55–64.

Lovett, S., Simmons, L. C., & Kali, R. (1999). Guanxi versus the market: Ethics and efficiency. *Journal of International Business Studies, 30*(2), 231–248.

Mäkelä, K., & Brewster, C. (2009). Interunit interaction contexts, interpersonal social capital, and the differing levels of knowledge sharing. *Human Resource Management, 48*(4), 591–613.

Mäkelä, L., Suutari, V., Brewster, C., Dickmann, M., & Tornikoski, C. (2016). The impact of career capital on expatriates' perceived marketability. *Thunderbird International Business Review, 58*(1), 29–40.

Myers, B., & Pringle, J. K. (2005). Self-initiated foreign experience as accelerated development: Influences of gender. *Journal of World Business, 40*(4), 421–431.

Nahapiet, J., & Ghoshal, S. (1998). Social capital, intellectual capital, and the organizational advantage. *Academy of Management Review, 23*(2), 242–266.

Nonaka, I., & Takeuchi, H. (1995). *The knowledge-creating company: How Japanese companies create the dynamics of innovation.* New York, NY: Oxford university press.

Park, S. H., & Luo, Y. (2001). Guanxi and organizational dynamics: Organizational networking in Chinese firms. *Strategic Management Journal, 22*(5), 455–477.

Parker, P., Khapova, S. N., & Arthur, M. B. (2009). The intelligent career framework as a basis for interdisciplinary inquiry. *Journal of Vocational Behavior, 75*, 291–302.

Peltokorpi, V. (2008). Cross-cultural adjustment of expatriates in Japan. *The International Journal of Human Resource Management, 19*(9), 1588–1606.

Peltokorpi, V., & Froese, F. J. (2009). Organizational expatriates and self-initiated expatriates: Who adjusts better to work and life in Japan? *The International Journal of Human Resource Management, 20*(5), 1096–1112.

Richardson, J. (2006). Self-directed expatriation: Family matters. *Personnel Review, 35*(4), 469–486.

Richardson, J., & Mallon, M. (2005). Career interrupted? The case of the self-directed expatriate. *Journal of World Business, 40*(4), 409–420.

Richardson, J., & McKenna, S. (2006). Exploring relationships with home and host countries. *Cross Cultural Management: An International Journal, 13*(1), 6–22.

Rodriguez, J. K., & Scurry, T. (2014). Career capital development of self-initiated expatriates in Qatar: Cosmopolitan globetrotters, experts and outsiders. *International Journal of Human Resource Management, 25*(7), 1046–1067.

Seibert, S. E., Kraimer, M. L., & Liden, R. C. (2001). A social capital theory of career success. *Academy of Management Journal, 44*(2), 219–237.

Selmer, J., & Lauring, J. (2010). Self-initiated academic expatriates: Inherent demographics and reasons to expatriate. *European Management Review, 7*(3), 169–179.

Selmer, J., & Lauring, J. (2011). Marital status and work outcomes of self-initiated expatriates: Is there a moderating effect of gender? *Cross Cultural Management: An International Journal, 18*(2), 198–213.

Singh, R., Ragins, B., & Tharenou, P. (2009). What matters most? The relative role of mentoring and career capital in career success. *Journal of Vocational Behaviour, 75*, 56–67.

Smart, A. (1993). Gifts, bribes, and guanxi: A reconsideration of Bourdieu's social capital. *Cultural Anthropology, 8*(3), 388–408.

Suutari, V., & Brewster, C. (2000). Making their own way: International experience through self-initiated foreign assignments. *Journal of World Business, 35*(4), 417–436.

Suutari, V., & Mäkelä, K. (2007). The career capital of managers with global careers. *Journal of Managerial Psychology, 22*(7), 628–648.

Tharenou, P., & Caulfield, N. (2010). Will I stay or will I go? Explaining repatriation by self-initiated expatriates. *Academy of Management Journal, 53*(5), 1009–1028.

Thorn, K. (2009). The relative importance of motives for international self-initiated mobility. *Career Development International, 14*(5), 441–464.

Tsang, E. W. K. (1998). Can guanxi be a source of sustained competitive advantage for doing business in China? *The Academy of Management Executive, 12*(2), 64–73.

Tseng, H. C., Chou, L. Y., & Yu, K. H. (2010). Current research paradigms in expatriate(s) research: A bibliometric approach. *The International Journal of Organizational Innovation, 2*(3), 22–39.

UNCTAD. (2015). *World investment report 2015, Reforming international investment governance.* United Nations, Geneva: United Nations Publication.

Vance, C. M. (2005). The personal quest for building global competence: A taxonomy of self-initiating career path strategies for gaining business experience abroad. *Journal of World Business, 40*(4), 374–385.

von Borell de Araujo, B. F., Teixeira, M. L. M., da Cruz, P. B., & Malini, E. (2014). Understanding the adaptation of organisational and self-initiated expatriates in the context of Brazilian culture. *The International Journal of Human Resource Management, 25*(18), 2489–2509.

Yao, C. (2013). The impact of cultural dimensions on Chinese expatriates' career capital. *The International Journal of Human Resource Management, 25*(5), 609–630.

Zhang, L., Liu, J., Loi, R., Lau, V. P., & Ngo, H. (2010). Social capital and career outcomes: A study of Chinese employees. *The International Journal of Human Resource Management, 21*(8), 1323–1336.

Chapter 5

Multiple Aspects of Readjustment Experienced by International Repatriates in Multinational Enterprises: A Perspective of 'Changes Occurring Over Time' and 'Changes due to Cultural Differences'

Yoko Naito

Abstract

Purpose — The purpose of this study is to understand the multiple aspects of readjustment of repatriates and to identify determinants relating to the readjustment, to enable MNEs (multinational enterprises) to utilize the advantages and retain the valuable knowledge that repatriates offer to the organization for talent management.

Methodology/approach — This study conducted a quantitative work involving questionnaire responses of 192 repatriates who returned to Japan after international assignments in MNEs.

Findings — Based on the results of the analysis using this Japanese data, the discussion is summarized in the following three points. First, it is important to seek determinants for the readjustment by focusing on all the aspects of 'repatriation adjustment' because the determinants of subordinate aspects are not always identical. Second, 'organizational factors — work duties' play a vital role in the readjustment to the organization different from the readjustment to daily life. Further, organizations benefit from providing assistance to both the

Global Talent Management and Staffing in MNEs
International Business & Management, Volume 32, 101–124
Copyright © 2016 by Emerald Group Publishing Limited
ISSN: 1876-066X/doi:10.1108/S1876-066X20160000032004

repatriates and the family of the repatriates to ensure that they are able to successfully readjust to life in the home country.

Originality/value – This study performed a comprehensive analysis of the subordinate concepts of the 'repatriation adjustment' dividing it into four aspects of job and private life. Factors related to the readjustment were classified into three factors by using a framework that analyses issues repatriates face by classifying these into *changes occurring over time* and *changes due to cultural differences*, and show a logical framework that elucidates the repatriation adjustment factors.

Keywords: Repatriation adjustment; job and private life; Japanese MNEs

5.1. Introduction

With the increases in activity including production, sales and other activities in foreign markets and the increases in the number of repatriates working in multinational enterprises (MNEs), the issue of how management strategies for international human resources is to be conducted has been analysed from a variety of viewpoints.

In general, expatriates are engaged in companies operating in different cultures, such as the company subsidiaries in overseas locations, and perform duties including disseminating management principles and policies of the headquarters, transferring technology, knowledge and skills, coordinating between organizations, conducting negotiations and building network in the locales they are dispatched to (Black, Gregersen, Mendenhall, & Stroh, 1999; Shiraki, 2006). While working overseas, expatriates gain knowledge and experience of different cultures through the work, and learn management skills and problem-solving there. Therefore, as a resource with potentially valuable knowledge and an established human network in the host country, repatriates are expected to play a leading role in and contribute to the global talent pool for the home organization after the return (Collings, 2014). Such talent management is the key of effective HRM conducting organizational success and performing a positive impact on return on investment on human capital (Sparrow, Scullion, & Tarique, 2014). Here, some studies have reported that many repatriates resign from their positions and companies after the return (e.g., Pattie, White, & Tansky, 2010) because they are unable to use their cross-cultural experience fully and face a range of problems in the process of the repatriation. They have to overcome these problems mainly by themselves (e.g., Black, 1992; Bossard & Peterson, 2005; Clague & Krupp, 1978; Lazarova & Caligiuri, 2001; Murray, 1973). Despite the problems faced by the repatriates, the company generally provides insufficient organizational support (e.g., Ishida, 1999; Newton, Hutchings, & Kabanoff, 2007).

The purpose of this study is to understand the multiple aspects of readjustment of repatriates and to identify determinants relating to the readjustment, focusing on the situation of repatriates upon and after the return. This study analyses issues related to the readjustment of repatriates to work duty aspects as well as to non-work aspects in the home country, in order to enable MNEs to utilize the advantages repatriates offer and to retain their knowledge in the organization and to manage the talent. The present study is mainly based on Naito (2012, in Japanese) that researched the 'readjustment to the organization/work', the study also partially uses Naito (2015, in Japanese) for the research of 'readjustment to daily life/non-work' and has translated the relevant parts presented here into English, for the combining 'readjustment to the organization/work' and 'readjustment to daily life/non-work' into 'repatriation adjustments'.

5.2. Literature Review

Considering the repatriation difficulty, Adler (1981) conducted an empirical study and suggested that companies should utilize the advantages repatriates offer. Also, since the study by Black and Gregersen (1991), research has become focused on improving the readjustment and on poor readjustment to the culture and company of the home country for repatriates, put differently, the focus of repatriation research has changed to an investigation of the *factors* which affect whether the readjustment could be successful or not. Recently, the focus has then narrowed further to the readjustment in the home organization rather than in the general society and culture of the home country, and many studies have focused on determinants possibly affecting readjustment to the job or company for repatriates (e.g., Chi & Chen, 2007).

Studies that analyse determinants for the repatriation adjustment provide valuable and important results of different kinds. This study treats two main issues in the development of the repatriation research, and as a result these issues tend to be overlooked. First, the approach to establishing the repatriation adjustment as outcomes that measure whether a repatriate is successfully readjusted or not. Reviewing previous studies that investigate the repatriation adjustment, the readjustment has been analysed by focusing on the following four aspects: 'job' directly related to the repatriates (Vidal, Valle, & Argon, 2007), the 'division/company' the repatriate belongs to (Chi & Chen, 2007; Kraimer, Shaffer, Harrison, & Ren, 2012) and 'companies' and their culture in general', as well as 'daily life in general' which traditionally form the country or regional culture and living environment in a place (Black, 1994; Black & Gregersen, 1991). In the previous studies, specific aspects, fragments, of the readjustment, have been examined and have not been examined comprehensively together. Considering that the repatriation adjustment is comprised of those aspects above, examining all aspects together with thinking about features of each element would contribute to a study with novel understanding. Then, based on this, it will be possible to develop policies for organizational support.

Second, in the approach to the determinants for the repatriation adjustment two points have been considered: (A) in previous studies determinants were used such as individual, job and organizational factors, however factors related to the intentions of the repatriates have not been examined sufficiently and (B) a new repatriation model is required, since the existing repatriation model (Black, Gregersen, & Mendenhall, 1992) was published more than two decades ago (Haslberger, Brewster, & Hippler, 2014). Reiche, Kraimer, and Harzing (2011, pp. 521−522) mentioned that 'despite the high risk of turnover, the factors that determine whether employees with international assignment experience choose to remain with their organizations are largely unclear'.

In the previous research the explanations of how to determine the factors of the repatriation adjustment are not clearly or unambiguously detailed. This study attempts to provide a wider perspective for repatriation adjustment research by elaborating the rationales for the factors influencing the repatriation adjustment more fully while investigating repatriation adjustment and the factors involved. This may contribute to improvements in the interpretation and practical understanding of the factors based on the nature of repatriation adjustment.

5.3. Repatriation Adjustment and its Factors

To provide insights as suggested above, I analyse the 'repatriation adjustment' from 'work duties/job' aspects ('readjustment to the organization') and 'daily life/non-work' aspects ('readjustment to daily life in general'), as is shown in Figure 5.1. Then, 'readjustment to the organization' is divided into three aspects: 'readjustment to the job', 'readjustment to the division/company' and 'readjustment to Japanese companies' culture in general'. First, the aspect of readjustment to the own job/work duties and the daily mission after repatriation (at organization) are most familiar to individuals. Second, the aspect of readjustment to the company or department/section in the company which the repatriates belong to. Third, the aspect of readjustment to the companies culture/style in general as a whole in the specific country or region. Further, the aspect of readjustment to daily life/non-work involves private life, it is 'readjustment to daily life in general'. To accommodate this, the 'repatriation adjustment' is analysed with these four aspects.

For the repatriation adjustment factors, the study examines the relationships between these four aspects and independent variables comprised of three factors. These three are 'individual factors', 'organizational factors related to the institution

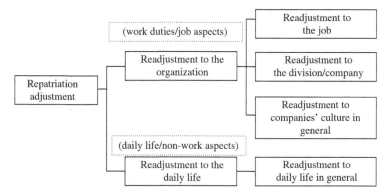

Figure 5.1: Multiple aspects of repatriation adjustment.

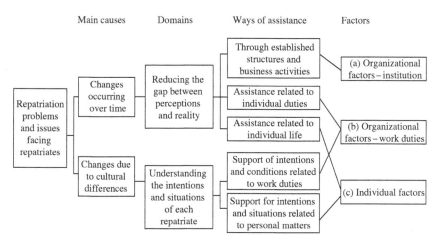

Figure 5.2: A framework of the readjustment factors deriving from repatriation problems and issues.
Source: Translated and revised from Naito (2013).

(organizational factors — institution)' and 'organizational factors related to the work duties (organizational factors — work duties)', and classified by extending a framework (Naito, 2012) that analyses factors deriving from *changes occurring over time* and *changes due to cultural differences* (Figure 5.2). Here it becomes necessary to describe and classify independent variables into the three factors while classifying the problems and tasks that individual repatriates face when returning to the home. Through this process, I identify factors that may affect the 'repatriation adjustment'.

There are numerous cases where repatriates after the completion of international assignments notice changes in the environment surrounding them and face re-entry shock, because both the repatriates themselves and society as well as the organizational environment in the home country have changed during the assignment in the foreign location (e.g., Martin & Nakayama, 2004). Developing a repatriation adjustment model and suggesting organizational practices for repatriates, this chapter applies the framework of *changes occurring over time* and *changes due to cultural differences* deriving from the repatriation adjustment issues and tasks facing individual repatriates when returning to the home country. Through this approach, the study shows the importance of 'practices for reducing the gap between perceptions and reality' and 'practices to understand and cope with individual intentions and situations' for the repatriation adjustment. Then, the necessity to distinguish factors relating to readjustment among the three factors is described, to be able to understand the necessary organizational support in more detail. Based on this approach, the independent variables that may be assumed to affect repatriation are identified.

5.3.1. A Framework of the Repatriation Adjustment Factors

This study revises the framework by Naito (2012) and applies the revised framework to the investigation of the factors influencing the readjustment to the home environment of repatriates as described below.

5.3.1.1. Changes Occurring Over Time
Repatriates face changes in the work and non-work environments in the home country that have occurred during the time of the assignments. This includes both organizational and societal changes that the repatriates must deal with, including matters such as value changes, interpersonal relationships, company-specific terminology, office relocation and more, as well as changes in the daily duties they are expected to engage in: procedures, technology and the like (e.g., Martin & Nakayama, 2004; Umezawa, 1994). Here, repatriates commonly pay little attention to such changes and commonly assume that it is easy to predict the situations they will encounter (e.g., Adler, 2002). As a result, there are gaps between the perceptions of repatriates and the reality surrounding them. The place where the repatriates have returned to is no longer the place they were familiar with even when the location is the same as where they used to live. This issue should not be mainly considered as the events of the host country, but be considered as the home country's circumstances and situation. That is, it is important to focus on the location where repatriates are. It is distinct from the *changes due to cultural differences* as described below.

Conventionally, practices for reducing the gap between the perceptions of individual repatriates and the surrounding reality from work to non-work facets, which may have appeared as *changes occurring over time*, have been investigated (e.g., Black, 1992; Hyder & Lövblad, 2007; Stroh, Gregersen, & Black, 2000). By expanding the findings there, I adopt the method that 'organizational factors' are investigated by separating the problems related to the institutions from those of the individual work assignments. This method may be more practicable or comprehensive, as it is based on the specific situation of a repatriate. Regarding 'organizational factors', I propose there are two approaches to reducing the gaps. One is going the organizational way and try to overcome the gap through institutional practices, for example training or guidance that provides uniform support for all repatriates to let them know about home and the organization. The other is dealing with issues in the job assignments of the repatriates and try to overcome the gap by providing individualized support in the daily work, for example by the manager paying special attention to the duties of a repatriate. Considering this, it would appear necessary to examine 'organizational factors' separately among the determinants for readjustment by distinguishing between 'organizational factors — institution' and 'organizational factors — work duties' when considering policies for organizational support. Further, repatriates also overcome the gaps in daily life/ non-work other than work duties which are classified as 'individual factors' in this treatment.

5.3.1.2. Changes Due to Cultural Differences
The repatriates have experienced dealing with cultural difference in the host country and overseas location of the international assignment. Then upon return to the home country they are again exposed to differences of a similar nature. Through an international assignment, repatriates are influenced by the culture of the host country' and acquire host culture traits. Their attitudes, perceptions, sense of values, beliefs, behavioural patterns, customs and identity become changed from what they were before the international assignment, whether they are aware of this or not. This is one reason why, even after an international transfer, when returning to the home country, it is not always straightforward to readjust to the culture of the home country (e.g., Adler, 1981; Gullahorn & Gullahorn, 1963).

At the time of repatriation, repatriates have some awareness that the conditions in the society of the home country, the home organization and the work duties are different from those in the host country. The awareness of these situations, due to cultural differences, is distinct from the '*changes occurring over time*' as described above. Even if there is an awareness of these differences, it is a challenge for repatriates to become immediately accustomed to the changes that arise from cultural differences.

To relieve these challenges and difficulties for repatriates, organizations should pay attention to the intentions and conditions of the repatriates, due to the possibility that they have been changed themselves by a different culture (Sussman, 2001) during the international assignment. This is both because the repatriates may be confused and surprised or even bewildered with their newly assigned organization and work (in the home country) due to the cultural changes in the repatriates themselves. However, while previous studies have paid attention to the situations of the repatriates in the search for readjustment, there is little evidence-based study focusing on repatriate intentions. Assuming that repatriates will have changed, it is necessary to determine accurate details of their intentions at the time when they return to the home country. Therefore, it is important for organizations to pay attention to repatriate intentions and wishes as they have changed as well as to know the situations of the repatriates. For that reason, it would be of valuable to verify whether repatriate intentions facilitate the readjustment. When examining individual intentions and situations, this should be analysed to show the intentions of individuals from two features: (1) the personal, individual features such as whether the employee wishes to return to the home country, these are categorized as 'individual factors' and (2) whether the company-centred features that relate to work such as whether the employee has particular wishes for the assignment on the return, these will be categorized 'organizational factors — work duties'. This distinction is suggested as previous studies have reported that the main problems encountered by repatriates are associated with a variety of job/work- and lifestyle/non-work-related problems (e.g., Clague & Krupp, 1978; Harvey & Novicevic, 2006; Naito, 2009).

5.3.2. Three Factors Facilitating Repatriation Adjustment

Repatriation adjustment requires effective organizational practices of assistance to the repatriates (Lazarova & Caligiuri, 2001). The repatriates need organizational assistance that meets the needs of the individual repatriate. Therefore, it is important to explore and identify possible factors that affect the repatriation adjustment by analysing specific details and variables related to repatriation.

When exploring these determinants, this chapter first focuses on factors contributing to the 'repatriation readjustment'. Next, the independent variables are identified and derived based on three facets: 'individual factors', 'organizational factors — institution' and 'organizational factors — work duties'. This chapter divides the 'organizational factors' into 'organizational factors — institution' and 'organizational factors — work duties' referred to '*A Framework of the Repatriation Adjustment Factors*'. As described in *Changes occurring over time*, variables that address the gap between the perceptions and reality are classified into 'organizational factors — institution', 'organizational factors — work duties' and 'individual factors'. As shown in *Changes due to cultural differences*, variables used to understand individual intentions and the situation surrounding the repatriates are classified into 'individual factors' and 'organizational factors — work duties'.

Based on these considerations, the three readjustment factors ((a)–(c) in Figure 5.2) are defined as follows. 'Individual factors' refer to factors related to individual attributes, individual intentions and situations and encompass family and private life. Generally, individual conditions and particulars are included here other than work duties. 'Organizational factors — institution' refers to factors that are determined by the organizations, related to the business operation and institutional matters of international assignments. This category then includes matters that organizations conduct and in general relate to all repatriates subject to organizational rules and regulations, and anything that arises due to impositions of the organization is included here. 'Organizational factors — work duties' refer to factors related to duties such as the daily work-related activities of the repatriate. This includes matters related to work duties where the intentions of an individual repatriate are reflected, and matters that are relatively simple to accede and handle by the organization depending on the needs/wishes of the individual repatriate.

Independent variables are identified from these three readjustment factors in the following section.

5.3.2.1. Individual Factors

It is assumed that the higher the 'age' of the repatriate, the better the readjustment is achieved, because older repatriates can be expected to have had more contact with the home country. Black (1994) and Gullahorn and Gullahorn (1963) suggest that 'age' will affect the readjustment and that repatriates will be readjusted more easily to daily life in the home country, the older they are. Therefore, 'age' presumably affects repatriation adjustment.

Black and Gregersen (1991) have found that the length of the period after the return to the home country, that is 'time back after an assignment' has a statistically significant relation with the readjustment: repatriates will readjust more easily to the home country the longer they have lived there. Also, studies of reverse culture shock after the return to the home country suggest that the mood and feelings of repatriates will improve, not immediately at repatriation but need time after the return (Adler, 2002; Gullahorn & Gullahorn, 1963).

'Family problems' refers to problems members of the family of repatriates face at the time of returning to the home country. It is inferred that such problems have a ripple effect on the repatriation adjustment. A further related variable, readjustment of spouses, has shown a statistically significant positive correlation with successful levels of repatriation adjustment (Gregersen & Stroh, 1997). As the research here is identifying the causes of the readjustment, it is considered to include problems experienced by spouses in the 'family problems' leading to poorer readjustment of family members.

It is often difficult for an expatriate, as an employee of a company, to decide the timing of the return to the home country. However, repatriates regard the life at the international assignment as a temporary situation, and many may desire to return to the home country for long durations, for a variety of reasons including conditions related to other members of the family and their own career matters, before receiving a notification of return from the company. As a result the readjustment may be assumed to be successful when their wishes are realized. For this reason, the 'desire to return' possibly affects the repatriation adjustment.

'Expectations for life/non-work' refers to the gaps between the expectations of the repatriates regarding life other than work duties before a return home and the actual situation after the return. Previous reports have suggested that expectations related to life affect the repatriation adjustment (Black, 1992; Gregersen & Stroh,

1997). Therefore it is assumed that if the expectation is matched with the reality, the readjustment is better.

Assuming these variables to be individual factors, it is presumed that these independent variables influence the repatriation adjustment. Therefore, the following Hypothesis 1 is proposed:

Hypothesis 1: Individual factors are significantly related to the repatriation adjustment.

5.3.2.2. Organizational Factors Related to the Institution

Related to 'repatriation training/guidance', Stevens, Oddou, Furuya, Bird, and Mendenhall (2006) have found that human resource (HR) practices including provisions for a reorientation programme has a statistically significant positive relation with on the degree of job satisfaction. Also, some studies suggest that companies provide training for repatriates to facilitate repatriation adjustment similar to the training prior to an international assignment before dispatching the employees (e.g., Black et al., 1999; Mesmer-Magnus & Viswesvaran, 2008; Stroh, Black, Mendenhall, & Gregersen, 2004).

Because returning to the home country is a long distance movement from one country to another, repatriates have to attend to many time-consuming tasks in the preparations, official formalities, the actual moving and the establishment of a base for the new life. To start uneventfully in a new environment requires sufficient and exhaustive preparations (Kim, 2001). Sussman (2001) has found that repatriates who are less well prepared suffer more fatigue upon return. In the case of personnel transfer by a company, specifically in the case of reassignments from an overseas country, the company will unofficially announce this to the employee in advance of the official notice of the repatriation date. If the reassignment is to another country, this announcement is usually given to the employee a few months in advance. It may be inferred that when the length of the period from the announcement to the repatriation day, the 'time for preparations of return', is shorter, the readjustment will be poorer.

Black and Gregersen (1991) and Black (1994) found that if the 'length of international assignment' is long, the repatriation adjustment will be more difficult because the repatriates will be less familiar with the present situations of the organization and conditions in the home country. In other words, the longer the period of the international assignment, the more difficult it will be to readjust to the home country environment (Shiraki & Nagai, 2002).

Concerning 'differences in the posts assigned', Vidal et al. (2007) focused on repatriate promotion, and suggested that repatriates who were promoted after the return show higher levels of job satisfaction. In many cases expatriates are assigned to higher ranking posts during the international assignments. It may then be assumed that problems arise in cases where repatriates are demoted or their authority is diminished after the return to the home organization (Cerdin & Le Pargneux, 2009; Umezawa, 1994). Therefore, repatriation adjustment may depend on whether repatriates are assigned higher or lower ranking posts after the international assignment.

'The frequency of visits to the home country (frequency of home visits)', that is, the frequency of temporary returns to the home country may affect the readjustment. This is because those who have had opportunities to return to the home country temporarily during the international assignment will have been able to obtain information about changes in the situation of the home country. Harvey and Novicevic (2006) and Stroh et al. (2004) suggest that taking a vacation to return to the home country, temporarily during the period of the assignment, will improve the readjustment after the completion of an international assignment.

Assuming these variables to be organizational factors related to the institution, it is presumed that these independent variables influence the repatriation adjustment. Therefore, the following Hypothesis 2 is proposed:

Hypothesis 2: Organizational factors related to the institution are significantly related to the repatriation adjustment.

5.3.2.3. Organizational Factors Related to the Work Duties

'Expectations for work duties' refers to gaps between the expectations the repatriates have had regarding the job/duties before the return to the home country and the actual situation after the return. Stroh, Gregersen, and Black (1998) suggest that reducing gaps related to the job contributes to improvements in the commitment to the organization, while Black (1992) and Naito (2011) also reported the positive relation of such met expectation with the readjustment to the organization.

For the communication with superiors or managers, if repatriates are adequately informed about their work duties by the managers after the return, that will make it easier for repatriates to engage in their duties. Naito (2011) has suggested that being informed about the job by their managers after the repatriation is statistically significant associated with the successful readjustment.

'Utilizing the repatriate experience' expresses that a company or organization takes advantage of repatriate knowledge and experience following the return. Previous studies have investigated this point by examining whether a company values the international experience, and suggested that this affects the repatriation adjustment. Here, examining whether a company utilizes the human resources of repatriates in reassigning duties may provide an effective avenue to develop HR policies.

'Consistency between the assigned duties/division and repatriate wishes (consistency — the job/division)' shows whether the type of work and assigned post in a company coincides with the wishes of a repatriate. Kraimer, Shaffer, and Bolino (2009) have highlighted that even if the wish of a repatriate is not fully met, providing information of career opportunities in the organization as a part of the organizational support reduces employee turnover intentions. It is inferred that 'consistency — the job/division' has a significant influence on the success of repatriation adjustment.

Assuming these variables to be organizational factors related to the work duties, it is presumed that these independent variables influence the repatriation adjustment. Therefore, the following Hypothesis 3 is proposed:

Hypothesis 3: Organizational factors related to the work duties are significantly related to the repatriation adjustment.

5.4. Methodology

5.4.1. Design of the Questionnaire

At the stage of this pilot survey to develop a questionnaire, the author visited eight Japan-based major companies where more than 300 employees were assumed to have been offered international assignments. Then the author discussed with the HR staff and repatriates working for these companies about the actual conditions of expatriates and repatriates. These discussions verified the accuracy of the terms, highlighted unclear or inappropriate statements and provided other details and opinions related to the questionnaire. After revision of the questionnaire based on the pilot survey, it received final confirmation by the respective HR departments of the companies.

5.4.1.1. Dependent Variables
Repatriation adjustment comprises four aspects (Figure 5.1). These are measured with the following five dependent variables: 'job satisfaction' (Black & Gregersen, 1990) as the readjustment to the job aspect, 'organizational commitment' (Jones, 1986; Mowday, Steers, & Porter, 1979) and 'retention(/turnover) intentions' as the readjustment to the division/company aspect, 'readjustment to Japanese companies' culture in general' (based on Black, 1992) as the readjustment to the companies' style in general aspect, and 'readjustment to Japanese daily life in general' (based on Black, 1992) as the readjustment to daily life in general aspect.

5.4.1.2. Independent Variables
The variables included in the survey are the following: 'age', 'time after return from assignment', 'family problems', 'desire to return', 'repatriation training/guidance', 'time for preparations of return', 'duration of the international assignment', 'differences in the posts assigned', 'frequency of home visits', 'expectations for work duties' (Black, 1992), 'expectations for life/non-work' (Black, 1992), 'communication with managers' (Naito, 2011), 'utilizing the repatriate's experience' (based on Lazarova & Caligiuri, 2001, Lazarova & Tarique, 2005, Suutari & Brewster, 2003) and 'consistency — the job/division'.

5.4.1.3. Control Variables

The following four control variables were employed: 'type of industry' (electric-appliance maker = 1, other = 0), 'type of occupation' (engineering = 1, other = 0), 'host country' (EU or North America = 1, other = 0) and 'number of times of international assignment'.

Further, four variables: 'desire to return', 'expectations for work duties', 'expectations for life/non-work' and 'consistency — the job/division' are reverse scoring items and were used to revise the data for the analysis.

5.4.2. Research Procedures

Along with the Nixon shock in 1971 and the Plaza Accord in 1985, direct investment in foreign countries by Japanese companies became active, and major Japanese corporations have become increasingly internationally oriented. Most companies have established offices or bases across the world, and gained recognition in the countries they operate in. With the activities of Japanese companies, international assignments have become common. Although there are numerous repatriates in MNEs in Japan, the research concerning repatriates in Japan is insufficient.

In this study a questionnaire survey was carried out targeting 233 repatriates who have worked for seven Japanese major MNEs classified as belonging to the manufacturing industry. The conditions for inclusion in the survey are repatriates who have had experience staying overseas for six months or longer in an international assignment and at the time of the survey two years or less have passed since the return to Japan. Repatriates as defined here means employees who had been assigned to duties in a country other than Japan by the employing company, and employees who were assigned overseas on "business trips" (assignments shorter than six months) were excluded. A total of 200 responses were collected, and the questionnaires were returned to the author. Among these, eight of the responses did not meet the requirements of the study, and the number of participants/respondents analysed was 192 (valid response rate: 82.40%).

5.5. Findings

5.5.1. Descriptive Statistics

The largest 'age' group was '41–45 years old', which comprised 33.33% ($n = 64$), and 99.48% ($n = 191$) were male. The average tenure with the company was 19.77 years (standard deviation (SD) = 7.47). The mean frequency of international assignments was 1.33 times ($SD = 0.61$). The main destinations included the United States (31.25%, $n = 60$), China (23.96%, $n = 46$) and Germany (8.85%, $n = 17$).

5.5.2. Correlations

Table 5.1 shows the correlations among the variables.

5.5.3. Multiple Regression Analysis

The multiple regression analysis was performed a total of five times using the 14 variables of the three factors and four control variables as independent variables, and the dependent variables including 'job satisfaction', 'organizational commitment', 'turnover intentions', 'readjustment to Japanese companies' culture in general' and 'readjustment to daily life in general' (Table 5.2). Based on Table 5.2, this section first describes the results seen from the independent variables and then, seen from the dependent variables.

These results showing significant relations are as follows. First, for the 'individual factors', it is found that a longer period after the return to the home country leads to better reported readjustment to company ($\beta = 0.25$) and daily life ($\beta = 0.25$). Repatriates with fewer family problems report higher job satisfaction levels ($\beta = 0.12$) and a better readjustment to daily life ($\beta = 0.13$). Repatriates with stronger wishes to return to the home country report better job satisfaction ($\beta = 0.14$). Repatriates who have more accurate expectations for non-work report better readjustment to daily life ($\beta = 0.39$). Thereby Hypothesis 1 is supported. Second, for the 'organizational factors — institution', the results show that repatriates with shorter periods of international assignments have higher job satisfaction levels ($\beta = -0.16$) and a better readjustment to company ($\beta = -0.34$) and life in general ($\beta = -0.32$), supporting Hypothesis 2. Third, for the 'organizational factors — work duties', the results show that repatriates with work expectations better meeting the actual conditions after the return ($\beta = 0.15$; 0.17; 0.19), and repatriates who report their skills as better utilized have better readjustment to the home organization ($\beta = 0.20$; 0.21; 0.23; 0.35). Repatriates who have better communication with superiors have higher levels of job satisfaction ($\beta = 0.23$) and organizational commitment ($\beta = 0.31$) and lower levels of intentions to resign ($\beta = 0.24$). Further, repatriates whose wishes related to work duties and reassigned posts better meet the actual conditions they encounter have higher levels of job satisfaction ($\beta = 0.18$). Thus Hypothesis 3 is supported.

5.6. Discussion

This chapter focuses on factors contributing to the readjustment of repatriates to identify organizational practices that would accommodate the needs and wishes of repatriates returning after international assignments. Based on the results of the analysis using the Japanese data reported here, I interpret the results considering two issues identified in the previous studies described in the section 'Introduction',

Table 5.1: Descriptive statistics and correlations among variables used in the study.

| | | | Individual Factors | | | | | Organizational Factors — Institution | | | | | Organizational Factors — Work Duties | | | | Readjustment | | | |
| | | | | | | | | | | | | | | | | | Organization | | | Non-work |
	M	SD	1 Age	2 Time after	3 Family	4 Desire to return	5 Expectations — life	6 Orientation	7 Prep.	8 Assign. duration	9 Position	10 Visits home	11 Expectations — duties	12 Commun.	13 Utilization	14 Consistency	15 Job satisfaction	16 Commit.	17 Turnover	18 Company	19 Daily life
1	–	–	1.00																		
2	12.97	6.78	-0.04	1.00																	
3	0.61	0.49	-0.04	-0.01	1.00																
4	2.77	1.24	0.07	0.01	-0.11	1.00															
5	1.95	0.68	0.01	-0.02	0.29	0.18*	(0.89)														
6	0.72	0.45	-0.03	0.00	0.10	0.10	0.25**	1.00													
7	4.29	3.27	-0.16*	0.05	0.02	0.05	0.00	-0.08	1.00												
8	52.50	32.47	0.22**	0.04	-0.27**	0.21**	0.21**	-0.14	0.02	1.00											
9	3.65	0.81	-0.24**	0.07	0.06	0.04	0.02	0.02	0.11	-0.18*	1.00										
10	4.16	4.61	0.18*	-0.12	-0.08	0.20**	-0.05	-0.02	-0.18*	0.31**	-0.18*	1.00									
11	2.73	0.61	0.00	-0.02	0.11	0.15*	0.25**	0.12	0.22**	-0.12	0.11	-0.16*	(0.77)								
12	3.80	1.03	-0.12	0.08	-0.05	0.06	0.20**	0.19**	0.06	-0.09	0.10	-0.20**	0.31**	(0.96)							
13	4.86	1.31	0.01	-0.03	0.03	0.09	0.15*	0.19**	0.16*	0.01	0.02	-0.04	0.32**	0.36**	(0.84)						
14	2.25	0.69	-0.14	0.05	0.00	0.05	0.17*	0.20**	0.07	-0.10	0.13	-0.15	0.20**	0.37**	0.35**	1.00					
15	4.30	1.10	-0.05	-0.04	0.14*	0.20**	0.32**	0.11	0.09	-0.23**	0.14	-0.07	0.42**	0.43**	0.50**	0.37**	(0.89)				
16	4.73	1.07	0.06	-0.01	0.10	0.18*	0.30**	0.01	0.16*	0.00	0.06	-0.04	0.35**	0.41**	0.36**	0.19*	0.62**	(0.92)			
17	4.63	1.37	0.07	-0.07	0.10	0.19*	0.25**	0.00	0.16*	-0.01	0.04	-0.01	0.35**	0.38**	0.36**	0.24**	0.58**	0.88**	(0.87)		
18	5.00	1.30	-0.04	0.24**	0.21**	0.04	0.43**	0.10	0.02	-0.32**	0.13	-0.13	0.33**	0.34**	0.34**	0.26**	0.50**	0.39**	0.36**	(0.92)	
19	5.58	1.13	-0.02	0.21**	0.34**	0.06	0.51**	0.16*	0.04	-0.37**	0.07	-0.12	0.15*	0.11	0.15*	0.16*	0.28**	0.18*	0.14	0.67**	(0.92)

$**p < .01$; $*p < .05$ (two-tailed).

M: mean; SD: standard deviation; $n = 192$; Time after: Time after return; Commun: Communication; Assign: Assignment; Prep: Preparation.

Cronbach's α coefficients are presented in parentheses, and show a relatively high degree of internal consistency.

Table 5.2: Regression results for variable relationships.

Independent Variables		Dependent Variables (Repatriation Adjustment)									
		Job		Readjustment to the organization (work duties/job aspects)						Readjustment to daily life in general (daily life/non-work aspects)	
				Division/Company				Companies in general		Daily life in general	
		Job satisfaction		Organizational commitment		Retention/Turnover intentions		Style of Japanese companies		Readjustment to daily life in general	
		β	t	β	t	β	t	β	t	β	t
Individual factors	Age	0.04	0.57	0.07	0.83	0.07	0.86	0.04	0.50	0.06	0.80
	Time after return	-0.05	-0.75	0.03	0.41	0.00	0.04	0.25	3.66***	0.25	3.81***
	Family problems	0.12	2.03*	0.10	1.33	0.09	1.18	0.09	1.37	0.13	1.98*
	Desire to return home	0.14	2.26*	0.07	1.00	0.09	1.28	0.06	0.86	0.09	1.30
	Expectations — life/non-work	—	—	—	—	—	—	—	—	0.39	5.57***
Organizational factors — institution	Orientation/Guidance	-0.04	-0.72	-0.08	-1.05	-0.10	-1.40	-0.04	-0.55	0.00	0.07
	Time for preparation	0.02	0.29	0.13	1.58	0.13	1.60	-0.11	-1.47	0.02	0.33
	Length of assignment	-0.16	-2.28*	0.04	0.51	0.01	0.16	-0.34	-4.24***	-0.32	-4.10***
	Differences of position	0.06	0.97	0.07	0.83	0.02	0.28	0.02	0.28	-0.01	-0.12
	Visits home	0.04	0.58	0.02	0.20	0.05	0.55	0.08	1.02	0.03	0.44

	Model 1		Model 2		Model 3		Model 4		Model 5	
Organizational factors — work duties										
Expectations — work duties	0.15	2.24*	0.17	2.07*	0.19	2.36*	0.17	2.17*	—	—
Manager communication	0.23	3.39***	0.31	3.78***	0.24	2.89**	0.15	1.90	-0.01	-1.36
Utilization of experience	0.35	5.28***	0.20	2.47*	0.21	2.60*	0.23	3.09**	0.08	1.12
Consistency of duties/wishes	0.18	2.75**	-0.01	-0.08	0.08	0.99	0.09	1.18	0.07	0.97
Control variables										
Type of industry	-0.04	-0.58	-0.09	-1.21	-0.09	-1.17	0.05	0.65	0.00	-0.01
Type of occupation	0.04	0.69	0.03	0.44	0.06	0.77	-0.03	-0.43	-0.05	-0.72
Host county	-0.08	-1.08	-0.14	-1.53	-0.10	-1.06	0.10	1.15	0.07	0.85
Time of international assignment	-0.04	-0.60	0.05	0.65	0.10	1.25	0.01	0.18	0.02	0.29
Adjusted R^2	0.47		0.25		0.25		0.32		0.37	
R^2	0.53		0.33		0.33		0.39		0.44	
F	9.68***		4.20***		4.28***		5.45***		6.77***	

$*p < .05; **p < .01; ***p < .001; n = 192.$

and propose details of what kinds of organizational support will be of benefit when extended to repatriates.

5.6.1. Four Aspects of the Repatriation Adjustment

Dividing the subordinate concept of the 'repatriation adjustment' into two: 'work duties/job' aspects and 'daily life/non-work' aspects, and the 'work duties/job' aspects further into three aspects, resulting in a total of four separate aspects (as in Figure 5.1). The results show that the determinants for each of these four aspects (five kinds of the readjustment) are different.

First, I will discuss 'readjustment to the organization'. While all of the three aspects of the 'readjustment to the organization' are related to 'organizational factors — work duties', 'readjustment to the division/company', one aspect of 'readjustment to the organization' is significantly associated only with the variables of 'organizational factors — work duties'. The 'readjustment to the job' and 'readjustment to Japanese companies' culture in general' are significantly related to several factors, and each has specific and different characteristic features. 'Readjustment to the job' is associated with 7 among the 13 independent variables. Since the job aspect is closest to the concerns of the individual on the work occasion, it may be supposed to be directly related to many factors and characteristics including the situations of family members. 'Readjustment to Japanese companies' culture in general' was related to four variables. This aspect tends to be the distance between the individuals themselves and the companies' culture in general rather than 'the job' which is related to everyday contacts, the cultural context is more abstract than the other aspects. This aspect ('readjustment to Japanese company culture in general') is also related to becoming reacclimatized to the home companies' culture and is closely related to changes occurring over time ('length of international assignment' and 'time after return from assignment'). A characteristic of this aspect is that it is somewhat difficult to take action to deal with situations related to this arising around the repatriate. 'Readjustment to the division/company' is an aspect which was related to only three variables of the 'organizational factors — work duties'. For Japanese companies, it may be a characteristic that only has restricting influences, and only few factors relate to 'organizational commitment' and 'turnover intentions' for repatriates, because the employing company is the same for the repatriate during the international assignment and after returning home, compared with other aspects.

Next, I examined the aspects related to the daily lives of repatriates. Here, 'Readjustment to Japanese daily life in general' was significantly related to the 'individual factors' and 'organizational factors — institution', but not to the 'organizational factors — work duties'. This suggests that this aspect may be simply related to factors regarding the individual and to changes occurring over time like 'readjustment to companies' culture in general'.

The above results suggest that when examining only one aspect of the readjustment of repatriates, determinants which are associated with other aspects are overlooked. Therefore, it is important to focus on all the results extracted here while still paying attention to the features that all of the aspects have in common as well as to the specific characteristics of each aspect. This suggests that this proposed framework is meaningful to investigate the repatriation adjustment. By verifying the factors related to each readjustment aspect, determinants for readjustment can be identified, and this will enable the development of appropriate policies for repatriation support. The next section will describe suggested policies for organizational support.

5.6.2. Practical Implications Based on the Determinants

First, the results of the analysis showed that among the three factors ((a)–(c) in Figure 5.2), 'organizational factors — work duties' may play the largest role in the 'readjustment to the organization'. Therefore, the study here suggests that the basic attitude for organizations to adopt to ensure successful repatriation adjustment is to focus on practices that deal with the individual work duties and the intentions/conditions of the work. Determinants classified into 'organizational factors — work duties' show that it is important for organizations to understand the wishes and intentions of repatriates about the duties and the division/group they are assigned to after the return, to assign repatriates to duties which utilize the advantages the repatriates offer, to ensure that arrangements for informing repatriates of their duties to enable them to predict the situation in advance and to create an environment where repatriates can discuss the new duties with their immediate managers. Because the sense of values and beliefs of individuals are changed by the overseas cultural experiences, organizations must pay attention to the attitudes of repatriates which have changed after the international assignments. When it is difficult to accede to the wishes or intentions of repatriates about the division/group to belong to and the duties they will be responsible for, the organization will benefit from making arrangements so that the repatriates will be able to understand the company perspective and understand that their specific skills are utilized in the organization for the long term. The findings described above support the view that the subjective evaluations of repatriates are important (Hyder & Lövblad, 2007; Zikic, Novicevic, Harvey, & Breland, 2006).

Second, the 'desire to return', 'family problems' and 'expectations for life/non-work' factors are significantly related to the repatriation adjustment. Here organizations will benefit from making effective arrangements for circumstances specific to each individual repatriate because the international experience can be a turning point in the life and career of a repatriate. In addition, as the family can ensure the provision of stability in daily life, and as this may affect the work performance of repatriates, it is also expedient to provide assistance that considers the other members of the family.

Third, two other determinants, 'length of international assignment' and 'time after return from assignment' are also related to the 'repatriation adjustment'. It may be inferred, and as also mentioned above, that 'readjustment to Japanese companies' culture in general' and 'readjustment to daily life in general' both are also related to *changes occurring over time*. The study finds both readjustments are originally parts of the same concept of cultural adjustment and are related to similar variables. This suggests that the readjustment of employees may be likened to a cyclic process: when dispatched to another country, the employees gradually acclimatize to the local culture, while they again get used to the culture of the home country when they are next assigned a post in the home country. Readjustment to the situation in the home country in general can be promoted by organizational practices assisting the repatriates, but it is also possible for this to take place over time, naturally, as a result of the length of the 'time after return from assignment'. For the 'length of international assignment', the longer the duration, the more important it is to provide this assistance, considering the changes that occur over time, as repatriates will become increasingly less familiar with the situations of their organization and the conditions in the home country. In particular, even when the employees are still on duty away from the home country, it is important for organizations to create regular opportunities where expatriates, managers and HR staff can discuss the wishes and intentions of the repatriates for their work duties and personal situation.

5.7. Conclusions

To take advantage of the skills and knowledge of the repatriates, the present study conducted research to identify determinants contributing to repatriation adjustment of Japanese MNEs from the perspective of *'changes occurring over time'* and *'changes due to cultural differences'*, and examined organizational practices of assistance extended to the repatriates that would be effective to alleviate the causes of repatriation problems. The study performed a comprehensive analysis of the subordinate concepts of the 'repatriation adjustment' dividing it into four aspects (Figure 5.1) and examined 'repatriation adjustment' from the 'organization/work' and 'private life/non-work' aspects separately. Then, the 'readjustment to the organization' was divided into 'the job', 'the division/company' and the 'country or regional companies' culture in general'.

Factors relating to the readjustment were classified into three: 'individual factors', 'organizational factors — institution' and 'organizational factors — work duties'.

The findings obtained from the analysis and the discussion are summarized into the following three points. First, it is important to seek determinants for the readjustment by focusing on all of the four aspects of the 'repatriation adjustment' which covers a wide range of concerns from the work aspect to the non-work aspect; this is because the determinants of each of the subordinate aspects are not always identical. By considering the non-work aspects in addition to the work aspects, it was found that the factors in the readjustment to daily life in general are different from the factors in readjustment to the organization. Then features of each aspect of the readjustment became clearer. Readjustment to 'the job' aspect is related to a wide range of factors, 'the division/company' aspect is only related to the work duties factor, and 'the companies' culture in general' aspect is related to 'time' (assignment's duration, time back) other than the work duties factors. The readjustment to 'daily life' aspect is related to 'duration' in addition to the factors reflecting the individual and excluding the work duties factor. Further, 'readjustment to companies' culture in general' and 'readjustment to daily life in general' have the subordinate concept of 'cultural readjustment' in common, and were both related to 'time'. Second, since 'organizational factors — work duties' plays a vital role in the readjustment to the organization rather than to the readjustment to daily life, organizations must try to know the intentions of repatriates and the situations related to their duties as well as the non-work aspects, to consider the details of the job, to assign posts utilizing the experience of the repatriates, to ensure accurate expectations for the duties is held by repatriates, and also that repatriates have opportunities to communicate with managers. Finally, organizations will benefit from providing assistance to both the repatriates and the family to ensure that they are able to readjust to life in the home country, specifically where the duration of the overseas assignment has been of long duration.

The results detailed above were obtained in this study; however, there are three main limitations and issues for future studies. First, because there are complicated relations among the variables in this study, I need to further elucidate details of these relationships. For that purpose, a qualitative study and longitudinal research should be performed for a better and more detailed understanding of what is involved in the readjustment. Second, it is also necessary to examine whether the three factors and determinants of readjustment shown in the study here can be applied to situations other than for repatriates, such as new employees and staff in domestic (in-country) transfers when assigned to new positions in different geographical locations. Third, the framework of *changes occurring over time* and *changes due to cultural differences* must also be further investigated by considering the circumstances. Using the framework to only Japanese companies of this study, it will be necessary to examine whether it would yield similar results also with companies and organizations based in other countries.

Acknowledgements

I am grateful for the comments from this books' reviewers, the participants of the 2015 Twelfth Annual JIBS (Journal of International Business Studies) Paper Development Workshop in June 2015, and the Association of Japanese Business Studies 27th Annual Conference in June 2014. The authors further appreciate the financial support provided by a Grant-in-Aid for Scientific Research (C), Japan Society for the Promotion of Science (Grant Number 26380531), and by a research granted from The Murafa Science Foundation.

References

Adler, N. J. (1981). Reentry: Managing cross-cultural transitions. *Group and Organization Studies, 6*(3), 341−356.

Adler, N. J. (2002). Cross-cultural transitions: Expatriate entry and reentry. In *International dimensions of organizational behavior* (4th ed., pp. 259−300). Mason, OH: South-Western.

Black, J. S. (1992). Coming home: The relationship of expatriate expectations with repatriation adjustment and job performance. *Human Relations, 45*(2), 177−192.

Black, J. S. (1994). Okaerinasai: Factors related to Japanese repatriation adjustment. *Human Relations, 47*(12), 1489−1508.

Black, J. S., & Gregersen, H. B. (1990). Expectations, satisfaction, and intention to leave of American expatriate managers in Japan. *International Journal of Intercultural Relations, 14*(4), 485−506.

Black, J. S., & Gregersen, H. B. (1991). When Yankee comes home: Factors related to expatriate and spouse repatriation adjustment. *Journal of International Business Studies, 22*(4), 671−695.

Black, J. S., Gregersen, H. B., & Mendenhall, M. E. (1992). Toward a theoretical framework of repatriation adjustment. *Journal of International Business Studies, 23*(4), 737−760.

Black, J. S., Gregersen, H. B., Mendenhall, M. E., & Stroh, L. K. (1999). *Globalizing people through international assignments.* Boston, MA: Addison-Wesley.

Bossard, A. B., & Peterson, R. B. (2005). The repatriate experience as seen by American expatriates. *Journal of World Business, 40*(1), 9−28.

Cerdin, J.-L., & Le Pargneux, M. (2009). Career and international assignment fit: Toward an integrative model of success. *Human Resource Management, 48*(1), 5−25.

Chi, S.-C. S., & Chen, S.-C. (2007). Perceived psychological contract fulfillment and job attitudes among repatriates: An empirical study in Taiwan. *International Journal of Manpower, 28*(6), 474−488.

Clague, L., & Krupp, N. B. (1978). International personnel: The repatriation problem. *Personnel administrator, 23*, 29−33.

Collings, D. G. (2014). Integrating global mobility and global talent management: Exploring the challenges and strategic opportunities. *Journal of World Business, 49*(2), 253−261.

Gregersen, H. B., & Stroh, L. K. (1997). Coming home to the arctic cold: Antecedents to Finnish expatriate and spouse repatriation adjustment. *Personnel Psychology, 50*(3), 635−654.

Gullahorn, J. T., & Gullahorn, J. E. (1963). An extension of the U-curve hypothesis. *Journal of Social Issues, 19*(3), 33−47.

Harvey, M., & Novicevic, M. M. (2006). The evolution from repatriation of managers in MNEs to 'patriation' in global organizations. In G. K. Stahl & I. Björkman (Eds.), *Handbook of research in international human resource management* (pp. 323−343). Cheltenham: Edward Elgar.

Haslberger, A., Brewster, C., & Hippler, T. (2014). Repatriation adjustment: Individual and organizational perspectives. In *Managing performance abroad: A new model for understanding expatriate adjustment* (pp. 161−181). New York, NY: Routledge.

Hyder, A. S., & Lövblad, M. (2007). The repatriation process: A realistic approach. *Career Development International, 12*(3), 264−281.

Ishida, H. (1999). *International business and the white color.* Tokyo: Chuo-keizai-sha (Kokusai keiei to howaitokara – in Japanese).

Jones, G. R. (1986). Socialization tactics, self-efficacy, and newcomers' adjustments to organizations. *Academy of Management Journal, 29*(2), 262–279.

Kim, Y. Y. (2001). *Becoming intercultural: An integrative theory of communication and cross-cultural adaptation.* Thousand Oaks, CA: Sage.

Kraimer, M., Shaffer, M., & Bolino, M. (2009). The influence of expatriate and repatriate experiences on career advancement and repatriate retention. *Human Resource Management, 48*(1), 27–47.

Kraimer, M. L., Shaffer, M. A., Harrison, D. A., & Ren, H. (2012). No place like home? An identity strain perspective on repatriate turnover. *Academy of Management Journal, 55*(2), 399–420.

Lazarova, M., & Caligiuri, P. (2001). Retaining repatriates: The role of organizational support practices. *Journal of World Business, 36*(4), 389–401.

Lazarova, M., & Tarique, I. (2005). Knowledge transfer upon repatriation. *Journal of World Business, 40*(4), 361–373.

Martin, J. N., & Nakayama, T. K. (2004). Understanding intercultural transitions. In *Intercultural communication in contexts* (3rd ed., pp. 266–302). New York, NY: McGraw-Hill.

Mesmer-Magnus, J. R., & Viswesvaran, C. (2008). Expatriate management: A review and directions for research in expatriate selection, training, and repatriation. In M. M. Harris (Ed.), *Handbook of research in international human resource management* (pp. 183–206). New York, NY: Lawrence Erlbaum Associates.

Mowday, R. T., Steers, R. M., & Porter, L. W. (1979). The measurement of organizational commitment. *Journal of Vocational Behavior, 14*(2), 224–247.

Murray, J. A. (1973). International personnel repatriation: Cultural shock in reverse. *MSU Business Topics, 21*(3), 59–66.

Naito, Y. (2009). Issues of international repatriation and organizational support: A study of repatriates at large Japanese multinational corporations. *Journal of International Business, 1*(1), 1–17. (in Japanese).

Naito, Y. (2011). Repatriation as an organizational re-socialization: An empirical study of an information acquisition model for repatriation adjustment in large Japanese MNCs. *Organizational Science, 45*(1), 93–110. (in Japanese).

Naito, Y. (2012). International repatriation: An empirical investigation of factors related to organizational readjustment. *The Japanese Journal of Labour Studies, 626,* 75–88. (in Japanese).

Naito, Y. (2013). Career management for repatriates after international assignments: Returnees in general and repatriates in organizations. In The Academic Association for Organizational Science (Ed.), *The review of organizational research: Dynamism of an organization and the staff* (pp. 47–89). Tokyo: Hakuto-shobo (in Japanese).

Naito, Y. (2015). Factors related to readjustment to daily life: A study of repatriates in Japanese multi-national enterprises. *Journal of the Faculty of Political Science and Economics, 47,* 159–177. Tokai University (in Japanese).

Newton, S., Hutchings, K., & Kabanoff, B. (2007). Repatriation in Australian organisations: Effects of function and value of international assignment on program scope. *Asia Pacific Journal of Human Resources, 45*(3), 295–313.

Pattie, M., White, M. M., & Tansky, J. (2010). The homecoming: A review of support practices for repatriates. *Career Development International, 15*(4), 359–377.

Reiche, S. B., Kraimer, M. L., & Harzing, A.-W. (2011). Why do international assignees stay? An organizational embeddedness perspective. *Journal of International Business Studies, 42*(4), 521–544.

Shiraki, M. (2006). *The comparative analysis of International HRM*. Experimental analysis of internal labor market in MNEs (pp. 33–102). Tokyo: Yuhikaku (Takokuseki naibu roudoushijou no jisshobunseki. Kokusai jintekishigenkanri no hikaku bunseki – in Japanese).

Shiraki, M., & Nagai, H. (2002). The research results of expatriates. *The Survey of Social Integration for International Transfer, 305*, 73–103. National Institute of Population and Social Security Research (Chosa kekka no gaiyo: Kaigai hakensha chosa kekka. *Kokusai idosha no shakaiteki togo ni kansuru kenkyu* – in Japanese).

Sparrow, P., Scullion, H., & Tarique, I. (2014). Introduction: Challenges for the field of strategic talent management. In P. Sparrow, H. Scullion, & I. Tarique (Eds.), *Strategic talent management: contemporary issues in international context* (pp. 3–35). Cambridge: Cambridge University Press.

Stevens, M. J., Oddou, G., Furuya, N., Bird, A., & Mendenhall, M. (2006). HR factors affecting repatriate job satisfaction and job attachment for Japanese Managers. *International Journal of Human Resource Management, 17*(5), 831–841.

Stroh, L. K., Black, J. S., Mendenhall, M. E., & Gregersen, H. B. (2004). Repatriating: Helping people readjust and perform. In *International assignments: An integration of strategy, research, & practice* (pp. 189–217). Mahwah, NJ: Lawrence Erlbaum Associates.

Stroh, L. K., Gregersen, H. B., & Black, J. S. (1998). Closing the gap: Expectations versus reality among repatriates. *Journal of World Business, 33*(3), 111–124.

Stroh, L. K., Gregersen, H. B., & Black, J. S. (2000). Triumphs and tragedies: Expectations and commitments upon repatriation. *International Journal of Human Resource Management, 11*(4), 681–697.

Sussman, N. M. (2001). Repatriation transitions: Psychological preparedness, cultural identity, and attributions among American managers. *International Journal of Intercultural Relations, 25*(2), 109–123.

Suutari, V., & Brewster, C. (2003). Repatriation: Empirical evidence from a longitudinal study of careers and expectations among Finnish expatriates. *International Journal of Human Resource Management, 14*(7), 1132–1151.

Umezawa, T. (1994). Expatriates' careers and motivation. In H. Ishida (Ed.), *International human resource management* (pp. 69–93). Tokyo: Chuo-keizai-sha (Kaigaihakennsha no kyaria to doukizuke. *Kokusai jinnji* – in Japanese).

Vidal, M. E. S., Valle, R. S., & Argon, M. I. B. (2007). Antecedents of repatriates' job satisfaction and its influence on turnover intentions: Evidence from Spanish repatriated managers. *Journal of Business Research, 60*(12), 1272–1281.

Zikic, J., Novicevic, M. M., Harvey, M., & Breland, J. (2006). Repatriate career exploration: A path to career growth and success. *Career Development International, 11*(7), 633–649.

Chapter 6

Why Expatriate Compensation Will Change How We Think about Global Talent Management

Yvonne McNulty

Abstract

Purpose — I build on a strong foundation of prior studies about expatriate compensation in general to provide an overview of changes in expatriate compensation, from home- to host-based approaches, during the past 10 years.

Methodology/approach — Underpinned by findings from academic and practitioner literature, I review and integrate studies of expatriate compensation and global talent management to outline the challenges and opportunities home- and host-based compensation approaches present to MNEs.

Findings — Home-based compensation is becoming an outdated and overly expensive model that is often ineffective in moving MNEs' global competitive advantage to where it needs to be, leaving host-based approaches as the only alternative. But the use of host-based "cheaper" compensation approaches can also lead to unintended outcomes for MNEs in terms of unforeseen opportunity costs (such as the loss of critical talent) arising from shortsighted compensation decisions.

Practical implications — I argue that expatriate compensation works best when it is not based on an employees' home-country status but instead on the role that he or she performs *locally*. I suggest a host-based compensation approach — global compensation — that is based on the worth of the position

Global Talent Management and Staffing in MNEs
International Business & Management, Volume 32, 125–150
ISSN: 1876-066X/doi:10.1108/S1876-066X20160000032005

rather than where the individual has come from. Such an approach is more equitable because it is performance-based thereby eliminating overpaying and perceived unfairness. It is much simpler to administer than home-based compensation because it represents an extension of most MNEs already existing domestic (home country) pay-for-performance model.

Originality/value — Despite more than 10 years of new compensation practices being implemented and reported by global mobility practitioners, very little has been studied or written by scholars about some of the recent changes in expatriate compensation over the past decade. The chapter addresses this gap in academic literature.

Keywords: Expatriate; compensation; balance-sheet; local-plus; localization; permanent transfers

6.1. Introduction

Attracting global talent in the form of expatriates is a competitive advantage for multinational enterprises (MNEs) as is developing, managing, and retaining them (Collings & Mellahi, 2009; De Cieri & Dowling, 2006; Vaiman & Collings, 2014). Expatriates are defined as,

> legally working individuals who reside temporarily in a country of which they are not a citizen in order to accomplish a career-related goal, being relocated abroad either by an organization, by self-initiation, or directly employed within the host country, some of whom are paid on enhanced terms and conditions to recognize their being foreigners in that country.

One area of importance in global talent management (GTM) is how expatriates are compensated (McNulty, De Cieri, & Hutchings, 2013; Warneke & Schneider, 2011). GTM is defined as the strategic integration of high-performing and high-potential employees on a global scale that includes their proactive identification, development, deployment, and retention. (Collings & Scullion, 2008; Farndale, Scullion, & Sparrow, 2010).

Studies show that compensation is a source of frustration for many MNEs (Chen, Choi, & Chi, 2002; Dowling, Festing, & Engle, 2013; Foote, 1977; Harvey, 1993a; Suutari & Tornikoski, 2001) regardless as to whether it is remunerating an organization-assigned expatriate (OE) or employing a locally hired foreigner already in the host-country location (see McNulty & Vance, 2016 for an overview of differences). While expatriate compensation has a long publication history dating back hundreds of years (Lay, 1925; Reynolds, 1997), and in the management literature dating back to the 1960s (Bader, 2014; Bonache & Fernandez, 1997; Foote, 1977; Gomez-Mejia & Welbourne, 1991; Harvey, 1993a; Hodgetts & Luthans, 1993; Lowe, Milliman, De Cieri, & Dowling, 2002; Phillips & Fox, 2003; Schollhammer, 1969; Stone, 1986, 1995; Suutari & Tornikoski, 2001), scholarly articles about changes in expatriate compensation over the past decade are lacking across most management disciplines (e.g., international human resource management, IHRM; international management, IM; and international business, IB). This is despite extensive coverage of changes in compensation approaches in the practitioner literature (e.g., AIR Inc., 2010, 2011, 2016; Brookfield Global Relocation Services, 2009a, 2015; Ernst & Young, 2010; Herod, 2009; KPMG, 2011; McNulty & Aldred, 2013; Mercer, 2006, 2010, 2014; ORC Worldwide, 2004a, 2008, 2009a; Reloc8 Asia Pacific Group, 2007; Stanley, 2009) and significant implications arising from these changes for GTM and global staffing practices that have emerged in recent extant literature (McNulty et al., 2013; Tait, De Cieri, & McNulty, 2014; Yanadori, 2014).

The most significant change in expatriate compensation over the past decade is the move from home- to host-based approaches resulting in large-scale reductions in the costs associated with expatriate remuneration more broadly (AIR Inc., 2011; Ernst & Young, 2010; ORC Worldwide, 2009a). The introduction of host-based approaches, such as local-plus, localization, and permanent transfers (AIR Inc., 2016; ORC Worldwide, 2004a; Stanley, 2009), has been shown to result in high strategic value for organizations by maximizing short-term talent management and cost containment (Brookfield Global Relocation Services, 2015; Herod, 2009). New evidence nonetheless suggests that short-term cost savings can also jeopardize MNEs' ability to achieve their *long-term* goals regarding talent management and knowledge sharing (McNulty et al., 2013; Reynolds, 2000). Whereas generous home-based compensation tends to bind expatriates to the MNE and increases their loyalty, host-based compensation has the opposite effect: it provides fewer ties that bind expatriates to the MNE financially (e.g., fewer allowances and benefits and often no pension or retirement plans) meaning that job movement in and out of the organization is facilitated with greater ease. There is, therefore, an inherent "opportunity cost" arising from host-based compensation that is often overlooked by MNEs and which remains virtually untouched as a research topic among expatriate compensation scholars, despite the prevalence with which it is being utilized in practice (Mercer, 2014; Stanley, 2009; Tait et al., 2014) and its likely impact on GTM. What we do know is that host-based compensation creates many problems for companies because, while short-term financial gains can become easier to attain for the MNE (via less expensive remuneration), it can be undermined by long-term strategic losses in talent (Ernst & Young, 2010).

In this chapter, I build on a strong foundation of prior studies about expatriate compensation in general (e.g., Bonache & Fernandez, 1997; Roth & O'Donnell, 1996; Sims & Schraeder, 2005; Tornikoski, 2011a), including solid evidence for the success of global rewards (Bonache & Stirpe, 2012; Fay, 2008; Festing & Perkins, 2008; Gomez-Mejia & Welbourne, 1991; Tornikoski, 2011b; Tornikoski,

Suutari, & Festing, 2014) and pay for performance (Lowe et al., 2002; Salimaki & Heneman, 2008), as well as global pay systems (Bloom & Milkovich, 1999; Dwyer, 1999; Festing, Eidems, & Royer, 2007; Stone, 1995; Suutari & Tornikoski, 2000; Warneke & Schneider, 2011; Watson & Singh, 2005) to provide, specifically, an overview of changes in expatriate compensation, from home- to host-based approaches, during the past 10 years. I outline the challenges and opportunities these changes present to MNEs in relation to GTM and in doing so suggest ideas for future scholarly inquiry.

The chapter contains five sections. The section that follows establishes a strong rationale for more scholarly studies about expatriate compensation. I then outline established terminology about expatriate compensation and clarify some new terminology and concepts that are used in practice but which has not yet been adopted in scholarly studies. This naturally provides an overview of the research base that has examined and informed expatriate compensation research to date by combining studies from within the scholarly domain with literature from practitioners. Next, the challenges that expatriate compensation presents to MNEs are canvassed, focusing on issues that pertain to GTM and how they can potentially be overcome. Concluding thoughts follow in which I outline a future research agenda.

6.2. Rationale: Why Expatriate Compensation Is Still Relevant

Despite more than 10 years of new compensation practices being implemented and reported by global mobility practitioners, very little has been studied or written by scholars about some of the recent changes in expatriate compensation over the past decade (cf. McNulty et al., 2013; Reynolds, 2000; Tait et al., 2014; Yanadori, 2014) which are outlined in Figure 6.1. My motivation for writing this chapter is based on this obvious gap and stems from two personal experiences. The first is my own journey as a corporate/academic expatriate (I am married to a corporate CEO). Our first international assignment in February 2000 was with *Oracle Corporation*, a US-headquartered company with subsidiary offices in all corners of the globe; the company asked my husband and I to relocate from our home country (Australia) to Chicago. We accepted the role on a fully localized basis meaning that, unlike our peers in other companies, we did not relocate with any of the typical benefits that expatriates could expect at the time — housing and car allowance, annual home leave, club membership, tax equalization, relocation bonus, cost of living allowance, school fees, and so on. My husband and I were unusual in that he did not relocate to the United States as a transferee of the Australian office but as a new employee of the US headquarters (on a H1B visa, having resigned his position in Australia). Thus, we were "localized" expatriates compensated entirely via salary and performance bonuses — and nothing else. While this was rare 17 years ago, today it is quite the norm.

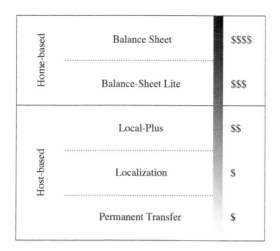

Figure 6.1: Overview of expatriate compensation approaches.

The second personal experience is based on an unsuccessful special issue on "expatriate compensation" in 2014 for which I acted as special issue editor (McNulty & Harvey, 2014). Despite the long-held view that there is much we still do not know about expatriate compensation, the special issue was (in all respects) a flop: the 12-month call for papers garnered only two useable submissions. In reflecting on this outcome, the general view held by senior scholars contacted at the time is that everything that has needed to be said about expatriate compensation has been said over the past 100 years and there is nothing more to add. Respectfully, I disagree, and so (it seems) do others. Bonache and Fernandez (1997, p. 457) observed nearly 20 years ago that,

> the aspect of expatriate management that has received the least amount of attention is compensation,

while Phillips and Fox (2003, p. 466) argued just over a decade ago that,

> this area is particularly worthy of attention.

Sims and Schraeder (2005, p. 107) similarly proffered that,

> it is apparent that the topic of expatriate compensation will be the focus of more research by the academic community, particularly with respect to systematic, empirical studies.

Yet personal experience shows that these long-standing calls within academia remain unheeded in spite of empirical evidence showing that new compensation approaches over the past decade are emerging that will dramatically change the expatriate management landscape (McNulty & Inkson, 2013; Reynolds, 2000). For example, AIR Inc. (2011, p. 1), a workforce globalization consultancy, in a recent commentary stated that,

> Local plus ... pay packages are not new to mobility, having been leveraged successfully in the financial and professional services industries for over a decade. Recently there has been a lot of interest in the local plus approach as a possible low-cost alternative to the traditional balance sheet. When used in the proper context, the host plus approach can be an effective and successful scheme for compensating expatriates. Knowing when and how best to use this method is the key to its successful implementation.

Dowling et al. (2013, p. 216) further argue that,

> Th[e] complexities, challenges and choices facing managers involved in global compensation decisions do not change two primary areas of focus. These individuals must manage highly complex and turbulent local details while concurrently building and maintaining a unified, strategic pattern of compensation policies, practices and values.

As my own family situation shows, there is irrefutable *practical* evidence that expatriate compensation is changing. Moreover, for a field such as IHRM which is so heavily tied to practice, it seems important not to ignore industry reports altogether when it shows there is an abundance of literature and issues demanding scholarly attention about this topic in particular (Bitten, 2001; Dwyer, 1999). If one were to ask, for instance, any global mobility practitioner 20 years ago about their compensation challenges, nearly all would have said the key issue is "fewer benefits" (Aschkenasy, 1997; Gould, 1999; Graham & Trevor, 2000; Kates & Spielman, 1995; Oemig, 1999; Reynolds, 2000); today, the biggest challenge is retaining global talent in an overwhelmingly cost-driven global mobility environment pushing to implement "localization" policies (Brookfield Global Relocation Services, 2012; Cartus, 2010; KPMG, 2003; Mercer, 2010; ORC Worldwide, 2004a) — an issue that has barely been looked at academically. The question then arises (among others), what does this mean in scholarly terms and how might it impact upon theories about expatriation? Undoubtedly, as the fierce competition for foreign talent increases, compensating expatriates is likely to become (if not already) more and more complex, with localization just the tip of the iceberg. A survey by Ernst and Young (2010), for example, found that 67 percent of mobility managers report "compensation packages" as the biggest area where expatriates' expectations are not met. This may in part be due to fluctuating exchange rates, inflation, challenging locations in emerging markets, variable income tax rates, and a range of new compensation practices — such as localization — being introduced (Dwyer, 1999; Phillips & Fox, 2003). Yet scholarly research suggests that expatriates do not seek or accept international assignments purely for financial reasons (Borstorff, Harris, Feild, & Giles, 1997; Dickmann, Doherty, Mills, & Brewster, 2008; McNulty, 2013). Indeed, there is compelling evidence that expatriates have many non-financial reasons for engaging in global mobility, with career enhancement and progression, seeking a personal or family adventure, and fulfilling a lifelong dream among them (Hippler, 2009). Why, then, is expatriate compensation such a challenging topic? And what is *localization* anyway? How could an understanding of this, and other, new compensation approaches impact positively on GTM and global staffing practices theoretically and strategically?

6.3. Overview of Expatriate Compensation Research and Approaches

6.3.1. Existing Terminology and Concepts

Expatriate compensation has a long history of well-established and accepted terms and concepts.

6.3.1.1. Balance-Sheet
The most commonly understood and longest-standing conceptualization is the home-based or balance-sheet approach defined as,

> providing an employee with the same standard of living in the host location as in the home location with no loss or gain ("no win, no loss"). The basic procedure involves covering for cost-of-living and housing cost differences to ensure maintenance of home country purchasing power. (Mercer, 2010, p. 4)

This approach is intended to keep an expatriate "whole" in relation to their home-country peers (Wentland, 2003) and to minimize changes in their standard of living resulting from an international assignment (Phillips & Fox, 2003; Sims & Schraeder, 2005; Tornikoski et al., 2014). For this reason, it is usually applied only to OEs on long-term assignments (Tornikoski et al., 2014), and particularly those who least want to be relocated abroad and thus need to be incentivized financially to go (Sims & Schraeder, 2005). In the 1980s and 1990s, research showed that a large majority of US companies employing OEs used the balance-sheet approach to compensate their expatriates (GMAC, NFTC, & SHRM Global Forum, 2004; Wentland, 2003).

The balance-sheet approach is conceived of four components: (1) *tax equalization* to alleviate an expatriate's assessed "tax burden," which guarantees that the expatriate pays neither more nor less in taxes than he or she would if they were to remain in their home country; (2) *housing allowance* which is calculated according to costs above or below those represented by an expatriate's home-country housing norm; (3) *goods and services* in relation to an expatriate's "purchasing power" in the host location for groceries, transportation, and medical care (among other items) compared to cost of living expenditure in the home country; and, (4) *reserve elements*, including pension contributions, savings, and investments all of which remain untouched (Mercer, 2010; ORC Worldwide, 2009b). The balance-sheet approach has also been referred to as the *net-to-net, home country, build-up* and *destination-based* approach (Dowling et al., 2013; Mercer, 2010; Sims & Schraeder, 2005).

The balance-sheet approach has many benefits including that, because compensation remains tied to the compensation system in the home country, it provides expatriates with lavish allowances and benefits (Stone, 1986) and MNEs with the ability to control who is sent to a particular host location with a reasonable assurance of their repatriation and/or re-assignment elsewhere (Dowling et al., 2013). It can be a useful retention tool, especially for high-potential employees that sit within

MNEs' global talent and succession planning initiatives. Nonetheless, it is not a "one size fits all approach" being costly and expensive to administer. Consider, for example, that in relative terms only a very small proportion of a company's overall *total* employee workforce (e.g., perhaps 5% of employees worldwide) could be incurring 60% or 70% of total salary costs. Arguments against using the balance-sheet approach are based largely upon those also made about executive compensation in general, that is, that top managers tend to be over-paid in comparison to the work they actually do (see Hope, 2004).

6.3.1.2. Balance-Sheet Lite
The expense of the balance-sheet approach, along with limited empirical evidence showing that higher pay results in better performance outcomes (see Hope, 2004; Locke, 2004), has resulted in a number of *hybrid* forms of home-based compensation such as the *cafeteria*, *mix-n-match* and *flexible plan* approaches (Sims & Schraeder, 2005; Wentland, 2003). These typically involve the higher of the home and host-country approaches being applied depending on the home/host location combination, or a home approach being used but with international (non-home-related) elements integrated, such as an international spendable income (Mercer, 2010). An *international headquarters* (or *regional*) approach can also be used where expatriates are compensated as if all originated from the same geographic headquarters and are being paid on the same balance-sheet program. Sims and Schraeder (2005) describe this approach as promoting perceptions of equity among expatriates from different nationalities working together in the same host location to ensure that each is not paid any more or less than expatriates already working in that location.

The balance-sheet approach has been shown to create considerable compensation disparity between the pay levels of OEs and host-country nationals (HCNs) who can be paid different amounts for performing the same or a similar role (Dowling et al., 2013). This has been identified as a key determinant of dissatisfaction and lower morale among local employees that work directly with expatriates resulting in feelings of resentment, inequity and unfairness (Bonache, Sanchez, & Zarraga-Oberty, 2009; Chen et al., 2002; Festing et al., 2007; Leung, Wang, & Hon, 2011; Leung, Zhu, & Ge, 2009).

6.3.2. New Terminology and Concepts

In contrast to home-based compensation, host-based compensation, in general, can be summarized according to two approaches — *local-plus* and *localization* — both of which are intended to integrate an employee into the local market structure of the host location by paying him or her a base salary according to the local market rate (Mercer, 2010; Yanadori, 2014). Host-based approaches are typically used as a cost containment measure and utilized when an assignment has a combination of: (a) a permanent position in the host country; (b) the assignment location is in the same region as an employee's home country; (c) there is not likely to be a suitable role in the home country for an employee to return to; and (d) cost reduction is a priority (Tait et al., 2014). Host-based approaches result in ties back to an expatriate's nominated home country being scaled back (for local-plus) or severed altogether (for localization) with he or she becoming a local (for the purposes of payroll) in the host country.

6.3.2.1. Local-Plus

Local-plus is an approach where expatriate employees are,

> paid according to the salary levels, structure, and administration guidelines of the host location, as well as being provided, in recognition of the employee's foreign status, with special expatriate benefits such as transportation, housing, and the costs of dependents' education. (Stanley, 2009, p. 2)

Expatriates compensated on local-plus,

> are usually responsible for paying all actual income taxes ... companies commonly keep assignees, where possible, on the home country pension or social security system, since local plus packages tend to be used for temporary assignments that can result in a return to the home country. (AIR Inc., 2011, p. 2)

Local-plus has also been described as *mutual benefit* (a reduced package of benefits) and *core plus* (a core of required benefits such as immigration and relocation costs to host country which can be added as needed depending on circumstances or as an incentive; Brookfield Global Relocation Services, 2009b).

Not all expatriates on local-plus receive the full range of additional benefits as these are at the discretion of the MNE and determined by a range of factors including the location of the assignment (e.g., hardship, emerging economy), position status and seniority, assignment type, and family size (Brookfield Global Relocation Services, 2009b). Stanley (2009) notes a steady rise in local-plus compensation in Asia as an alternative to the traditional balance-sheet approach, with AIR Inc. (2011) reporting that, of the companies that offer local-plus policies, approximately one-third of expatriates are compensated in this way. McNulty et al. (2013), in their study of 31 OEs in Asia found that, consistent with other surveys (e.g., Brookfield Global Relocation Services, 2016; ORC Worldwide, 2004b, 2009a), local-plus compensation was the most common form of remuneration.

An important benefit for firms when using local-plus is the inherent flexibility to tailor each "plus" component (i.e., to add or remove a benefit) according to a variety of MNE objectives (Burns, 2003). These "top ups" or "uplifts" can be delivered either as cash directly to the expatriate (in the host-country currency) or as in-kind benefits directly to a supplier (e.g., a landlord, airline, or school; AIR Inc., 2011). Local-plus is particularly beneficial for OEs being sent from and to developed economies where home and host-country locations are comparable in terms of wages and standard of living, but less appropriate for OEs that are sent into low wage, developing, or hardship countries where lower levels of affinity between the home and host country exist. In contrast, local-plus can be particularly suited to locally hired foreigners employed by MNEs in low wage and emerging economies directly from local labor markets who may already be adjusted to lower levels of affinity and for whom "keeping them whole" is not a requirement (AIR Inc., 2011).

6.3.2.2. Localization

Localization is similar to local-plus with the exception that it involves the removal or absence of an OEs "expatriate" status but only from a policy and payroll stand-point in terms of benefits and allowances (ORC Worldwide, 2004a). Mercer (2010, p. 5) defines localization as,

> the process of transferring an employee who used to be under expatriate terms and conditions to local conditions.

Localization almost always involves replacing a salary package (e.g., base salary, incentives, allowances, perquisites, social security, and retirement plans) with compensation comparable to that offered to local citizens of the host country and/or in accordance with minimum salary levels required by law for locally hired foreigners employed on work visa. Localization has also been described as the *going rate* and *market rate* approach (Dowling et al., 2013).

It is important to note that there has been some confusion in academic literature about the exact meaning of the term "localization" in reference to expatriation. Some articles refer to localization as the,

> extent to which jobs originally held by expatriates are filled by local employees who are competent to perform the job (Selmer, 2003, p. 43),

or,

> displacing expatriate managers with local talent. (Fryxell, Butler, & Choi, 2004, p. 269)

These definitions assume that "local employees" are nationals of the host country, where localization is linked to their career development (i.e., they are offered a job that an expatriate used to do). Technically, this is not correct given that localization as defined and practiced among mobility consulting firms determines that "local employees" are *both* nationals of the host country *and* localized expatriates (i.e., locally hired foreigners). Localization is not, therefore, the replacing of expatriates with nationals of the host country, but the transitioning of OEs that are originally deployed on home-based compensation onto host-based local terms and conditions, who then join the local workforce as locally employed foreigners.

Local-plus and localization is offered in one of two ways. It can be *delayed* where an expatriate commences an international assignment on a balance-sheet (or lite) approach and, after a period of between three to five years, then transitions to local-plus or is fully localized directed by either the employer or employee (ORC Worldwide, 2004a). Some expatriates relocate, for example, with full knowledge that local-plus will be offered or localization will occur after two years in the host country as pre-determined in their contract whereas other expatriates will be transitioned onto host-based compensation on completion of an initial assignment but with little prior warning. Transitioning to a reduced compensation package usually involves a phasing out period where expatriate benefits (such as transportation, housing, health care, and school fees) are reduced over a wind-back period (e.g., 50% phased out in Y1, and 50% in Y2). For fully localized expatriates, it is essential for them to resign from his/her home country office for payroll and tax purposes and to be formally hired by the host country office of the same company. This is also a typical requirement for local-plus expatriates, but not always enacted.

6.3.2.3. Permanent Transfers

Localization and local-plus which is offered *immediately* at the onset of an assignment is typically in the form of a permanent (or one-way) transfer. In this scenario, employees know from the outset that they will be on local-plus or fully localized once they arrive in a host location and will be required to operate as a "local" whilst there (Mercer, 2010; Tait et al., 2014). A permanent transfer is one in which an employee resigns from their home country office and is hired by the host country office of the same company, but for which there is no return (repatriation) to the home country and no guarantee of company-sponsored re-assignment elsewhere (Mercer, 2010; Tait et al., 2014; Yates, 2011). When a permanent transfer is used, host-country compensation and benefits are applied with relatively few, if any, typical expatriate package benefits made available over the long term (ORC Worldwide, 2004a). In some instances, a local-plus compensation package may be offered to a permanent transferee during an initial transfer period of up to two years to facilitate their transition. Importantly, and excepting only on the payroll, employees undertaking a permanent transfer are still expatriates in every sense of the literal meaning of the word because of their non-immigrant status and lack of citizenship of the host country (see McNulty & Brewster, 2016).

The prevalence of permanent transfer opportunities among companies is on the rise. Reports by EY (2016), KPMG (2003) and ORC Worldwide (2004a) show, for example, that more than three-quarters of companies have some form of permanent transfer and localization policy in place. Brookfield Global Relocation Services (2012) found that more than one-third of the 123 participating firms in their survey used permanent transfers as a cost effective alternative to the balance-sheet approach. Indeed, it (along with others, e.g., EY, 2016) found that half of the firms in their survey were switching employees to localized conditions, with a marked increase in permanent transfer and localization activity overall. A survey by Cartus (2010) identified skills shortages in host-country locations as an additional reason for using permanent transfers.

The upside of host-based approaches for MNEs is that it reduces global mobility costs, widens talent pool and sourcing opportunities, and provides employees with more job opportunities in international labor markets. In other words, it offers an alternative, less expensive solution to global staffing, buoyed by the availability of more employees willing to accept partial or full host terms and conditions in exchange for valuable international experience. A further key advantage for MNEs, especially in relation to localization, is that it can facilitate a strategy of local responsiveness particularly when there is a need to demonstrate long-term commitment to a particular host country or region. It is worth noting, however, that companies do not always drive host-based compensation practices. Employees are increasingly seeking out permanent transfers as a step toward fulfilling their own career development abroad (Collings, Scullion, & Morley, 2007), even though doing so may not increase the financial rewards they receive as substantially as their balance-sheet colleagues.

6.4. Expatriate Compensation and Global Talent Management

The transitioning by many MNEs from home- to host-based compensation approaches illustrates that expatriate compensation is undergoing significant, and some would argue necessary, evolution. The subsequent impact on GTM is undeniable, largely because GTM is predominantly a *human* activity and compensation is an inherently *personal* hygiene factor in the MNE-expatriate employment relationship. Moreover, while MNEs will never stop using monetary rewards as the primary solution to motivate and reward their employees (Pfeffer, 1997), including expatriates, what remains critical is *how* it is used to ensure the success of GTM and global staffing practices. MNEs face three challenges when compensating expatriates: issues arising from the normalization of global mobility, balancing extrinsic versus intrinsic rewards, and managing the increasing irrelevance of repatriation.

6.4.1. Normalization of Global Mobility

The "normalization" of global mobility as a typical, rather routine, and even expected part of one's career progression is a major challenge for GTM due to an increasing availability of more employees willing to relocate abroad in order to gain valuable international experience (Cerdin & Brewster, 2014), particularly younger employees, which has been a key reason for the steady decline in home-based compensation approaches in regions such as Asia, where host-based packages are in the majority (Diez & Vierra, 2013; ORC Worldwide, 2008). In certain regions and across particular industries, the heightened competition for global talent has not driven expatriate salaries up as one would logically expect but has actually driven salaries down. This means that it is increasingly more difficult for MNEs to attract, and then retain, global talent via the compensation it offers them. While on the one hand this can be seen as a legitimate reason for MNEs to utilize cost-reducing host-based compensation approaches in lieu of more expensive home-based approaches (because it is not necessary to pay more for some segments of the talent pool), it also means that MNEs have fewer tools at their disposal to find the *right* talent at precisely the time it is required. This challenge has been shown to feed into a "buy" versus "build" dilemma for MNEs (McNulty, 2013; Minbaeva & Collings, 2013; Stahl et al., 2012), where the building of a global talent pool through developmental and career enhancement activities is likely to be a far more successful long-term GTM strategy, than the short-term focus of poaching talent from competitors with expensive and over-inflated salaries.

6.4.2. Intrinsic versus Extrinsic Rewards

Another major challenge facing MNEs is that, while decades of research about expatriates has assumed that the fundamental driver for them to undertake an international assignment is for financial (extrinsic) gains, recent studies show a strong bias toward intrinsic rewards as a key motivator (Cappellen & Janssens, 2010a; Dickmann et al., 2008; Dickmann & Harris, 2005; Hippler, 2009). Warneke and Schneider (2011), for example, found that the five top criteria for relocating includes base salary (71%) and a location bonus (to incentivize the move; 32%), as well as accompanying partner support to assist in adjustment and the dual-career issue (finding employment; 60%), re-integration guarantees for an expatriate's career (58%), and the quality of schooling for children (41%). This suggests that financial rewards as the primary motivator to relocate are waning (Crowley-Henry & Collins, 2016; McNulty & Inkson, 2013), particularly when competitor organizations can match or exceed an expatriate's host-based remuneration package as a means of poaching them. Instead, non-monetary factors such as job guarantees and family support seem to play an increasingly important role, with the potential to impact on intent to leave and turnover (McNulty et al., 2013).

The shift in motivators has come at an important time in expatriate management. Decades of conventional wisdom aside, studies have recently shown that higher pay does not guarantee improved performance, instead being linked to a number of unintended and negative consequences such as manipulating performance measures (e.g., revenues) and excessive risk taking (e.g., Enron immediately comes to mind; Pfeffer, 1998; Pierce & Aguinis, 2013; Sanders & Hambrick, 2007). In other words, to fully link global mobility to GTM, MNEs need to deploy an appropriate compensation approach in combination with other non-monetary rewards that engages and motivates their expatriates *intrinsically* and which is aligned, rather than in conflict, with its broader GTM objectives. Recent research (e.g., Haslberger & Brewster, 2009; McNulty & Inkson, 2013) suggests this can be achieved using the psychological contract — an individual's subjective belief about the terms of his or her exchange agreement with an employer, usually in an indirect, unwritten form of communication between them (Inkson & King, 2011; Rousseau, 2004). This involves moving away from a transactional approach to compensation and rewards (i.e., motivating an OE to undertake an assignment using financial incentives) to instead adopting a relational approach that fosters harmonious and committed relationships through mutual respect and understanding (e.g., family and career support). Studies show that transitioning from transactional to relational psychological contracts can positively impact on expatriate retention and the success of MNEs' GTM programs (McNulty & De Cieri, 2016; McNulty et al., 2013). Whether this is achieved via home- or host-based compensation is dependent on the MNEs short- and long-term GTM objectives (e.g., where host-based compensation is more likely to facilitate short-term talent management objectives and home-based compensation much longer term goals).

For host-based compensation, it requires that MNEs carefully manage expatriates to ensure they are not treated like HCNs or domestic employees. It means acknowledging that *all* expatriates, regardless of the compensation approach used to employ them, incur more substantial expenses and greater disruption to their lives than employees who choose not to work abroad. As such, they need to be rewarded accordingly and subjected to a different set of policies, but only insofar as the compensation approach remains appropriate to the job that the expatriate actually does, rather than the status he or she holds because of their home-country ties. In addition to formal policy elements, attention must be paid as to how expatriates are adjusting to their new status of being semi- or permanently integrated among a local workforce. It includes issues related to an "organizational hierarchy" or "pecking order" that typically arises when MNEs treat employees differently on the basis of those considered "true expatriates" versus those who are "locals" from a policy and payroll standpoint (Tait et al., 2014; see also Mellahi & Collings, 2010). Expatriates on home-based compensation, for example, typically represent the elite class of foreign employees being of higher strategic value, while expatriates on host-based compensation are often viewed as lower-order foreign employees stuck beneath a type of expatriate glass ceiling — a limbo status of being neither a "true expatriate" nor a "true" local employee. This glass ceiling frequently results in strategic and operational restrictions for localised expatriates in terms of frustration with their career advancement that has recently been shown as a predictor of turnover (McNulty et al., 2013).

6.4.3. Repatriation Is Increasingly Irrelevant

A third challenge for MNEs is that home-based compensation is based on a repatriation model that insists on maintaining a link to expatriates' nominated home country or headquarters, despite increasing evidence that a growing number of expatriates may never return there (Cappellen & Janssens, 2010b; Stahl, Miller, & Tung, 2002). Thus, the increasing irrelevance of repatriation is a factor that must be considered when deciding on a compensation approach. If home-based compensation, for example, is strategically geared toward an expatriate who will one day return to their home country but who never does, or who does so infrequently and intermittently, this compensation approach is likely to be unnecessarily expensive, and potentially cost-prohibitive over the long-term, nor is it likely to effectively support a GTM program that is reliant on the continual movement of expatriates across borders — often over decades — to help build the MNEs competitive advantage. Host-based compensation then becomes the only viable alternative, and along with it various opportunity costs as outlined above that MNEs might be unprepared for. What is needed is a strategic level of GTM in the MNE (see Collings & Mellahi, 2009), to determine the most effective global staffing "mix" that combines the different types of expatriates (see McNulty & Brewster, 2016; McNulty & Vance, 2016) with appropriately aligned home- or host-based compensation approaches, that can then effectively support the MNEs broader objectives as appropriate to the demands of its global operation (see Hartman, Feisel, & Schober, 2010). Clearly, this is easier said than done given that it requires a level of strategic GTM planning that many MNEs struggle to implement in practice (Collings, 2014; Minbaeva & Collings, 2013; Scullion, Collings, & Gunnigle, 2007; Stahl et al., 2012).

6.5. Future Research Agenda: Expatriate Compensation

The study of expatriate compensation has the potential to extend and build on prior research about expatriate management in general, including changes to reward and benefits structures applicable to international employees. Although this chapter has provided an overview of recent changes in expatriate remuneration, more systematic and empirical research is needed to increase our understanding of the specific challenges MNEs face when compensating expatriates and how they can be overcome. I propose a number of research questions that will help advance conceptual and empirical development related to these challenges.

One of the major issues facing MNEs is how to link global mobility to GTM and how compensation acts as a moderator or predictor variable for the success of global mobility and GTM in general. In their insightful article about the seven myths of global talent management, Minbaeva and Collings (2013) show that the connection between global mobility activities (including expatriate compensation) and talent pool acquisition remains weak: many MNEs seem to engage in global mobility without linking it to developing future global leaders or to meeting expatriates' career development expectations (see Collings, 2014; Cerdin & Brewster, 2014). Yet GTM is often the program through which many individuals hope to realize their international career aspirations and goals. McNulty and De Cieri (2016, p. 4) define the link between global mobility and GTM as one that is,

> focused on international mobility as a planned and deliberate career move for expatriates that has clear long-term benefits for the individual ... as well as for the employer, i.e., successful GTM outcomes.

These "outcomes" are undeniably linked to expatriates' performance which prior research suggests can be impacted by the MNEs compensation and reward structure (Evans, Pucik, & Bjorkman, 2011; Locke, 2004; Malhotra, Budhwar, & Prowse, 2007). The importance of GTM success lies not just in getting the mobility piece right but also in overall global strategic success across all aspects of the MNEs business operation (Boudreau & Dowling, 2003; Cui, 2006). Research on GTM has nonetheless paid very little attention to the mobility and/or relocation of individuals as part of the MNEs overall GTM initiative (see Collings & Mellahi, 2009 for a review), with virtually no research linking GTM and expatriate compensation. Given the many problems MNEs face in compensating expatriates (Ernst & Young, 2010; McNulty et al., 2013), there is an urgent need to rethink international compensation (see Milkovich & Bloom, 1998 for an early call) and to address the challenges it presents in relation to GTM. Important topics worthy of further examination are thus:

RQ1. To what extent do MNEs link global mobility and GTM? What are the barriers and how can they be overcome?

RQ2. Which compensation models encourage, and conversely discourage, expatriate performance?

RQ3. To what extent, and by how much, does expatriate compensation impact on GTM outcomes? Which compensation models are more or less effective in helping MNEs achieve GTM success?

In light of recent changes to expatriate compensation as outlined earlier in the chapter, there is still little empirical data to explain why, and how, MNEs adopt home- versus host-based compensation beyond the simplistic reasoning of "cost considerations." Moreover, do MNEs apply strategic decision-making when deciding on a compensation approach for expatriates or do operational considerations take precedence? Engle and Mendenhall (2004) suggest that pay for expatriates should be based on strategic choices related to type of job (skill-based, developmental, knowledge transfer, governance and control, oversight) and seniority, while Gomez-Mejia and Welbourne (1991) argue that the unit of aggregation is an important consideration (e.g., individuals, groups, business units, pay/skill grade). An over-riding concern in the literature relates to pay equity and fairness (hierarchical vs. egalitarian; Engle & Mendenhall, 2004), especially in comparison to HCNs (Bonache et al., 2009; Festing et al., 2007; Leung et al., 2011). Yet practitioner literature suggests that practical choices related to ease of administration and standardization of pay practices (by avoiding a complicated number of home-host combinations for the balance-sheet, or having to deal with numerous "local" systems for host-based approaches) can over-ride the desire to engage in strategic decision-making (Brookfield Global Relocation Services, 2015; Ernst & Young, 2010). When deciding on an expatriate compensation approach, tension often exists between MNEs strategic necessity and the contextual requirements of the host location: while pay standardization is expensive (e.g., balance-sheet), host-based compensation is complex (with many versions across geographies) but more flexible and responsive to diverse business conditions (Dowling et al., 2013). Related to the diversity MNEs face are differences in the types of expatriate employed (see McNulty & Brewster, 2016; McNulty & Vance, 2016 for an overview of different types), given that how newer types of expatriates are attracted to work for, and compensated by, the MNE differs significantly from approaches used in the past (Shaffer, Kraimer, Chen, & Bolino, 2012). These new types of expatriates constitute a broad array of different types, e.g., employed self-initiated expatriates (SIEs) that are characterized as taking control of their career outside of the confines of the organization thereby abandoning corporate intervention and its relative security in favor of autonomy and flexibility (Doherty, Richardson, & Thorn, 2013). Scholars suggest that employed SIEs may be ideally suited to host-based compensation (Froese & Peltokorpi, 2013; McNulty, 2013), hence the link between global mobility, GTM and compensation is clearly evident but remains under-researched. Thus:

RQ4. How do MNEs decide on a home- versus host-based compensation approach for expatriates? Which criteria are used (strategic, operational, administrative, financial) to determine a compensation approach for expatriates?

RQ5. What are the MNE drivers (strategic, operational, administrative, financial) for changing compensation approach (e.g., from home- to host-based and vice versa)?

RQ6. Which types of expatriates are more or less suited to home- versus host-based compensation, and why?

A further challenge for MNEs is addressing the opportunity costs that arise when changes in expatriate compensation occur. Virtually nothing is known about the opportunity costs arising from these changes, especially from home- to host-based compensation, to both MNEs and the expatriates they employ, despite recent commentaries suggesting that these costs can be high (McNulty et al., 2013; McNulty & Inkson, 2013). When, exactly, should host-based compensation be introduced and implemented? Expatriates who are compensated on host-based approaches from the start or transitioned at some point during an assignment but who know to expect it have been found to adjust better in the host location (Tait et al., 2014) than those who do not undertake an international assignment with a host-based approach in mind but who inevitably find themselves with less remuneration that they originally intended (McNulty, 2013). In the latter case, expatriates will no longer have access to allowances and incentives resulting in unplanned lost income and financial disadvantages. A recent study found that this then impacts on perceived fulfillment of the psychological contract, leading to resentment, thoughts of leaving, and decreases in engagement (McNulty & De Cieri, 2016; McNulty et al., 2013).

Prior research (e.g., Festing & Müller, 2008; Haslberger & Brewster, 2009; McNulty & Inkson, 2013; Pate & Scullion, 2010) suggests that the psychological contract "currency" for expatriates generally falls into two categories: (1) *economic* currency in benefits like tax equalization, bonuses, paid home leave, housing and education costs, and medical insurance; and, (2) *development* currency in the form of, for example, increased levels of job autonomy and challenge, and mobility opportunities (including re-assignment) that can help them to build an international or global career. When companies reduce expatriate compensation they are shrinking the psychological contract "pie" by asking (or forcing) expatriates to re-define their value to the MNE, possibly their lifestyle, and probably their commitment to the organization. While some expatriates welcome the opportunity to engage in international work experience irrespective of the compensation approach applied (Crowley-Henry & Collins, 2016; Doherty et al., 2013), research has shown that there are many who accept host-based compensation because they perceive there is no alternative (McNulty, 2013; McNulty et al., 2013). Here, the temporal dimension becomes critical in terms of when, and how, host-based compensation is introduced. A recent study found, for example, that expatriates are not necessarily dissatisfied with their need to transition to local-plus or localization but with the *process* by which it is implemented (McNulty et al., 2013). The most significant issue is transitioning during an assignment rather than waiting until the end of the contract to allow better personal budgeting and financial planning to take place. Others were found to resent that once they were established as "career" expatriates, the compensation "goal posts" were then moved at the point of re-assignment or assignment extension by the MNE in the full knowledge that expatriates have few alternative employment opportunities in their home country. These practices create a heightened sense of unjustified loss among expatriates. Issues of job embeddedness (Feldman & Ng, 2007) as a predictor of employee retention (Holtom & O'Neill, 2004), and job mobility preparedness activities (e.g., obtaining information about job opportunities, developing networks of contacts about job information, keeping an updated resume, benchmarking compensation with other employers, and considering the next position that is desired; Kossek, Roberts, Fisher, & Demarr, 1998) are likely to emerge. McNulty (2013) recommends that the best way to alleviate tension relating to the implementation of host-based compensation is to engage in a much closer dialogue with expatriates and to ensure absolute transparency about the process. Thus:

RQ7. What is the opportunity cost(s) to (a) MNEs, and (b) expatriates when changes in compensation approach occur (e.g., from home- to host-based)?

RQ8. How do changes in expatriate compensation (e.g., from home- to host-based) impact on expatriates' perceptions of psychological contract fulfillment?

RQ9. To what extent do changes in expatriate compensation (e.g., from home- to host-based) impact on outcomes related to (a) expatriate performance and (b) GTM.

Recent commentaries suggest that a global compensation model (Bloom & Milkovich, 1999; Phillips & Fox, 2003; also referred to as "global pay" and "universal pay," Dowling et al., 2013) could help MNEs achieve global strategic success. A global compensation model is based on remunerating expatriates as related to the role that he or she performs as opposed to their home-country status (Harvey, 1993b). This is because it is the *worth of the position* that needs to be aligned to GTM, not whether an employee has expatriate status or where the individual has come from. The shift in focus from "expatriate" to "global" compensation reflects a shift in mindset (see Milkovich & Bloom, 1998); while expatriates clearly perform in an international context, many are nonetheless employed in jobs similar to those of HCNs, or in jobs that HCNs can also do at some point in the future. The distinction, then, is to focus less on "expatriate status" as the defining criteria for compensation and more on the international nature of the job (Freeman & Kane, 1995). In this way, a global compensation approach enables MNEs to find the most appropriate candidate and then compensate them accordingly, not because of who they are but according to what they are expected to achieve for the MNE in relation to their performance and other GTM expectations. A global compensation approach, then, is more equitable because it is performance-based, thereby eliminating overpaying and perceived unfairness (Engle & Mendenhall, 2004; Hope, 2004). Global compensation is much simpler to administer than a balance-sheet approach because it represents an extension of most MNEs already existing domestic (home country) pay-for-performance model (Dowling et al., 2013; Salimaki & Heneman, 2008).

While a global compensation approach will, in some instances, also reduce expatriates' compensation when host-based approaches are used, one advantage is that it allows MNEs to expand their global talent pool by targeting candidates' eager to pursue international and global careers; that is, candidates who are willing to expatriate not just because of the compensation being offered, but often in spite of it. This includes career expatriates and other locally hired foreigners for whom many have already acquired the intercultural competencies, cultural intelligence, and language abilities necessary to succeed in an international role, and who also have the necessary desire, skills, and attitudes (Froese & Peltokorpi, 2013; Thomas & Inkson, 2009). A further advantage is that it is inherently more flexible than that of the balance-sheet because, being based on pay-for-performance, it can continue even after an employee decides to relinquish their expatriate status: global compensation is not necessarily location or status-specific to the MNE but can be leveraged over the long term to facilitate the retention of expatriates as a means of ensuring a better return on investment from global mobility and GTM programs. Systematic field studies about global compensation are lacking, but sorely needed. Thus:

RQ10. How common is the global compensation model in practice? What are the drivers for MNEs to implement a global compensation model?

RQ11. Is a global compensation model more or less (a) expensive and (b) effective than other home- and host-based compensation approaches (e.g., balance-sheet, balance-sheet lite, local-plus, localization and permanent transfer)?

6.6. Conclusion

My goal in this chapter has been to build on a strong foundation of prior studies about expatriate compensation by providing a detailed overview of changes in expatriate compensation during the past 10 years and the implications arising from these changes for global mobility and GTM in practice. One such implication is that the move to host-based compensation approaches is both increasing and undoubtedly permanent. This means that the situation is likely to get worse before it gets better for MNEs struggling to find the right global talent. In other words, the balance-sheet approach is likely to be proven as an outdated and overly expensive model that is ineffective in moving MNEs' global competitive advantage to where it needs to be, leaving host-based approaches as the only alternative. But the use of host-based "cheaper" compensation approaches that seem appealing to many MNEs can also lead to unintended outcomes in terms of unforeseen opportunity costs (such as the loss of critical talent) arising from "shortsighted decisions" about home- versus host-based expatriate compensation strategies (Tait et al., 2014). While I have outlined these and other challenges and opportunities that recent compensation changes present to MNEs in relation to GTM, my hope is that by identifying significant gaps in our understanding of these new compensation trends over the past decade, future researchers have the opportunity to contribute to studies that will help MNEs across a wide range of communities and industries to address the complex issues associated with remunerating an increasingly diverse and inclusive expatriate workforce.

References

AIR Inc. (2010). *Diverse expatriate populations — Alternative remuneration packages.* Cambridge, MA: AIR Inc.
AIR Inc. (2011). *Local-Plus: Tips, tools and trends.* Cambridge, MA: AIR Inc.
AIR Inc. (2016). *Mobility outlook survey.* Cambridge, MA: AIR Inc.
Aschkenasy, J. (1997). Culture shock: Expatriate benefits are getting squeezed as companies tighten their belts. *International Business, 10,* 20–27.
Bader, B. (2014). The power of support in high-risk countries: Compensation and social support as antecedents of expatriate work attitudes. *The International Journal of Human Resource Management, 26*(13), 1712–1736.
Bitten, J. (2001). Compensation strategies for international assignments: Alternatives to the balance sheet. *HR Professional, 18*(2), 29–31.
Bloom, M., & Milkovich, G. (1999). A strategic human resource management perspective on international compensation and rewards. In G. Ferris (Ed.), *Research in personnel and human resource management.* Vol. Supplement 4. Greenwich, CT: JAI Press.
Bonache, J., & Fernandez, Z. (1997). Expatriate compensation and its link to the subsidiary strategic role: A theoretical analysis. *The International Journal of Human Resource Management, 8*(4), 457–475.
Bonache, J., Sanchez, J., & Zarraga-Oberty, C. (2009). The interaction of expatriate pay-differential and expatriate inputs on host country nationals' pay unfairness. *The International Journal of Human Resource Management, 20*(10), 2135–2149.

Bonache, J., & Stirpe, L. (2012). Compensating global employees. In G. Stahl & I. Björkman (Eds.), *Handbook of research in international human resource management* (2nd ed., pp. 162–182). Cheltenham: Edward Elgar.

Borstorff, P., Harris, S., Feild, H., & Giles, W. (1997). Who'll go? A review of factors associated with employee willingness to work overseas. *Human Resource Planning, 20*(3), 29–40.

Boudreau, J., & Dowling, P. (2003). Global talentship: Toward a decision science connecting talent to global strategic success. In W. Mobley & P. Dorfman (Eds.), *Advances in global leadership* (pp. 63–99). Oxford: Elsevier Science.

Brookfield Global Relocation Services. (2009a). *Global relocation trends survey report.* Woodridge, IL: Brookfield Global Relocation Services.

Brookfield Global Relocation Services. (2009b). *International mobility: Introducing flexibility into policy structures.* Woodridge, IL: Brookfield Global Relocation Services.

Brookfield Global Relocation Services. (2012). *Global relocation trends survey report.* Woodridge, IL: Brookfield Global Relocation Services.

Brookfield Global Relocation Services. (2015). *Global relocation trends survey report.* Woodridge, IL: Brookfield Global Relocation Services.

Brookfield Global Relocation Services. (2016). *Global mobility trends survey: Breakthrough to the future of global talent mobility.* Woodridge, IL: Brookfield Global Relocation Services.

Burns, S. (2003). Flexible international assignee compensation plans. *Compensation and Benefits Review, 35*(3), 35–44.

Cappellen, T., & Janssens, M. (2010a). The career reality of global managers: An examination of career triggers. *The International Journal of Human Resource Management, 21*(11), 1884–1910.

Cappellen, T., & Janssens, M. (2010b). Enacting global careers: Organizational career scripts and the global economy as co-existing career referents. *Journal of Organizational Behavior, 31*, 687–706.

Cartus. (2010). *Global mobility policy & practices survey: Navigating a challenging landscape.* Wilmington, NC: Cartus.

Cerdin, J.-L., & Brewster, C. (2014). Talent management and expatriation: Bridging two streams of research and practice. *Journal of World Business, 49*(2), 245–252.

Chen, C., Choi, J., & Chi, S. (2002). Making justice sense of local-expatriate compensation disparity: Mitigation by local references, ideological explanations, and interpersonal sensitivity in China-foreign joint ventures. *Academy of Management Journal, 45*(4), 807–817.

Collings, D. (2014). Integrating global mobility and global talent management: Exploring the challenges and strategic opportunities. *Journal of World Business, 49*(2), 253–261.

Collings, D., & Mellahi, K. (2009). Strategic talent management: A review and research agenda. *Human Resource Management Review, 19*(4), 304–313.

Collings, D., & Scullion, H. (2008). Resourcing international assignees. In M. Dickmann, C. Brewster, & P. Sparrow (Eds.), *International human resource management: A European perspective* (pp. 87–106). Abingdon: Routledge.

Collings, D., Scullion, H., & Morley, M. (2007). Changing patterns of global staffing in the multinational enterprise: Challenges to the conventional expatriate assignment and emerging alternatives. *Journal of World Business, 42*(2), 198–213.

Crowley-Henry, M., & Collins, M. (2016). Millennial expatriates. In Y. McNulty & J. Selmer (Eds.), *The research handbook of expatriates.* (forthcoming). London: Edward Elgar.

Cui, C. (2006). International compensation: The importance of acting globally. *WorldatWork, 15*(4), 18−23.

De Cieri, H., & Dowling, P. (2006). Strategic human resource management in multinational enterprises: Developments and directions. In G. Stahl & I. Björkman (Eds.), *Handbook of research in international human resource management* (pp. 15−35). Cheltenham: Edward Elgar.

Dickmann, M., Doherty, N., Mills, T., & Brewster, C. (2008). Why do they go? Individual and corporate perspectives on the factors influencing the decision to accept an international assignment. *The International Journal of Human Resource Management, 19*(4), 731−751.

Dickmann, M., & Harris, H. (2005). Developing career capital for global careers: The role of international assignments. *Journal of World Business, 40*(4), 399−408.

Diez, F., & Vierra, K. (2013). *Why companies in Asia are changing their approach to pay*. Scottsdale, AZ: WorldatWork.

Doherty, N., Richardson, J., & Thorn, K. (2013). Self-initiated expatriation: Career experiences, processes and outcomes. *Career Development International, 18*(1), 6−11.

Dowling, P., Festing, M., & Engle, A. (2013). *International human resource management* (6th ed.). London: Cengage.

Dwyer, T. (1999). Trends in global compensation. *Compensation and Benefits Review, 31*(4), 48−53.

Engle, A., & Mendenhall, M. (2004). Transnational roles, transnational rewards: Global integration in compensation. *Employee Relations, 26*(6), 613−625.

Ernst & Young. (2010). *Global mobility effectiveness survey*. London: Ernst & Young.

Evans, P., Pucik, V., & Bjorkman, I. (2011). *The global challenge: International human resource management*. Boston, MA: McGraw Hill.

EY. (2016). *Global mobility effectiveness survey*. London: Ernst & Young.

Farndale, E., Scullion, H., & Sparrow, P. (2010). The role of the corporate HR function in global talent management. *Journal of World Business, 45*(2), 161−168.

Fay, C. (2008). The global convergence of compensation practices. In L. Gomez-Mejia & S. Werner (Eds.), *Global compensation: Foundations and perspectives* (pp. 131−141). Oxon: Routledge.

Feldman, D., & Ng, T. (2007). Careers: Mobility, embeddedness, and success. *Journal of Management, 33*(3), 350−377.

Festing, M., Eidems, J., & Royer, S. (2007). Strategic issues and local constraints in transnational compensation strategies: An analysis of cultural, institutional and political influences. *European Management Journal, 25*(2), 181−231.

Festing, M., & Müller, B. (2008). Expatriate careers and the psychological contract: An empirical study on the impact of international human resource management. In M. Festing & S. Royer (Eds.), *Current issues in international human resource management and strategy research* (pp. 92−118). Hamburg: München and Mering.

Festing, M., & Perkins, S. (2008). Rewards for internationally mobile employees. In M. Dickmann, C. Brewster, & P. Sparrow (Eds.), *International human resource management: A European perspective* (pp. 150−173). Oxon: Routledge.

Foote, M. R. (1977). Controlling the cost of international compensation. *Harvard Business Review, 55*(6), 123−132.

Freeman, K., & Kane, J. (1995). An alternative approach to expatriate allowances: An international citizen. *The International Executive, 37*(3), 245−259.

Froese, F., & Peltokorpi, V. (2013). Organizational expatriates and self-initiated expatriates: Differences in cross-cultural adjustment and job satisfaction. *The International Journal of Human Resource Management, 24*(10), 1953–1967.

Fryxell, G., Butler, J., & Choi, A. (2004). Successful localization programs in China: An important element in strategy implementation. *Journal of World Business, 39*(3), 268–282.

GMAC, NFTC, & SHRM Global Forum. (2004). *Ten years of global relocation trends: 1993–2004.* Oakbrook, IL: GMAC.

Gomez-Mejia, L., & Welbourne, T. (1991). Compensation strategies in a global context. *Human Resource Planning, 14*(1), 29–41.

Gould, C. (1999). Expat pay plans suffer cutbacks. *Workforce, 78*(9), 40–46.

Graham, M., & Trevor, C. (2000). Managing new pay program introductions to enhance the competitiveness of multinational corporations. *Competitiveness Review, 10*(1), 136–154.

Hartman, E., Feisel, E., & Schober, H. (2010). Talent management of western MNCs in China: Balancing global integration and local responsiveness. *Journal of World Business, 45*(2), 169–178.

Harvey, M. (1993a). Empirical evidence of recurring international compensation problems. *Journal of International Business Studies, 24*(4), 785–799.

Harvey, M. (1993b). Designing a global compensation system: The logic and a model. *Columbia Journal of World Business, 28*(4), 56–72.

Haslberger, A., & Brewster, C. (2009). Capital gains: Expatriate adjustment and the psychological contract in international careers. *Human Resource Management, 48*(3), 379–397.

Herod, R. (2009). *Expatriate compensation strategies.* Alexandria, VA: SHRM.

Hippler, T. (2009). Why do they go? Empirical evidence of employees' motives for seeking or accepting relocation. *The International Journal of Human Resource Management, 20*(6), 1381–1401.

Hodgetts, R., & Luthans, F. (1993). US multinationals' expatriate compensation strategies. *Compensation and Benefits Review, 25,* 57–62.

Holtom, B., & O'Neill, B. (2004). Job embeddedness: A theoretical foundation for developing a comprehensive nurse retention plan. *Journal of Nursing Administration, 34*(5), 216–227.

Hope, M. (2004). An interview with Geert Hofstede. *Academy of Management Executive, 18*(1), 75–79.

Inkson, K., & King, Z. (2011). Contested terrain in careers: A psychological contract model. *Human Relations, 64*(1), 37–57.

Kates, S., & Spielman, C. (1995). Reducing the cost of sending employees overseas. *The Practical Accountant, 28*(2), 50–58.

Kossek, E., Roberts, K., Fisher, S., & Demarr, B. (1998). Career self-management: A quasi-experimental assessment of the effects of a training intervention. *Personnel Psychology, 51*(4), 935–962.

KPMG. (2003). *International assignment policies and practices survey.* New York, NY: KPMG.

KPMG. (2011). *Global assignment policies and practices survey.* Geneva: KPMG.

Lay, T. (1925). *The foreign service of the United States.* New York, NY: Prentice Hall.

Leung, K., Wang, Z., & Hon, A. H. Y. (2011). Moderating effects on the compensation gap between locals and expatriates in China: A multi-level analysis. *Journal of International Management, 17*(1), 54–67.

Leung, K., Zhu, Y., & Ge, C. (2009). Compensation disparity between locals and expatriates: Moderating the effects of perceived injustice in foreign multinationals in China. *Journal of World Business, 44*(1), 85–93.

Locke, E. (2004). Linking goals to monetary incentives. *Academy of Management Executive*, *18*(4), 130–133.

Lowe, K., Milliman, J., De Cieri, H., & Dowling, P. (2002). International compensation practices: A ten-country comparative analysis. *Human Resource Management*, *41*(1), 45–66.

Malhotra, N., Budhwar, P., & Prowse, P. (2007). Linking rewards to commitment: An empirical investigation of four UK call centres. *The International Journal of Human Resource Management*, *18*(12), 2095–2127.

McNulty, Y. (2013). Are self-initiated expatriates born or made? Exploring the relationship between SIE orientation and individual ROI. In V. Vaiman & A. Haslberger (Eds.), *Talent management of self-initiated expatriates: A neglected source of global talent* (pp. 30–58). London: Palgrave Macmillan.

McNulty, Y., & Aldred, G. (2013). Local plus: Winning the compensation battle but losing the talent war. *Strategic Advisor*, *4*(9), 1–5.

McNulty, Y., & Brewster, C. (2016). The concept of business expatriates. In Y. McNulty & J. Selmer (Eds.), *The research handbook of expatriates* (forthcoming). London: Edward Elgar.

McNulty, Y., & De Cieri, H. (2016). Linking global mobility and global talent management: The role of ROI. *Employee Relations*, *38*(1), 8–30.

McNulty, Y., De Cieri, H., & Hutchings, K. (2013). Expatriate return on investment in Asia Pacific: An empirical study of individual ROI versus corporate ROI. *Journal of World Business*, *48*(2), 209–221.

McNulty, Y., & Harvey, M. (2014). *Call for papers: Is it just about the money? New perspectives on expatriate compensation*. Bingley, UK: Emerald Group Publishing Limited.

McNulty, Y., & Inkson, K. (2013). *Managing expatriates: A return on investment approach*. New York, NY: Business Expert Press.

McNulty, Y., & Vance, C. (2016). Dynamic global careers: A new conceptualization of expatriate career paths. *Personnel Review*, forthcoming.

Mellahi, K., & Collings, D. (2010). The barriers to effective global talent management: The example of corporate elites in MNEs. *Journal of World Business*, *45*(2), 143–149.

Mercer. (2006). *Global compensation planning report: The information you need to develop your worldwide compensation strategy*. Geneva: Mercer.

Mercer. (2010). *Mercer localization practice survey: China, Hong Kong and Singapore*. Geneva: Mercer.

Mercer. (2014). *Mercer HR worldwide survey of international assignment policies and practices survey*. Geneva: Mercer.

Milkovich, G., & Bloom, M. (1998). Rethinking international compensation. *Compensation and Benefits Review*, *30*(1), 15–23.

Minbaeva, D., & Collings, D. (2013). Seven myths of global talent management. *The International Journal of Human Resource Management*, *24*(9), 1762–1776.

Oemig, D. (1999). When you say 'we'll keep you whole', do you mean it? *Compensation and Benefits Review*, *30*(4), 40–47.

ORC Worldwide. (2004a). *Survey of localization policies and practices*. New York, NY: ORC Worldwide.

ORC Worldwide. (2004b). *Worldwide survey of international assignment policies and practices*. New York, NY: ORC Worldwide.

ORC Worldwide. (2008). *Survey on local-plus packages in Hong Kong and Singapore*. New York, NY: ORC Worldwide.

ORC Worldwide. (2009a). *Survey on local-plus packages for expatriates in China.* New York, NY: ORC Worldwide.

ORC Worldwide. (2009b). *Understanding the balance sheet approach to expatriate compensation.* New York, NY: ORC Worldwide.

Pate, J., & Scullion, H. (2010). The changing nature of the traditional expatriate psychological contract. *Employee Relations, 32*(1), 56−73.

Pfeffer, J. (1997). Pitfalls on the road to measurement: The dangerous liaison of human resources with the ideas of accounting and finance. *Human Resource Management, 36*(3), 357−365.

Pfeffer, J. (1998). Seven practices of successful organizations. *California Management Review, 40*(2), 96−124.

Phillips, L., & Fox, M. (2003). Compensation strategy in transnational corporations. *Management Decision, 41*(5−6), 465−476.

Pierce, J., & Aguinis, H. (2013). The too-much-of-a-good-thing effect in management. *Journal of Management, 39*(2), 313−338.

Reloc8 Asia Pacific Group. (2007). *Survey of relocation trends: A snapshot of the tend to "lopat"/local/hybrid terms and "localisation" for international assignments in the Asia Pacific region.* Sydney: Reloc8 Australia.

Reynolds, C. (1997). Expatriate compensation in historical perspective. *Journal of World Business, 32*(2), 118−132.

Reynolds, C. (2000). Global compensation benefits in transition. *Compensation and Benefits Review, 32*(1), 28−38.

Roth, K., & O'Donnell, S. (1996). Foreign subsidiary compensation strategy: An agency theory perspective. *Academy of Management Journal, 39*, 678−703.

Rousseau, D. (2004). Psychological contracts in the workplace: Understanding the ties that motivate. *Academy of Management Executive, 18*(1), 120−127.

Salimaki, A., & Heneman, R. (2008). Pay for performance for global employees. In L. Gomez-Majia & S. Werner (Eds.), *Global compensation: Foundations and perspectives* (pp. 158−168). Milton Park: Routledge.

Sanders, W., & Hambrick, D. (2007). Swinging for the fences: The effects of CEO stock options on company risk-taking and performance. *Academy of Management Journal, 50*, 1055−1078.

Schollhammer, H. (1969). Compensation of international executives. *Michigan State University Business Topics, 17*(1), 19–30.

Scullion, H., Collings, D., & Gunnigle, P. (2007). International human resource management in the 21st century: Emerging themes and contemporary debates. *Human Resource Management Journal, 17*(4), 309−319.

Selmer, J. (2003). Staff localization and organizational characteristics: Western business expatriates in China. *Asia Pacific Business Review, 10*(1), 43−57.

Shaffer, M., Kraimer, M., Chen, Y.-P., & Bolino, M. (2012). Choices, challenges, and career consequences of global work experiences: A review and future agenda. *Journal of Management, 38*(4), 1282–1327.

Sims, R., & Schraeder, M. (2005). Expatriate compensation: An exploratory review of salient contextual factors and common practices. *Career Development International, 10*(2), 98−108.

Stahl, G., Björkmann, I., Farndale, E., Morris, S., Paauwe, J., Stiles, P., & Wright, P. (2012). Leveraging your talent: Six principles of effective global talent management. *MIT Sloan Management Review, 53*(2), 25−42.

Stahl, G., Miller, E., & Tung, R. (2002). Toward the boundaryless career: A closer look at the expatriate career concept and the perceived implications of an international assignment. *Journal of World Business, 37*(3), 216–227.

Stanley, P. (2009). Local-plus packages for expatriates in Asia: A viable alternative. *International HR Journal, 3*(Fall), 9–11.

Stone, R. (1986). Compensation: Pay and perks for overseas executives. *Personnel Journal, 64*, 67–69.

Stone, R. (1995). Expatriation remuneration practices: A survey of Australian multinationals. *International Journal of Management, 12*(3), 364–372.

Suutari, V., & Tornikoski, C. (2000). Determinants of expatriate compensation: Findings among expatriate members of SEFE. *Finnish Journal of Business Economics, 49*(4), 517–539.

Suutari, V., & Tornikoski, C. (2001). The challenge of expatriate compensation: The sources of satisfaction and dissatisfaction among expatriates. *The International Journal of Human Resource Management, 12*(3), 389–404.

Tait, E., De Cieri, H., & McNulty, Y. (2014). The opportunity cost of saving money: An exploratory study of permanent transfers and localization of expatriates in Singapore. *International Studies of Management and Organization, 44*(3), 79–94.

Thomas, D., & Inkson, K. (2009). *Cultural intelligence: Living and working globally* (2nd ed.). San Francisco, CA: Berrett-Koehler.

Tornikoski, C. (2011a). Expatriate compensation: A theoretical approach. In C. Antoni, X. Baeten, R. Lucas, S. Perkins, & M. Vartiainen (Eds.), *Pay and reward systems in organizations: Theoretical approaches and empirical evidence* (pp. 38–67). Lengerich: Pabst Science Publishers.

Tornikoski, C. (2011b). Expatriates' affective commitment: A total reward perspective. *Cross Cultural Management: An International Journal, 18*(2), 214–235.

Tornikoski, C., Suutari, V., & Festing, M. (2014). Compensation package of international assignees. In D. Collings, G. Wood, & P. Caligiuri (Eds.), *The Routledge companion to international human resource management* (pp. 289–307). Oxon: Routledge.

Vaiman, V., & Collings, D. (2014). Global talent management. In D. Collings, G. Wood, & P. Caligiuri (Eds.), *The Routledge companion to international human resource management* (pp. 210–225). Oxon: Routledge.

Warneke, D., & Schneider, M. (2011). Expatriate compensation packages: What do employees prefer? *Cross Cultural Management: An International Journal, 18*(2), 236–256.

Watson, B. W. J., & Singh, G. (2005). Global pay systems: Compensation in support of a multinational strategy. *Compensation and Benefits Review, 37*, 33–36.

Wentland, D. (2003). A new practical guide for determining expatriate compensation: The comprehensive model. *Compensation and Benefits Review, 35*(3), 45–50.

Yanadori, Y. (2014). Compensation and benefits in the global organization. In D. Collings, G. Wood, & P. Caligiuri (Eds.), *The Routledge companion to international human resource management* (pp. 190–209). Oxon: Routledge.

Yates, J. (2011). Putting down roots: How localization can help reduce expatriate program costs. *Mobility, 32*, 92–97.

Chapter 7

Global Talent Management and Corporate Entrepreneurship Strategy

Vanessa Ratten and Joao Ferreira

Abstract

Purpose – The aim of this chapter is to focus on the role human capital, innovative recruitment practices and cross-cultural staffing policies have on organizational performance. This facilitates a better understanding about how entrepreneurial thinking is encompassed into an organizational context by utilizing global talent management practices.

Methodology/approach – The chapter discusses the linkage between global talent management and corporate entrepreneurship literature by providing a number of research propositions.

Findings – The chapter highlights how it is important for entrepreneurial organizations to focus on global talent management for their global competitiveness.

Research limitations/implications – This conceptual paper is based on corporate entrepreneurship as the underlying theoretical framework for global talent management, which means the results should be interpreted from an entrepreneurial perspective.

Practical implications – Global talent management is becoming increasingly popular as a way to integrate organizations corporate entrepreneurship goals with their strategic objectives.

Global Talent Management and Staffing in Mnes
International Business & Management, Volume 32, 151–165
Copyright © 2016 by Emerald Group Publishing Limited
ISSN: 1876-066X/doi:10.1108/S1876-066X20160000032006

Social implications – More organizations are taking a social perspective that encompasses a global mindset for talent management in order to facilitate more entrepreneurial thinking.

Originality/value – This chapter stresses the importance placed on hiring and retaining talented individuals who can contribute to innovative and risk taking outcomes in global organizations.

Keywords: Corporate entrepreneurship; global talent management; international entrepreneurship; human resource strategy

7.1. Introduction

Scholars and practitioners in human resource management are essentially involved in global talent management (Collings, Scullion, & Vaiman, 2015). The employee perspective instead of the managerialist orientation of talent management has been receiving more attention due to the increase in individuals seeking international assignment (Farndale, Avinash, Sparrow, & Scullion, 2014). Talent is managed differently depending on the firm-specific knowledge required and utilized by an organization (Doherty & Dickmann, 2013). Managers need to coordinate the use of individuals employed at an organization to ensure their skills are best utilized. This requires human resource managers to control how and where talented individuals work in the international context. The international environment is sometimes hard to monitor due to the cultural and personal differences in each employee. Global talent management has been referred to as smart talent management due to the focus on the efficient use of resources in the international environment.

In this chapter, global talent management is defined as the effective management of human resources in an international enterprise. Global talent management is an important part of a company's entrepreneurship strategy particularly for large multinational enterprises. Traditional business operations have been changed from the shift in the global economy to more dynamic trading agreements (Turner & Pennington, 2015). Global companies have to continually adjust to the trading market in terms of managing, hiring and recruiting talented professionals. This has meant that in the global competitive environment more companies are changing how they staff their operations in order to maximize resources (Morris, Kuratko, & Covin, 2011). The effective management of people is important to an organizations success and is a key part of human resource management (Collings, 2014).

Talent management incorporates the way organizations hire, recruit and retain important people who have specific skills necessary for success. Despite the popularity of talent management by human resource management scholars and practitioners there is still confusion as to its meaning and application (Mellahi & Collings, 2010). Most definitions of talent management focus on human capital and the development of expertise for a specific purpose (Cappelli, 2008). This means that talent is seen as a source of success for an organization depending on how it is managed (Mellahi & Collings, 2010).

Talent management is important for global organizations for two main reasons. Firstly, individuals with a high level of talent can help develop an organizations strategic direction. The talent inherent in individuals is measured by their ability, knowledge and skill to add value to an organization (Vance & Vaiman, 2008). This means that some talented individuals will be employed to provide leadership and direction based on the corporate strategy of an organization. Secondly, there are human resource management techniques that are used to manage talented individuals. These include specific procedures and policies that help talented individuals succeed as part of a company's strategic direction (Tarique & Schuler, 2012). Employees who possess specialized knowledge are necessary for organizational development particularly when entrepreneurship is required (Tarique & Schuler, 2012). The skills in demand individuals have helps mobilize resources within an organizational setting. This can lead to attracting more talented individuals who fill job roles designed to enable an organization to move into innovative markets.

Recently, more human resource management research has linked talent management to corporate strategy (e.g., Collings & Scullion, 2009; Farndale, Scullion, & Sparrow, 2010; Kim & Scullion, 2011). This is due to the linkage of talent management with strategy as it is involves a set of activities, which includes identifying and selecting talent from the labour market (Sparrow, Hird, & Balain, 2011). The talent can come from the external or internal labour market as long as it has special features that are important to an organization. Some organizations focus on developing employees who show features of becoming talented individuals in their field of expertise. Due to the decreased restrictions in the global labour market, more talented individuals are moving across regions and countries for work. Managing the flow of talented individuals into different geographical contexts has become increasingly important for organizations. Often companies will structure their labour force based on the expertise and experience they need in the global market. This management of talent helps ensure key employees are retained and utilized at optimal efficiency.

Part of the importance of global talent management derives from its inclusion in an organizations knowledge capital (Vaiman, Haslberger, & Vance, 2015). Knowledge is important for many global companies as the way they generate and apply information is part of the learning process. In addition, the acquisition and transfer of knowledge can be increased when human capital disseminates to their international networks. The competition for human capital has meant companies have aggressive strategies to recruit top talent (Tarique & Schuler, 2012). This includes formulating management strategies designed to entice talented individuals to organizations. Some organizations also utilize creative approaches to recruiting talent based on policies they have in place. The next section will further discuss the importance of global talent management in human resource management strategy.

7.2. Literature Review

Human resource management strategies designed to provide career support to talented individuals are becoming increasingly popular ways to incorporate corporate objectives for a global organization. Other strategies involve tailoring talented individuals with organizations that require specific language or aptitudes. This is due to an important source of organizational talent being the recruiting of host-country nationals abroad that can be repatriated. This helps attract talented individuals who wish to return to their home country due to personal or family reasons.

Some sought after qualities for talented workers include the ability to adjust to the host environment. As countries transition from developing or transitional economies to market-based ones it becomes more attractive for workers to return home. In addition, there is less risk involved when recruiting a talented individual to their home country as they will require less management involvement. By recruiting talented individuals to their home country they can teach others their skills and also help networking activities (Vance & McNulty, 2014). This is important for global companies in building a local support system that encourages talent development.

Social networking sites that provide information about related individuals and their connections are helpful in sourcing talent for global companies. This is important when human resource managers are seeking to hire specific talented individuals that are hard to find. The valuable connections talented individuals have can be in their personal networks and social connections making it easier for global companies to perform better in the marketplace. Organizations that have a proactive approach to managing talent set clear expectations about work requirements. This helps when mentoring and support systems are in place that enables talented individuals to develop corporate entrepreneurship with their organization. The provision of housing and banking assistance is also useful in enabling talented professional's transition to a different country environment.

There are many assumptions about talent management, which has been referred to as human resource planning, talent strategy and succession management (Lewis & Heckman, 2006). The process of managing people in organizations means ensuring the right people are in the appropriate positions when needed (Creelman, 2004). This involves that there is continuity in the key positions making the systematic advancement of corporate strategy. By having a deliberate and systemic approach to managing the flow of human capital in an organization it should encourage better corporate strategy (Pascal, 2004).

The supply and demand of talent is an important part of succession and human resource planning. Talent management centres on the management of employee talent in an effective and timely manner. There are a variety of different alternatives organizations have in terms of how they manage the careers of employees. This includes acquiring and selecting appropriate staff, which is a mindset organizations have for talent management (Cheloha & Swain, 2005). In order to ensure everyone works at their optimal efficiency it is important to manage talented individuals (Aston & Morton, 2005). Talent management is strategically important to organizations as it is a collection of activities, functions and practices including human resource management departments. The development of talent is made easier by technology for human resource managers who can use enterprise systems as part of the process (Mercer, 2005).

The traditional way of recruiting and developing staff is changed by talent management, which focuses on productivity (Olsen, 2000). The training and development of staff is made easier by leadership development programs (Byham, 2001). The growing of talent helps ensure appropriate use of compensation and performance management processes. The term talent management has replaced the traditional term of human resources (Lewis & Heckman, 2006). This has been due to the change in the focus of human resource management departments to be more on the flow of employees within an organization (Pascal, 2004). Organizations need to forecast and plan for staffing needs, which can occur through internal processes. This means understanding the internal workforce and career changes that are organized by anticipated needs.

The way an individual enters and exists in a position can determine the perception of future hires to an organization. The term 'talent' refers to high performing and large impact individuals who can help an organization perform its corporate strategic objectives. Some researchers refer to talent as being top performers and are more important than other types of individuals due to their ability to work strategically. The strategic importance of human capital to an organization is part of their overall ability to meet and exceed market expectations. High quality human resource practices depend on the people strategies adopted by an organization (Lepak & Snell, 2002). In addition, the environmental context of an organization influences the association between staffing practices and profitability (Terpstra & Rozell, 1993).

7.3. Research Propositions

Corporate entrepreneurship strategy involves building an entrepreneurial strategic vision, a pro-entrepreneurship architectural structure and having entrepreneurial processes within an organization (Ireland, Covin, & Kuratko, 2009). The entrepreneurship and strategic management literature emphasizes the importance of corporate entrepreneurship for organizational competitiveness (Crawford & Kreiser, 2015). This is due to the link of corporate entrepreneurship with organizational strategy, which integrates individuals in a firm with firm's external environmental conditions (Crawford & Kreiser, 2015). Corporate entrepreneurship strategy focuses on the reliance on behaviour that reinvigorates an organization (Ireland et al., 2009). This entrepreneurial behaviour shapes an organization by recognizing and exploiting opportunities (Morris et al., 2011). An organization needs to have a commitment to values and beliefs that have an entrepreneurial philosophy (Kuratko, 2009). This enables key attributes of an organization to manifest in an organizations strategic vision, which is communicated through entrepreneurial endeavours. This encourages an organization to support entrepreneurship that guides management strategy. The willingness of an organization to focus on entrepreneurship is driven by their internal structures, which can foster and maintain innovation (Hornsby, Kuratko, Shepherd, & Bott, 2009). Sometimes this will involve organizations being reliant on entrepreneurial processes to maintain their competitiveness. This can take the form of behaviours that evolve based on the strategic approach by the organization.

The adoption of an entrepreneurial strategy is important for a firm's competitive advantage (Ireland et al., 2009). Corporate entrepreneurship involves the use of entrepreneurial actions and initiatives that transform an organization into having more emphasis on dynamic capabilities (Goodale, Kuratko, Hornsby, & Covin, 2011). Part of this transformation for an organization can involve pursuing new business opportunities (Turner & Pennington, 2015). This strategic renewal process can extend an organization into new markets (Guth & Ginsberg, 1990). For many global organizations corporate entrepreneurship enables them to adapt and innovate to develop knowledge that can be utilized more effectively (Morris et al., 2011).

The increasingly complex global market means that innovation is important in developing new processes and programs that can increase an organization's competitiveness (Turner & Pennington, 2015). The development of innovation for global organizations needs to integrate with specific conditions that make change an economically viable outcome (Kuratko, 2009). This enables innovation to emerge in an organization and in a structured business environment. As many global organizations are changing the concept of what a traditional organization looks like it is important to have an entrepreneurial orientation. The entrepreneurial usages of global talent management include alternative recruitment strategies based on technological innovations. Examples of these entrepreneurial usages are to base recruitment decisions on direct connections from online networking sites or the utilize data analytics to find the most appropriate individual for the job. Sometimes these entrepreneurial usages require organizations to use more detailed hiring practices that incorporate alternative approaches. When there is more innovation and forecasting completed by an organization this is likely to help performance in the long term. This leads to the first research proposition:

Research Proposition 1. Entrepreneurial usages of global talent management will positively influence organizational performance.

As more global organizations face disruptive competition a corporate entrepreneurial strategic approach needs to be taken in terms of global talent management. An organization can be transformed by innovative ways linking complex organizational networks. Corporate entrepreneurship occurs when organizational networks share their knowledge and learning. This involves an organization focusing on the information processing within a network relationship to see entrepreneurial potential (Falbe, Dandrige, & Kumar, 1998). The ability to act entrepreneurially within an organization may involve providing better ways to share information.

Organizations are looking at their organizational networks for innovative potential about market opportunities (Turner & Pennington, 2015). The ability to generate knowledge is a prerequisite for innovation. The way in which an organization values knowledge will enable more financial and human capital objectives to be fulfilled. Some organizations need to utilize their networks to build scale and scope in the global environment (Castrogiovanni, Combs, & Justis, 2006). Corporate entrepreneurship is characterized by the innovation emerging from knowledge sharing and organizational learning (Turner & Pennington, 2015). The ability to leverage an organizations entrepreneurial strategy is linked to its motivation towards learning new practices (O'Reilly & Tushman, 2011). Corporate entrepreneurship enhances productivity and induces innovation in an organization (Zahra, 2015). Organizations achieve growth when they utilize corporate entrepreneurship for revitalizing their performance. There are a variety of antecedents to corporate entrepreneurship including external environment, organizational culture and industry conditions (Miller, 1983). These antecedents provide incentives for organizations to focus on ways to be more entrepreneurial in the global business environment (Zahra & Covin, 1995). The advantage for organizations with a corporate strategy is in the knowledge creating potential of these entrepreneurial initiatives (Zahra, 2015).

Global talent management can be shaped by the formal and informal corporate entrepreneurship strategy existing in an organization. Knowledge creation is important in corporate entrepreneurship as it can include the creative recombination of information (Zahra, 2015). This means that organizations discover ways of developing new knowledge to benefit future outcomes. Corporate entrepreneurship is a strategy, which can help organizations cope with the realities of global competition (Kurtako, Hornsby, & Hayton, 2015). All functions of management can be transformed by taking a strategic approach (Govindarajan & Trimble, 2005). This enables innovation in a range of business activities, which incorporate entrepreneurial leadership (Kurtako et al., 2015).

Organizations need to nurture global competitive advantages in order to increase innovation capacity. Many successful organizations take a corporate entrepreneurial strategic approach as it is viewed as a flexible approach to competing when there is uncertainty in the global business world. For some organizations, the implementation of corporate entrepreneurship is hard as it requires simultaneously evaluating business opportunities with creating an innovation ecosystem (Kurtako et al., 2015).

Organizations have been faced with challenges for survival as global market conditions change based on labour market requirements. This has meant some organizations have grown in different ways including by placing more emphasis on innovation activities. More emphasis is being placed on fostering conditions for creating corporate innovative activities (Kurtako et al., 2015). A better understanding of corporate entrepreneurship within an organization is helpful to global talent management. This is especially evident in innovative management practices built from the usage of global talent management. As individuals within an organization are recruited and retained based on their talent regardless of their nationality, this will lead to increased levels of corporate entrepreneurship. As more individuals are attracted to an organization due to its ability to a global workforce this helps increase the number of individuals with diverse experiences and backgrounds. This leads to the second research proposition:

Research Proposition 2. Innovative management practices will lead to increased levels of human capital.

Corporate entrepreneurship is an area for human resource managers to focus on as part of their recruitment strategies for global talent management. Some individuals will be attracted to organizations that have a higher level of corporate entrepreneurial strategy as they may perceive better employment prospects. In addition, the external socio-cultural environment will influence the development of corporate entrepreneurship within an organization (Hornsby et al., 2009). This is due to the social and cultural conditions of workplaces influencing the propensity to engage in entrepreneurial activities. This includes the use of personal networks that individuals have in the workplace which help develop corporate entrepreneurship (Hayton & Kelley, 2006).

An organization with a corporate entrepreneurial strategy will have an intent to continuously create entrepreneurial opportunities (Covin & Miles, 1999). By deliberately focusing on entrepreneurship an organization can see advantages to their business (Shane & Venkataraman, 2000). The vision for corporate entrepreneurship strategy is the reliance on innovation as a key asset for growth purposes. In order to develop competitive advantages, corporate entrepreneurship will be the strategic focus for most organizations (Narayanan, Yang, & Zahra, 2009). This means that the accumulation of knowledge is important for an organizations corporate entrepreneurship strategy as it helps to understand potential opportunities (Kurtako et al., 2015).

Corporate entrepreneurship occurs across many different organizational configurations but is mostly associated with large firms (Phan, Wright, Ucbasaran, & Tan, 2009). Entrepreneurial initiatives emerge within established firms due to the resources and opportunities available (Nason, McKelvie, & Lumpkin, 2015). Entrepreneurship within organizations is seen as a necessity rather than option due to its impact on performance (Nason et al., 2015). This has lead to the focus of much research about corporate entrepreneurship being around ventures and the role leadership plays in innovation (Sharma & Chrisman, 1999). The diversity of objectives within corporate entrepreneurship has meant it has focused more on the duration of ventures for performance outcomes (Narayanan et al., 2009). Organizational-level entrepreneurship has increased in popularity due to its role in increasing competitive advantage for firms (Nason et al., 2015). Many organizations long term success is a result of corporate entrepreneurship being directed by top leaders (Ireland et al., 2009). Corporate entrepreneurship requires the effective management of people, which is why human resource management is important (Hayton, 2005). Individuals are important sources of corporate entrepreneurship activities (Sharma & Chrisman, 1999).

Talent management at multinationals involves the use of both domestic and international employees in staffing foreign operations. Al Ariss (2014) discussed the role of company assigned expatriates as a form of global talent management who have knowledge about strategic direction. High potential talent development is important especially in fields where brand name and reputation is key to corporate entrepreneurship. As more individuals are willing to work globally depending on pay rates the management of global careers is increasing (Cerdin & Brewster, 2014).

A source of global talent is expatriates who are linked to the organization regardless of geographic location. Global talent management is complex due to the interdependencies between individual, family and culture within an organizational setting (Minbaeva & Collings, 2013). This has led to an exponential growth in the interest in global talent management due to the difficulties for incorporating societal change into corporate strategy (Burning & Tung, 2013). Organizations need to achieve a balance between local and global employees who are coordinated based on level of talent. Some organizations do this by integrating their business processes with their talent management practices to achieve the best performance (Farndale et al., 2014).

Some individuals favour an overseas experience, which contributes to the management of a global workforce (Nolan & Morley, 2014). Some business professionals utilize their international experience to help them develop career prospects in the local market (Fitzgerald & Howe-Walsh, 2008). This has lead to global talent management occurring in a variety of industries including academia, in which specialized skills and performance outcomes are important (Isakovic & Whitman, 2013). Some research has focused on self-initiated expatriates for global talent management (Doherty, 2013). Self-initiated expatriates see themselves as citizens of the world and move depending on career prospects. This has enabled individuals to have more international mobility, which enables companies to make use of their talent (Cerdin & Selmer, 2014).

Self-initiated expatriates are defined at opting to relocate by choice internationally due to skilled and professional qualifications (Cerdin & Selmer, 2014). The offer of regular employment intentions means individuals choose their geographical location depending on work conditions (Welch & Worm, 2006). Some individuals have intentions to stay temporarily and relocate based on job prospects. Self-initiated expatriates help facilitate global talent management in organizations by providing necessary skills and an international outlook. The cross-cultural understanding of self-initiated expatriates helps encourage a collaborative environment in their workplaces (Al-Ariss, 2010). Organizations with an international outlook fostered by collaborative individuals are better able to adapt and change to suit business conditions. Due to increased globalization there have been increasing numbers of individuals working outside their home country due to employment opportunities. This has resulted in organizations having to understanding different cultures and take alternative viewpoints in managing their global workforce. When global talent is management well using a cross-cultural perspective there will be greater diversity in organizations. It is expected that these alternative points of views based on different cultures and backgrounds will encourage more entrepreneurial strategies for organizations. This leads to the third research proposition:

Research Proposition 3. Cross-cultural talent management leads to increased entrepreneurial strategies.

Taking into consideration this literature review, we hereby propose the following research conceptual model (Figure 7.1) for studying the processes and practices inherent to global talent management their relationship with corporate entrepreneurship.

7.4. Managerial Implications

Talent management practices have been changing from their dysfunctional practices to becoming important strategic planning processes (Cappelli, 2008). This is due to the focus on talent management being on the anticipation of setting a plan for meeting human capital requirements (Cappelli, 2008). The importance of global talent

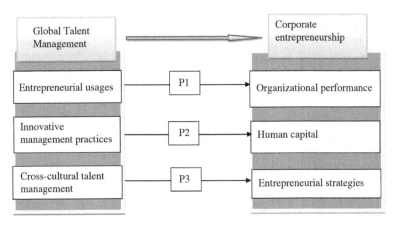

Figure 7.1: Conceptual Model.

management has been supported by the Global Competitiveness Index, which indicates companies with better human resource management practices perform better (Lanvin & Evans, 2013). This is supported by Furusawa and Brewster (2015) who suggests there are international staffs who by birth or experience are capable of working in more than one culture.

In uncertain global markets, there is more emphasis on development talent management strategies to help attract the best talent (Khilji, Tarique, & Schuler, 2015). Talent management is decisive in determining an organizations long term success (McDonnell, 2011). In the past many organizations took a reactive approach to talent management by hiring strategically after finding a need for a specific person. This has changed to be more proactive with organizations anticipating needs particularly in terms of corporate entrepreneurship where innovative practices are important. As more organizations focus on lean and agile management practices, the structure of talent management is changing from being bureaucratic to more matrix like in decision making style. This allows for better forecasting and succession planning that enables talent to be managed in a global economy.

The global economic crises have meant that economic downturns have affected talent pipelines. This has been influenced by devaluation of some countries currencies, which makes other geographic locations due to their exchange rates more attractive places to work in. Some large organizations have invested in talent development in order to encourage entrepreneurial leadership. PepsiCo and General Electric have become known for being academy companies, which is a term for breeding talented individuals (Cappelli, 2008). Organizations want to recruit talent away from their competitors but at the same time retain their own talent. This can be difficult in the global business environment as it becomes more competitive amongst organizations to keep talented individuals.

Some larger organizations may focus on internal talent development as their workforce planning to meet long term succession demands. Some groomed successors are developed in organizations based on their ability to fit with entrepreneurship goals. As management teams change the strategies and organizational charts for developing talent becomes important. The tactical objectives a company has can support overall strategic outcomes, which essentially involve corporate entrepreneurship. The costs and benefits associated with talent management practices are important to global managers. The costs include individuals expecting to change job positions unlike previous lifetime employment practices.

7.5. Conclusion

This paper has discussed the importance of global talent management to the field of human resources and corporate entrepreneurship. As this chapter focused on the theoretical linkages between global talent management and corporate entrepreneurship more research could develop statistical models that test the relationship. This means using multiple levels of analysis at the industry, organization and individual level to evaluate the perceptions of global talent management and corporate entrepreneurship. The impact of talent management decisions in an organization could be tested based on geographic locations to see the linkage of culture with entrepreneurial decision making strategies.

Talent architectures in high technology industries that are rapidly changing need to be evaluated with corporate entrepreneurship management processes. An understanding of successful high technology organizations with world recognized talent management practices such as those occurring at Google need to be compared to other cultural conditions to see the changing nature of corporate entrepreneurship in developing and transition economy contexts. The linkage of human resource management and corporate entrepreneurship is a crucial linkage for understanding appropriate strategies for organizations in the global environment.

The main contribution of this chapter is to integrate global talent management with corporate entrepreneurship. More human resource management scholars and practitioners are focusing on entrepreneurship as a way to compete in the global marketplace. As it is becoming easier and more common for individuals to work internationally, corporate entrepreneurship is an enticement for talented managers in organizations. Many international organizations with corporate entrepreneurship share common strategies, which perceive the recruitment and retention of talent as being important.

The fostering of global talent management is an innovative and proactive approach to organizations corporate strategies. The management of shortages and surpluses of global talent is crucial in helping organizations perform better. Our discussion provides guidance to academics in the human resource management and entrepreneurship literature about the role of human capital. The chapter suggested that global talent management is also important for entrepreneurs as they seek to include corporate strategy.

References

Al-Ariss, A. (2010). Modes of engagement: Migration, self-initiated expatriation and career development. *Career Development International, 15*(4), 338–358.

Al Ariss, A. (Ed.). (2014). *Global talent management: Challenges, strategies and opportunities.* New York, NY: Springer.

Aston, C., & Morton, L. (2005). Managing talent for competitive advantage: Taking a systematic approach to talent management. *Strategic HR Review, 4,* 28–31.

Burning, N. S., & Tung, R. L. (2013). Leadership development and global talent management in the Asian context: An introduction. *Asian Business & Management, 12*(4), 381–386.

Byham, W. C. (2001). Are leaders born or made? *Workspan, 44*(12), 56–60.

Cappelli, P. (2008). Talent management for the twenty-first century. *Harvard Business Review, March,* 1–9.

Castrogiovanni, G., Combs, J., & Justis, R. (2006). Resource scarcity and agency theory predictions concerning the continued use of franchising in multi-outlet networks. *Journal of Small Business Management, 44*, 27–44.

Cerdin, J.-L., & Brewster, C. (2014). Talent management and expatriation: Bridging the two streams of research and practice. *Journal of World Business, 49*(2), 245–252.

Cerdin, J.-L., & Selmer, J. (2014). Who is a self-initiated expatriate? Towards conceptual clarity of a common notion. *International Journal of Human Resource Management, 25*(9), 1281–1301.

Cheloha, R., & Swain, J. (2005). Talent management system key to effective succession planning. *Canadian HR Reporter, 18*(17), 5–7.

Collings, D. G., Scullion, H., & Vaiman, V. (2015). Talent management: Progress and prospects. *Human Resource Management Review, 25*(3), 233–235.

Collings, D. G. (2014). Toward mature talent management: Beyond shareholder value. *Human Resource Development Quarterly, 25*(3), 301–319.

Collings, D. G., & Scullion, H. (2009). Global staffing. *International Journal of Human Resource Management, 20*(6), 1249–1272.

Covin, J. G., & Miles, M. P. (1999). Corporate entrepreneurship and the pursuit of competitive advantage. *Entrepreneurship Theory and Practice, 23*(3), 47–64.

Crawford, G. C., & Kreiser, P. M. (2015). Corporate entrepreneurship strategy: Extending the integrative framework through the lens of complexity science. *Small Business Economics, 45*, 403–423.

Creelman, D. (2004). *Return on investment in talent management: Measures you can put to work right now*. Washington, DC: Human Capital Institute.

Doherty, N. (2013). Understanding the self-initiated expatriate: A review and directions for future research. *International Journal of Management Reviews, 15*(4), 447–469.

Doherty, N., & Dickmann, M. (2013). Self initiated and assigned expatriates: Talent management and career considerations. In V. Vaiman & A. Haslberger (Eds.), *Managing talent of self-initiated expatriates: A neglected source of the global talent flow* (pp. 234–255). London: Palgrave MacMillan.

Falbe, C. M., Dandrige, T. C., & Kumar, A. (1998). The effect of organizational context on entrepreneurial strategies in franchising. *Journal of Business Venturing, 14*, 125–140.

Farndale, E., Avinash, P., Sparrow, P., & Scullion, H. (2014). Balancing individual and organizational goals in global talent management: A mutual benefits perspective. *Journal of World Business, 49*(2), 204–214.

Farndale, E., Scullion, H., & Sparrow, P. (2010). The role of the corporate human resource function in global talent management. *Journal of World Business, 45*(2), 161–168.

Fitzgerald, C., & Howe-Walsh, L. (2008). Self-initiated expatriates: An interpretative phenomenological analysis of professional female expatriates. *International Journal of Business and Management, 3*(10), 156–175.

Furusawa, M., & Brewster, C. (2015). The bi-cultural option for global talent management: The Japanese/Brazilian Nikkeijin example. *Journal of World Business, 50*, 133–143.

Goodale, J. C., Kuratko, D., Hornsby, J. S., & Covin, J. G. (2011). Operations management and corporate entrepreneurship: The moderating effect of operations control on the antecedents of corporate entrepreneurial activity in relation to innovation performance. *Journal of Operations Management, 29*(2), 116–127.

Govindarajan, V., & Trimble, C. (2005). Building breakthrough businesses within established organizations. *Harvard Business Review, 83*(5), 58–68.

Guth, W. D., & Ginsberg, A. (1990). Corporate entrepreneurship. *Strategic Management Journal, 11*(Special Issue), 5–15.

Hayton, J. C. (2005). Competing in the new economy: The effect of intellectual capital on corporate entrepreneurship in high technology new ventures. *R&D Management, 35*(2), 137–155.

Hayton, J. C., & Kelley, D. (2006). A competency-based framework for promoting corporate entrepreneurship. *Human Resource Management, 45*(3), 407–427.

Hornsby, J. S., Kuratko, D. F., Shepherd, D. A., & Bott, J. P. (2009). Managers corporate entrepreneurial actions: Examining perception and position. *Journal of Business Venturing, 24*(3), 236–247.

Ireland, R. D., Covin, J. G., & Kuratko, D. F. (2009). Conceptualizing corporate entrepreneurship strategy. *Entrepreneurship Theory and Practice, 33*(1), 19–46.

Isakovic, A. A., & Whitman, M. F. (2013). Self-initiated expatriate adjustment in the United Arab Emirates: A study of Academics. *Journal of Global Mobility, 1*(2), 161–186.

Khilji, S. E., Tarique, I., & Schuler, R. (2015). Incorporating the macro view in global talent management. *Human Resource Management Review, 25*, 236–248.

Kim, C. H., & Scullion, H. (2011). Exploring the links between corporate social responsibility and global talent management: A comparative study of the UK and Korea. European *Journal of International Management, 5*(5), 501–523.

Kuratko, D. F. (2009). The entrepreneurial imperative of the 21st century. *Business Horizons, 52*, 421–428.

Kurtako, D., Hornsby, J., & Hayton, J. (2015). Corporate entrepreneurship: The innovative challenge for a new global economic reality. *Small Business Economics, 45*, 245–253.

Lanvin, B., & Evans, P. (2013). *The global talent competitiveness index 2013*. Paris, France: Human Capital Leadership Institute, INSEAD.

Lepak, D. P., & Snell, S. A. (2002). Examining the human resource architecture: The relationships among human capital, employment, and human resource configurations. *Journal of Management, 28*(4), 517–543.

Lewis, R. E., & Heckman, R. J. (2006). Talent management: A critical review. Human Resource *Management Review, 16*, 139–154.

McDonnell, A. (2011). Still fighting the 'War for Talent'? Bridging the science versus practice gap. *Journal of Business and Psychology, 26*(2), 169–173.

Mellahi, K., & Collings, D. G. (2010). The barriers to effective global talent management: The example of corporate cities in MNEs. *Journal of World Business, 45*(2), 143–149.

Mercer, S. R. (2005). Best-in-class leadership. *Leadership Excellence, 22*(3), 17.

Miller, D. (1983). The correlates of entrepreneurship in three types of firms. *Management Science, 29*(7), 770–791.

Minbaeva, D., & Collings, D. G. (2013). Seven myths of global talent management. *The International Journal of Human Resource Management, 24*(9), 1762–1776.

Morris, M. H., Kuratko, D. F., & Covin, J. G. (2011). *Corporate entrepreneurship and innovation* (3rd ed.). Southwestern: Cengage.

Narayanan, V. K., Yang, Y., & Zahra, S. A. (2009). Corporate venturing and value creation: A review and proposed framework. *Research Policy, 38*(1), 58–76.

Nason, R. S., McKelvie, A., & Lumpkin, G. T. (2015). The role of organizational size in the heterogenous nature of corporate entrepreneurship. *Small Business Economics, 45*, 279–304.

Nolan, E., & Morley, M. J. (2014). A test of the relationship between person-environment fit and cross-cultural adjustment among self-initiated expatriates. *International Journal of Human Resource Management, 25*(11), 1631–1649.

Olsen, R. (2000). Harnessing the internet with human capital management. *Workspan, 45*(11), 24–27.

O'Reilly, C. A., & Tushman, M. L. (2011). Organizational ambidexterity in action: How managers explore and exploit. *California Management Review, 53*(4), 5–22.

Pascal, C. (2004). Foreword. In A. Schweyer (Ed.), *Talent management systems: Best practices in technology solutions for recruitment, retention and workforce planning.* Canada: Wiley.

Phan, P., Wright, M., Ucbasaran, D., & Tan, W. (2009). Corporate entrepreneurship: Current research and future directions. *Journal of Business Venturing, 24*, 197–205.

Shane, S., & Venkataraman, S. (2000). The promise of entrepreneurship as a field of research. *Academy of Management Review, 25*, 217–226.

Sharma, P., & Chrisman, J. J. (1999). Toward a reconciliation of the definitional issues in the field of corporate entrepreneurship. *Entrepreneurship Theory and Practice, 23*(3), 11–28.

Sparrow, P., Hird, M., & Balain, S. (2011). *Talent management: Time to questions the tablets of stone?* White Paper 11/01, CPHR, Lancaster University Management School.

Tarique, I., & Schuler, R. (2012). *Global talent management literature review.* A special report for SHRM Foundation. SHRM.

Terpstra, D. E., & Rozell, E. J. (1993). The relationship of staffing practices to organizational level measures of performance. *Personnel Psychology, 46*(1), 27–48.

Turner, T., & Pennington, W. W. (2015). Organizational networks and the process of corporate entrepreneurship: How the motivation, opportunity, and ability to act affect firm knowledge, learning and innovation. *Small Business Economics, 45*, 447–463.

Vaiman, V., Haslberger, A., & Vance, C. M. (2015). Recognizing the important role of self-initiated expatriates in effective global talent management. *Human Resource Management Review, 25*(3), 280–286.

Vance, C. M., & McNulty, Y. (2014). Why and how women and men acquire expatriate career development experience: A study of American expatriates in Europe. *International Studies of Management and Organization, 44*(2), 34–54.

Vance, C. M., & Vaiman, V. (2008). Smart talent management: On the powerful amalgamation of talent management and knowledge management. In V. Vaiman & C. Vance (Eds.), *Smart talent management: Building knowledge assets for competitive advantage* (pp. 1–15). Northampton, MA: Edward Elgar.

Welch, D. E., & Worm, V. (2006). International business travelers: A challenge for IHRM. In G. K. Stahl & I. Bjorkman (Eds.), *Handbook of research in international human resource management* (pp. 283–301). Cheltenham: Edward Elgar.

Zahra, S. A. (2015). Corporate entrepreneurship as knowledge creation and conversion: The role of entrepreneurial hubs. *Small Business Economics, 44*, 727–735.

Zahra, S. A., & Covin, J. G. (1995). Contextual influence on the corporate entrepreneurship performance relationship: A longitudinal analysis. *Journal of Business Venturing, 10*(1), 43–58.

Chapter 8

The Effects of Work Values and Organisational Commitment on Localisation of Human Resources

Justin Williams and Ramudu Bhanugopan

Abstract

Purpose — This study examines the interactive effects of work values and organisational commitment on localisation.

Methodology/approach — This study draws on human capital theory, and reports on a survey of 200 expatriate managers working in Qatar.

Findings — We find that localisation is negatively associated with work values and positively associated with organisational commitment. Furthermore, work values appear to influence organisational commitment.

Originality/value — Despite a surfeit of literature on localisation of human resources, few studies previously have explored its relationship with work values and organisational commitment. This chapter presents empirical research on the issue from Qatar, a country in a region which remains under-researched in the literature.

Keywords: Organisational commitment; work values; localisation; Qatar

Global Talent Management and Staffing in Mnes
International Business & Management, Volume 32, 167–188
Copyright © 2016 by Emerald Group Publishing Limited
ISSN: 1876-066X/doi:10.1108/S1876-066X20160000032007

8.1. Introduction

The dependence on foreign labour and expertise has long been recognised as a problem in the Gulf Cooperation Council (GCC) Countries (Al-Lamki, 1998; Kapiszewski, 2005; Looney, 2004; Rees, Mamman, & Braik, 2007) as it tends to present challenges to the economic, political and social costs that impact the reliant states in the long term (Al-Lamki, 1998; Looney, 2004). The governments of the GCC countries have attempted to implement several mechanisms to increase workforce participation of HCNs. Saudiisation, Emritisation, Kuwaitisation, Baharainisation, Omanisation and Qatarisation all attempt to address workforce imbalance (Al-Dosari, Rahman, & Yusuf, 2006; Forstenlechner, 2008). Localisation initiatives have primarily relied on quotas, thus ensuring priority for nationals in public sector jobs. For example, most state-owned organisations, such as Saudi Aramco, have strict employment rules around employing nationals. In addition, government human resource development (HRD) initiatives have played an indirect role and there has also been a significant increase in educational institutions for nationals (Forstenlechner & Rutledge, 2010; Mellahi & Al-Hinai, 2000; Muysken & Nour, 2006; Randaree, 2009; Rutledge, Al Shamsi, Bassioni, & Al Sheikh, 2011). These efforts combine to provide what would appear to be (but are not) effective localisation policies.

The distribution of oil wealth has traditionally been broader and through different channels than in most other economic regions. For example, vast oil revenues have allowed governments to support policies and practices associated with no income tax, free education and medical care, and a generous social system which has significantly reduced the pressure on GCC nationals for employment. (Forstenlechner, 2010; Rees et al., 2007).

Despite improved efforts in many areas to decrease the number of expatriates, expatriation — as noted earlier — has continued to increase (Forstenlechner & Rutledge, 2010). In fact, the trend towards international employment has increased even at the height of localisation efforts (Kapiszewski, 2006; Lee, 2005; Sadi & Al-Buraey, 2009). This chapter is structured as follows: firstly we review the literature relating to localisation of human resources, work values (WV) and Organisational Commitment (OC). Secondly, we present the research methods adopted in the study. Finally we discuss the results, implications and avenues for future research.

8.1.1. Qatar: Country Background and Profile

Qatar is a small country on the Arabian Peninsula and is one of the world's wealthiest nations. With an indigenous population of 300,000 nationals, it boasts the highest per capita income in the world of US$100,000 per annum, which places the nation first among the industrialised nations in terms of income. The small country also boasts the third largest oil and gas reserves in the world, with 15 per cent of the world's proven gas reserves. Like the rest of the GCC countries, it is a Muslim nation.

Qatar is a significant State in the Arab Gulf Region for several reasons. It is, like most of the Gulf governments, a constitutional monarchy with the Emir acting as the head of state. However, the constitution of Qatar has provisions for democracy and has started to implement elections for some government posts. The political structure is oriented around the Emir and the 45-member advisory council.

In addition, it is a staunch ally of the United States of America (US) and served as a launching point for the second Gulf War. The largest US army base in the Middle East is located in Qatar, less than 20 kilometres from downtown Doha, the capital.

8.1.2. The Labour Force

There are several challenges for Qatar in terms of its labour force. Like much of the GCC, Qatar has a high number of nationals employed in the public sector, leaving the private sector relatively devoid of nationals. An extremely high dependence on expatriate workers and an education system that is not comprehensively in line with labour market needs represent troubling trends. Combined, these issues could present significant challenges to the small nation in the future.

Unlike many other Gulf States, Qatar has an extremely low unemployment rate for nationals. The unemployment rate has decreased dramatically since 2001, when it was approximately 4 per cent, to 0.3 per cent in 2009. The total number of unemployed nationals in 2009, the time of the last census, was only 4000. This indicates rising employment across all sectors of the labour force, however, it is important to note that according to the Qatar government, Qatari nationals only make up 8 per cent of the national workforce and only 1 per cent of the private sector. This trend of decreasing unemployment is not consistent with the rest of the GCC, where unemployment among young, educated nationals is a growing concern (Forstenlechner, 2010; Harry, 2007).

Although education appears to be a challenge in much of the GCC, it does not appear so in Qatar, at least from the results of the 2009 Labour Force Survey. Seventy-two per cent of unemployed nationals have secondary level education or higher. For the unemployed in Qatar, education does not appear to be a contributing factor to unemployment. Over 64 per cent of the unemployed cite low job opportunities or lack of suitable work as being the main reasons for unemployment. However, in line with the work of Forstenlechner and Rutledge (2010), Harry (2007) and Rees et al. (2007), the type of education may be more important than the level, as would the type of suitable prospects. The challenges in attaining accurate and reliable statistics as indicated earlier by Harry (2007) may also be evident here.

Perhaps more telling is that 96 per cent of Qataris reported that they had not been offered a private sector job. However, in a departure from other studies on nationals' attitudes to private sector employment (Al-Lamki, 1998; Harry, 2007; Rees et al., 2007), almost 50 per cent of Qataris indicated that they would be willing to take a private sector position if offered. The other 50 per cent indicated that they would not be willing to take a job in the private sector due to the perception of lower wages and perhaps most interestingly, low 'social status'. This supports the work current literature in much of the Gulf on perceptions of work, status and employment (Achoui, 2009; Forstenlechner & Rutledge, 2010; Harry, 2007; Shaban, Assad, & Al-Qudsi, 1995). Essentially, it is preferable to remain unemployed rather than take undesirable employment in the private sector.

Like the rest of the GCC, the cultural distaste for low status jobs is also prevalent in Qatar with rising career aspirations among young Qataris (Stasz, Eide, & Martorell, 2007). As Harry (2007) and Shaham (2009) point out, the rise in the domestic labour force in low status positions such as maids and drivers is an increasing trend in the GCC. There is evidence that this may also be the case in Qatar. Between 2008 and 2009, the number of females (non-Qatari) in the workforce who performed domestic positions increased from 58.6 per cent to 60 per cent.

One of the largest changes has been in the employment of Qatari women. In 2001, women represented the highest number of unemployed with approximately 22 per cent unemployment. Only eight years later, this had declined to 1.9 per cent, with only 2400 females unemployed in 2009.

This is in direct contrast with the rest of the GCC where one sector of the workforce that is completed underrepresented is that of females (2006, 2007, 2008, 2011). For example, female Emiratis account for less than 12 per cent of the workforce (Randaree, 2009). Ironically, women generally have higher education attainment than men in the GCC; for example, over two-thirds of university graduates in the Emirates are women (Randaree, 2009).

The rapid growth of the past decade has, to a significant extent, been reliant on expatriate labour. Highly skilled, Western-trained managers have key positions in the oil and gas sector and education, while low skilled immigrant workers from the Asian sub-continent have taken more menial positions (Berrebi, Martorell, & Tanner, 2009, p. 428). Both have fuelled the rapid growth and now Qatar, much like the rest of the GCC, is in a position where it is becoming increasingly necessary to balance the workforce to avoid the excess reliance on foreign nationals for safety and cultural reasons (Berrebi et al., 2009).

8.1.3. Qatarisation

The Qatarisation program was brought into place in 2000. The Qatarisation program was introduced in much the same manner as the localisation movement in the rest of the GCC; through political, legal and quantitative methods (Forstenlechner, 2010), and a combination of quotas and government incentives (preferential treatment of Qataris).

The Qatarisation program has, since 2000, attempted to meet employment goals of 50 per cent in key positions in the energy and industrial sectors. The Qatarisation project for example, combines the quota system with professional training initiatives. Its goal is to achieve 50 per cent local employment in the energy sector (currently at 28 per cent) within five years. It is based on the active participation of leading companies in the energy sector in processes of locating, training and employing Qatari nationals with the support of the government (Ministry of Interior, June 12, 2013).

The Qatarisation program originally proposed a quota of 50 per cent Qataris in key positions in oil and gas industries, and 100 per cent of all non-specialist positions in government to be staffed by nationals (Kamrava, 2009). However, these goals, as in other regions in the GCC, are not being met (Kamrava, 2009).

Many organisations in Qatar are hopeful of progress in Qatarisation. In fact, some claim to have achieved high levels of Qatarisation, up to 85 per cent for senior positions.

This low attrition rate was attributed to very careful monitoring of Qataris, including career progression, and training and development programs (*Al Bawaba Newspaper*). The issue of attrition and subsequently organisational commitment (OC) may be an important factor in localisation.

Certainly, a key component of successful localisation is the implementation of effective HR strategies. As Forstenlechner (2010) and Forstenlechner and Mellahi (2010) point out, the political, legal and quantitative approaches to localisation are only as effective as the implementation. Qatarisation appears to be achieved most effectively through effective training programs, human resource practices (HRP) such as career planning and efficient training development that constantly monitor and provide guidance to nationals, and a high level of job security (Forstenlechner, 2010).

There is now increasing evidence that there will be a more aggressive stance by the government to ensure that the Qatarisation goals are met. This may be driven by the perception of many nationals that Qatarisation is not working effectively. There appears to be increasing animosity between nationals and expatriates, fuelled in part by a perception of inequality by nationals. Many nationals believe that they are prejudiced against by expatriates, and this is undermining the Qatarisation program. This has further lead to a deep sense of hostility from nationals around their position in society, and their views on expatriates.

8.2. Work Values

Since the recognition that work values are an important component of work, researchers have endeavoured to find out the value and depth of the relationship. The need to review the work values' construct has been limited primarily to Western

Europe and North America, leaving the fundamental question of how work values are impacted by culture unanswered.

Hofstede (2001) proposes that work values are important because they are an excellent measure of a national culture. Further, work values are shaped more heavily by culture and society than by individual factors. Of equal importance is the notion that work values affect a number of work-related behaviours (Matic, 2008).

The recognition that work values are important, and a measure of culture prompted additional research into the effects of culture on the construct. However, the impacts of culture and the research into culture, specifically relating to Hofstede (1980), were virtually non-existent (Robertson, Al-Khatib, & Al-Habib, 2002). The cultural values of the Middle East were grouped into one lump by Hofstede as there was little statistical difference. Based on, 1991s dimensions, the Middle East scored high in uncertainty avoidance, masculinity and power distance, and low in individualism.

However, work values in the Middle East have received limited academic attention (Ali & Al-Kazemi, 2005) despite their impact on work practices. The behaviour of nationals at the individual level, and the relationship between their actions and localisation may be related to each other.

8.3. Organisational Commitment

OC is the topic of significant research in academic literature. The nature of the relationship between the employee and the employing organisation has fascinated researchers' since its inception as a field of research. OC has been described as the heart of all research into human resource management (HRM) and as such is the central point in HRM discussions (Muthuveloo & Raduan, 2005).

Although several definitions exist (Becker, Randal, & Riegel, 1995; Meyer, Herscovitch, & Topolnytsky, 2002; Mowday, Steers, & Porter, 1979), the concept of OC can be described as the degree of affinity one has in voluntarily staying with an organisation. One of the most powerful forms is affective organisational commitment (AOC). AOC can be described as the employee's want and desire to be attached to an organisation and to identify with the organisation (Meyer & Allen, 1990).

The importance of AOC to turnover, productivity, absenteeism and a host of other work-related behaviours has been heavily researched (Meyer & Allen, 1991; Meyer & Herscovitch, 2001; Meyer, Allen, & Smith, 1993; Muthuveloo & Raduan, 2005). Its implications have been perhaps one of the most researched areas. Further, research has looked at the antecedents of AOC, both in terms of personal characteristics, and organisational statistics (Bernardi & Guptill, 2008; Naumann, 1993). Further still, some researchers have reviewed the effects of nationality and other factors in determining the effects of cultural values on employee commitment (Suliman & Al-Junaibi, 2010).

As pointed out by Forstenlechner (2010), Harry (2007), Godwin (2006), Budhwar and Mellahi (2007) and Rees et al. (2007), localisation in the Middle East is of increasing concern for the region. The demographic shifts including increasing unemployment, rising costs, higher educational attainment and expectations of nationals, coupled with ever-increasing expatriate workers, will lead to significant and ongoing challenges to the area unless effectively addressed. Localisation will need to become more than a numbers game; it will require the genuine effective participation of nationals in both the private and public sectors.

Although there are some statistics regarding Qatarisation, they are difficult to obtain and specific numbers may be difficult to verify. There are conflicting perceptions between expatriates and nationals about what Qatarisation is, and how successful it has been to date. Further investigation into the success of Qatarisation is warranted on an industry and business-specific level.

The claims made by nationals that there is no support for localisation requires further investigation (Suliman & Al-Junaibi, 2010). There is some irony in the fact that in order to perform one's job, one must train one's replacement. Conversely, the belief that nationals are not equipped to perform at the same level as expatriates is evident as a barrier in localisation programs (Rees et al., 2007; Wong & Law, 1999). Indeed, while there may be merit to this view, the responsibility falls on the expatriate to act as mentor and coach to the national in order to bring them up to international standards (Selmer, 2004). However, as has been recognised by Forstenlechner (2008) and others, the differences in localisation between GCC countries and other localisation efforts may have an impact on the effectiveness of organisational actions. The level of motivation and employee commitment may play a pivotal role in GCC localisation efforts (Forstenlechner, 2010). If national employees are not engaged, they will be less responsive to mentoring and coaching.

It is widely recognised that localisation initiatives achieve greater success when expatriates are supportive of the process and willing and able to work with nationals toward the goal of localisation (Selmer, 2004; Wong, Hui, & Law, 1995). It is becoming generally recognised in the GCC that leadership, including expatriate leadership, is essential in achieving localisation goals. Likewise, it falls on nationals to perform at an acceptable and competitive level.

However, there have been challenges to localisation initiatives. There is the perception that nationals are not consistently and properly equipped in either experience or skills to effectively replace expatriate management in terms of productivity and performance (Suliman & Al-Junaibi, 2010). The work values of nationals have been suggested as being less focused on productivity than those of expatriates. Further, AOC, which is identified in the current literature as having a positive relationship with productivity, is related to culture (Froese & Xiao, 2012). The link between these three constructs has not been evaluated in this diverse cultural environment.

8.4. The Relationship between Localisation, Work Values and Organisational Commitment

Localisation is a pressing problem in the GCC, one that can potentially lead to significant economic and social instability (Harry, 2007). The aim of the current study was to investigate and test the relationship between the three constructs of localisation, work values and OC. The relationship represented in the structural model between the three constructs represents a new contribution to the literature around localisation. While the relationship between the two constructs of work values and OC has been demonstrated in other environments, no relationship is evident in the current literature on the relationship between localisation, work values and OC. Therefore, it is hypothesised that:

H1. *The work values exhibited by expatriates will have a significant negative influence on localisation.*

H2. *The organisational commitment exhibited by expatriates will have a significant negative influence on localisation.*

H3. *The work values exhibited by expatriates will have a significant positive influence on organisational commitment.*

H4. *There is a significant positive relationship between localisation, Work Values and organisational commitment for expatriates.*

8.5. Research Methods

8.5.1. Population and Sampling

The questionnaire was distributed to approximately 200 expatriates in Qatar via email. The 200 email addresses were from a number of different industry sources including education (specifically College of the North Atlantic-Qatar, University of Calgary-Qatar, Weill-Cornell in Qatar, Northwestern University in Qatar, Carnegie Mellon in Qatar and Georgetown University in Qatar) as well as a number of contacts in other industries such as oil and gas (Shell, Total, Qatargas, Rasgas and Qatar Petroleum). The email was also sent to a number of contacts in organisations such as local newspapers, banks, and consulting companies.

The email was distributed with a request to forward the link to electronically distribute the questionnaire to five expatriate contacts. The email included a link to a Vovici software site that housed the online survey.

Although an Arabic country, the most common language spoken in Qatar is English, and was the language selected for the survey for both expatriates and nationals. Because of the international nature of the population, with expatriates from many Western nations, English is the lingua franca of the region. Further, because the survey targets individuals in professional or administrative positions, English is the most likely common language. The use of English also avoided inadvertent Arabic translation errors, which would have added risk to the research.

Two pilot studies determined whether there were any issues with the survey language. One included 20 expatriates. The participants suggested two minor changes to the survey language — from British English to American English. For example, a suggested and approved change was exchanging the word 'brief' for 'stay'. In context, the statement, 'My brief here includes training a national as my replacement' was changed to, 'My stay here includes training a national as my replacement'.

8.6. Measures

8.6.1. Localisation

The research instrument for localisation was based on Selmer's (2004). Expatriates are predominantly the messengers of localisation at the front line. The generic nature of the study (looking at the unwillingness or inability of expatriates to support localisation efforts) identified two necessary components of successful localisation — willingness and ability to facilitate localisation. Therefore, the survey instrument was deemed to have measures that were generic enough to be relatively void of cultural bias. The participants were asked to rate how much they agreed or disagreed with the survey statements using a five-point Likert scale. For example, 1 *strongly disagree*, 5 *strongly agree*.

8.6.2. Work Values

The concept of work values was evaluated using a measurement scale developed by Matic (2008). The instrument was originally used to compare the work values of American and Croatian undergraduate students. The theoretical underpinning of the survey was based on Hofstede's (1980) IBM survey. The scale was selected because it has been used previously in an international context to explore the differences between the work values of different nationalities.

The validated research instrument asked expatriates to estimate the importance of 10 work values using a five-point Likert scale. For example, respondents were asked to rate the importance of having little stress on the job, with 1 = *not important at all*, 5 = *very important*.

8.6.3. Affective Organisational Commitment

Meyer and Allen's OC scale is one of the pre-eminent models of the construct. AOC, the desire to remain with a company due to a genuine caring for the organisation, is considered to be one of the most significant predictors of productivity. Internal consistency (alpha co-efficient) of this model has been well documented (Meyer & Allen, 1991; Meyer & Herscovitch, 2001; Meyer et al., 1993) and demonstrates internal reliability with Cronbach alpha scores of .75 to .89.

The statements asked expatriates and nationals to provide feedback on their level of AOC using a five-point Likert scale, with 1 = *strongly disagree*, 5 = *strongly agree*.

8.7. Control Variables

A number of demographic variables were collected in the survey:

- gender
- age
- educational background
- position level
- years in Qatar (expatriates only).

8.8. Organisational Variables

In addition to demographic variables, a number of organisational variables were also collected:

- number of employees
- industry
- business type (multinational/joint-venture/government, etc.).

8.8.1. Data Analytic strategies

While it was noted earlier that the deductive approach follows a series of steps, this is mirrored, or rather demonstrated, in the data analytic plan. A multi-step approach was used in data analysis as recommended by Anderson and Gerbing (1988). The purpose of using a multi-step approach was to test the fit between the theoretical model and the empirical findings emerging from the research. The data analysis plan was based on a multi-step approach incorporating tests of reliability, factor analysis and regression techniques. Statistical analysis was performed using the SPSS software package and LISREL for the SEM component.

There are several challenges to the research in quantitative analysis. Threats to internal and external validity must be addressed (Creswell, Plano Clark, Gutmann, & Hanson, 2003). The first step in the process was to determine validity using a variety of standard techniques including Pearson's r, and Chronbach's alpha. Once data had been determined, acceptable data analysis was employed.

The second step was to employ EFA using SPSS 20.0. The purpose of using EFA was to determine if an underlying factor structure existed among the variables. This grouped questions based on their degree of correlation. Each construct — work value, OC or localisation — was examined individually.

The third stage was to identify and group questions based on their correlations. This step employed CFA to confirm the relationships, followed by SEM using LISREL software (Jöreskog & Sörbom, 1996).

Finally, regression analysis was applied again, using SPSS 20.0, to identify the demographic and organisational variables factors affecting localisation, as the factors were measured in relation to the demographic variables. Regression analysis was used to interpret the relationships between the demographic and organisational variables and the latent variables established in the EFA and CFA.

8.9. Results

We calculated means, standard deviation, and scale reliabilities and interscale correlations for all the variables. All the variation inflation factors (VIF) were below 1.9, indicating multicollinearity was not an issue in the present study.

In order to test the hypotheses, CFA was used to test the relationships. This was done using SEM and LISREL 8.80 software. The model consisted of 21 items to measure localisation (LOCE1, LOCE2, LOCE4, LOCE6, LOCE7, LOCE9, LOCE10, LOCE11, LOCE12, LOCE13, LOCE14 and LOCE15, LOCE16, LOCE18, LOCE19, LOCE21, LOCE22, LOCE23, LOCE24, LOCE26 and LOCE27) and eight items to measure work values (WV2, WV3, WV4, WV5, WV6, WV7, WV9 and WV10) and seven items to measure OC (OCN1, OCN3, OCN4, OCN5, OCN6, OCN7 and OCN8).

Absolute fit indices determine how well the model fits the sample data and which one represents the best fit (Hooper, Coughlan, & Mullen, 2008). Although there is some debate as to what acceptable fit levels are, estimates range from 0.80 to 0.90 (Hu & Bentler, 1999). According to Marsh, Hau, and Grayson (2005), the CFI (0.71), the NFI (0.69), the NNFI (0.69) and the IFI (0.71) were not within acceptable ranges and determined the GFI. In addition, the chi-square was 2766.25. Further, the RMSEA was 0.135, well above the acceptable range of 0.05 to 0.10 (with levels below 0.05 representing a perfect fit).

Several items were dropped from the scale in order to ensure model fit. The final model consisted of eight items to measure localisation (LOCE2, LOCE3, LOCE7, LOCE8, LOCE9, LOCE10, LOCE22 and LOCE23) and eight items to measure work values (WV2, WV3, WV4, WV5, WV6, WV7, WV9 and WV10) and seven items to measure OC (OCN1, OCN3, OCN4, OCN5, OCN6, OCN7 and OCN8). The final acceptable model used was selected based on the GFI statistics. This model yielded high values for many of the indices that are considered indicative of a good fit. The NFI was 0.87, the NNFI was 0.92, the CFI was 0.93 and the IFI was 0.93. These were all within acceptable limits.

The RMSEA is considered to be one of the best indictors of model fit. According to Hooper et al. (2008) and Hu and Bentler (1999), RMSEA points below 0.05 indicates a perfect fit and an acceptable range is between 0.05 and 0.10. The best fit indicated an RMSEA of 0.73. Using standard GFI measures to evaluate the model, it converged on the second attempt.

The results of the structural model are presented in Figure 8.1. The final structural model provides evidence that the path estimate between obstacles to localisation and work values is neither positive nor significant. However, the path estimate between work values and OC is positive and mildly significant. Further, the path estimate between OC and obstacles to localisation is also positive and but insignificant.

The conundrum of localisation in the GCC raises many questions. Namely, that despite significant investment in time and money, the number of expatriates keeps increasing while unemployment and underemployment remains high among nationals in most of the GCC. While it is recognised that localisation must take place in the context of other considerations such as globalisation, social environment and competitiveness (Rees et al., 2007), the increase in expatriates despite incentives to the contrary required investigation. The resulting SEM model for the obstacles to localisation for expatriates demonstrates that there is a positive relationship between OC and a reluctance to facilitate localisation. Further, that there is a positive relationship between work values and AOC. However, there is a negative relationship between work values and the obstacles to localisation. These relationships will be discussed below.

Work values generally indicate what values and expectations an individual has about their work. In this study, the work values that were selected as most desirable for expatriates were those of harmony and autonomy: harmony meaning a workplace where there was minimal unhealthy conflict; and autonomy meaning that employees could perform at a high level on their own with minimal supervision.

The expatriate respondents' work values had a negative relationship with the obstacles to localisation. Because the localisation statements focused on obstacles (negative), this is a positive result. To put it differently, expatriates with the work values of harmony and autonomy support localisation policies and initiatives if they are the objectives of the organisation. Work values then are negatively related to the obstacles to localisation.

The positive association between work values and the importance of engaging expatriates in localisation efforts is congruent with the qualitative research of Rees et al. (2007). Employees with high work values would be more inclined to support

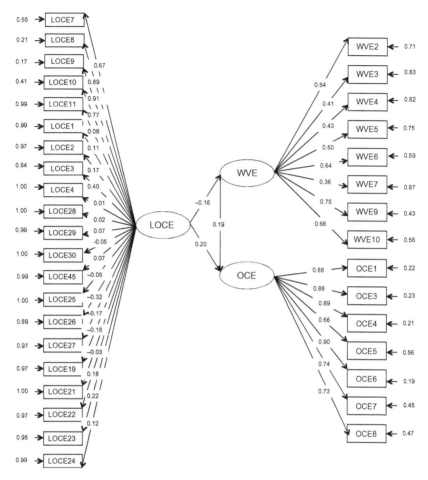

Figure 8.1: The model showing the relationship between localisation (LOCE), work values (WV) and organisational commitment (OCE) (expatriates).

localisation policies if these were performance goals. This is reflected in Selmer's (2004) research, who notes that performance and incentives related to localisation are important to its success. When expatriate employees are communicated the importance of localisation, and localisation goals were set up early in the expatriate's employment as organisational goals, then the employees with high work values were more inclined to support localisation.

The postulated relationship between work values as an antecedent to OC has found support in the literature that there is a significant and direct relationship between work values and OC (Fischer & Mansell, 2009; Froese & Xiao, 2012).

The literature indicates a relationship between the two constructs (Fischer & Mansell, 2009; Putti, Aryee, & Ling, 1989); however, it is also recognised that these relationships are weak. This also supports the work of Yunus, Mazlan, Rahim, and Shabudin (2012) in the Middle East, who found that work values were moderately related to OC. This study supports the earlier works and confirms that while there is a positive relationship for expatriates, and statistically insignificant.

The relationship between OC and obstacles to localisation is also positive, as originally postulated, however it is statistically insignificant. Although no research has been forthcoming on the relationship between AOC and localisation, it is not surprising that the higher the AOC, the less likely a job incumbent would be willing to relinquish their position. What is also interesting is the nature of the questions in the resulting SEM model. Several of the questions from the obstacles to localisation construct are affective in nature, for example, 'I like my job and want to keep it', clearly relates to AOC; however, several others are more closely related to continuance commitment ('if I lose my job I have nowhere to go'). This is also reflected in findings by Rees et al. (2007), who uncovered a reluctance to support localisation among expatriates in the UAE.

Suliman and Al-Juanaibi (2010) studied the relationship between intention to quit and OC. They found that there is a significant negative relationship between the two constructs. It would logically follow that a high degree of affective commitment would hinder governmental and organisational attempts at localisation, as it would mean ultimately severing the employee/organisational relationship. While most companies attempt to create a positive work environment with high levels of OC, this may in fact hinder localisation if not implemented with AOC in mind.

Expatriates with high degrees of AOC are generally more productive and engaged. Previous research suggests that while these are the type of employees who foster productivity and organisational performance, as discussed earlier, they may also be the same employees who resist localisation. In a region with high pay, low tax and other extrinsic benefits, it is not surprising that employees, and in particular expatriate employees, value their jobs.

8.9.1. Theoretical and Managerial Implications

The overarching objective of this research was to provide an interactive model of localisation, work values and OC. The gap between the quota system and localisation was recognised at the onset of this research, as was the premise proposed that work values were intrinsically tied to localisation via AOC, as the best predictor for employee productivity (Matic, 2008) and localisation. The final results of this research provided interesting results on the relationship between work values and OC.

In relation to the development of theory around work values and OC, Kidron (1978) and Putti et al. (1989) in identifying a link between work values and OC studies, found that intrinsic factors played a more instrumental role than extrinsic factors (Elizur, 1996). Consequently, job satisfaction is essential in retaining qualified employees (Al-Zu'bi, 2010) and enabling organisational performance (Chen & Francesco, 2003; Meyer et al., 2002). The results from this study revealed only a weak link between work values and localisation for nationals, this was somewhat contrary to Palich, Horn, and Griffeth (1995), who found that values were linked to satisfaction and OC.

For expatriates, a weak but positive relationship was found between work values and OC and a weak but positive relationship between localisation and OC. In terms of theory, these findings add to the small body of work on localisation in the region, and the greater body of work on OC and work values internationally.

In terms of practice, the implications of this combined research are significant. From an expatriate perspective, increased training, enhanced career planning and a recruitment and selection process that emphasises localisation are important components. Work values did not appear to have a strong influence on OC or localisation. Further, the link between OC and localisation was also very weak.

8.10. Limitations

The first limitation was sample size. While a larger sample size would have been preferable, the challenges in gaining a large sample size in this socioeconomic environment were many. A transient population of expatriates, a culture that promotes privacy, and language issues were all impediments to research. Nonetheless, a larger sample size would strengthen the statistical results.

A second limitation was the fact that the research was conducted only in Qatar. The sample was limited to expatriates in only one country, and did not include expatriates in the greater Arab Gulf region, or further abroad. A broader study including Bahrain, Saudi Arabia and other Gulf States in the GCC or further in the Middle East or Middle East North Africa (MENA) region would have helped to limit the risk of homogeneity.

Another limitation was common method bias. Common method bias is a common method of error in research and much attention has been focused on limiting it (Sanchez, Spector, & Cooper, 2006). Common method variance may come from a number of different errors and can lead to misleading conclusions. As with others, this study was at risk of common method bias. However, steps were taken to mitigate such bias as much as possible. First, questionnaires were distributed online, thus minimising influences such as social desirability, leniency effects, halo effects, acquiescence. This also allowed respondents to answer questions anonymously, which further limited the many types of biases at risk in qualitative research. In addition, as identified by Wong et al. (1995), common method bias was a major risk for other studies on localisation, including Law, Wong, and Wang (2004) and Selmer (2004), as these researchers collected data from a single source. This study endeavoured to ensure that the sample was as broad as possible and that a number of organisations were represented. It is difficult to limit all potential biases, but further efforts were made to reduce ambiguity and bias through a pilot study.

8.11. Directions for Future Research

This research has a number of limitations, suggesting areas for further research. This section provides an overview of the directions for further research arising from this body of knowledge.

This research has provided a starting point for further research into localisation in the State of Qatar and further for localisation efforts in the region. Content analysis is proposed to support the theoretical distinctiveness of localisation in this cross-cultural context. Furthermore, a longitudinal study is required to further explore the temporal dynamics of the localisation models and the validity of the nomological network of the latent variables. Collectively, this study was intended to stimulate the need for research in localisation in the GCC, and to demonstrate empirically, while drawing scholarly attention to, the obstacles to localisation among employees in the Middle East, particularly in Qatari organisations. Also, the results of this study identify opportunities for more comprehensive future research in light of the new models tested in this study.

It would be useful to determine if the factors for the five latent dimensions would be applicable for expatriates in other parts of the Gulf, for example, testing perceptions on localisation in Saudi Arabia or the UAE using the same scales for each construct. This would help to determine the differences between the countries but perhaps more importantly, highlight overlapping contributions to theory.

Further, a study using the same scales, but also including nationality in the variables would be valuable. In identifying another dimension of demographic variables such as nationality, further data would be added to the current research.

In addition, a more comprehensive, expanded study providing a view of localisation across the GCC would be of value. As mentioned earlier, the scholars contributing to the literature generally focus on one region, such as Forstenlechner (2008, 2010) who focuses on the UAE, specifically, identifying organisations where localisation is effectively managed and identifying specific success factors for this success. Thus far, few studies have focused on more than one country. Perhaps one approach would be a large-scale project that investigates localisation across the GCC.

Thinking larger, a study testing the latent factors of localisation uncovered from this research, from an expatriate perspective, as well as a nationals' perspective, would be useful. The former would help in uncovering any obstacles to localisation in the GCC. The wilful and supportive participation of expatriates is essential in supporting and implementing localisation. The development of specific expatriate management policies that are supportive of localisation and recognise the value of expatriate support would be useful and in fact, are essential in implementing localisation in this context.

A study involving a number of countries would provide valuable information in both evaluating and developing localisation tools. For nationals, a study garnering additional insight into their perspective would provide managers and scholars with more information into the motivation and beliefs of nationals, and may also help to identify organisations and industries that are particularly successful in localisation.

One of the most important areas for further exploration would be the research and development of a tool that measures localisation. Localisation thus far has, for the most part, focused on the quantitative approach, rather than an approach that measures employee performance with linkages to organisational performance. A more meaningful approach would be the measurement of localisation using metrics that are performance related, and evaluate nationalisation from a performance-based approach as suggested by Harry (2007) and Forstenlechner (2008).

Finally, one of the areas that require attention is the refinement of HRM and HRD techniques that attract and retain nationals. Based on a larger study, as discussed earlier, a review of nationalisation HRD techniques could create and enhance a performance-based localisation environment. The concept of employee work values continues to provide opportunities for further research. Arguably, nowhere is this truer than internationally, in a non-Western context. An interesting opportunity for further research arising from this study would be the testing of these work value models in other regions.

As with the other constructs, a longitudinal study on work values in the region would be interesting and provide long-term results. Further, it would be beneficial to the field of work values to uncover differences between the different expatriate nationalities evident in the region. As well, the addition of other demographic information such as marital status and nationality would add to the existing body of knowledge.

It would also be interesting to expand and further research if a relationship exists between work values and AOC. By applying the same measures and models for other areas, a more comprehensive set of data would help to provide evidence regarding the relationship.

At the onset it was recognised that OC receives significant attention in the current literature. The implications for OC, and in particular for AOC, are significant for organisations. The results of this study have significant implications for managing HR and localisation in Qatari organisations.

The results of this study provide scholars with a critical baseline for further research in the area and further abroad. These key differences offer crucial information on the differences between the two control groups and identify a base from which new research can be explored. Further, application of the factors uncovered in this research and tested in other regions in the GCC, and further abroad would provide interesting data into the construct in a non-Western environment. A review of the OC of nationals over time would have the potential to provide rich data and test the current research.

Finally, a study that was able to identify the similarities and differences between the different expatriate groups would greatly add to the body of literature. A review of the AOC among expatriate groups in this cultural context would provide interesting data to the field of OC.

8.12. Conclusion

Despite the implications of youth unemployment and underemployment, the issue has received limited attention in the literature. Further, localisation has been called one of the most dire HR issues in the GCC. This pioneering study was to identify obstacles to localisation, and determine if a relationship exists between the obstacles to localisation, work values and the OC of the national and expatriate workforce using multivariate techniques.

The State of Qatar has one of the most unbalanced labour participation rates in the world. Facing a wave of immigration, nationals in Qatar are minorities in both the workforce (making up just 10 per cent) and in total population. Qatar depends highly on the expatriate population to fulfil ambitious development plans. However, an underlying problem exists whereby nationals face significantly less pressure to join the workforce through a generous social contract.

This chapter proposed and tested a theoretical model where the underlying challenge to localisation is expatriate resistance, work values and an overarching relationship between these variables and OC. This research uncovered some of the latent factors acting as obstacles to localisation, work values and OC. Further, the study evaluated the factor structure of the obstacles to localisation, work values and OC of expatriates.

The results of this study revealed that expatriates perceived a number of obstacles such as lack of training, succession planning and resistance due to satisfaction in the workplace. The length of stay had strong predictive value in relation to expatriate resistance to localisation.

The findings from this study offer new perspectives on the workforce profile in Qatar Although the overall relationship model uncovered using SEM reveals statistically insignificant findings, the results suggest that relationships indeed exist between the different variables and that a nomological relationship exists thus offering a unique and valuable contribution to the literature on all three constructs.

Finally, this study provided valuable baseline data for HRD in Qatar by drawing on participants from a broad range of industries and demographic backgrounds. The predictive power of these organisational and demographic variables provide scholars and practitioners with new perspectives and data that bear implications for HRD in this unique context.

References

Achoui, M. M. (2009). Human resource development in Gulf countries: An analysis of the trends and challenges facing Saudi Arabia. *Human Resource Development International*, *12*(1), 35–46.

Al-Dosari, A., Rahman, S., & Yusuf, A. (2006). A communicative planning approach to combat graduate unemployment in Saudi Arabia. *Human Resource Development International*, *9*(3), 397–414.

Al-Lamki, S. (1998). Obstacles to Omanization in the private sector: The perceptions of Omani graduates. *The International Journal of Human Resource Management*, *9*(2), 377–400.

Al-Zu'bi, H. A. (2010). A study of relationship between organizational justice and job satisfaction. *International Journal of Business & Management*, *5*(12), 102–109.

Ali, A., & Al-Kazemi, A. (2005). The Kuwaiti manager: Work values and orientations. *Journal of Business Ethics*, *60*(1), 63–73.

Anderson, J. C., & Gerbing, D. W. (1988). Structural equation modeling in practice: A review and recommended two – Step approach. *Psychological Bulletin*, *103*, 411–423.

Becker, T. E., Randal, D. M., & Riegel, C. D. (1995). The multidimensional view of commitment and theory of reasoned action: A comparative evaluation. *Journal of Management*, *21*(4), 617–638.

Bernardi, R. A., & Guptill, S. T. (2008). Social desirability response bias, gender, and factors influencing organizational commitment: An international study. *Journal of Business Ethics*, *81*(4), 797–809.

Berrebi, C., Martorell, F., & Tanner, J. (2009). Qatar's labor market at a crucial crossroad. *The Middle East Journal*, *63*(3), 421–442.

Budhwar, P., & Mellahi, K. (2007). Introduction: Human resource management in the Middle East. *The International Journal of Human Resource Management*, *18*(1), 2–10.

Chen, Z., & Francesco, A. (2003). The relationship between the three components of commitment and employee performance in China. *Journal of Vocational Behavior*, *62*, 490–510.

Creswell, J. W., Plano Clark, V. L., Gutmann, M. L., & Hanson, W. E. (2003). Advanced mixed methods research designs. *Handbook of Mixed Methods in Social and Behavioral Research* (pp. 209–240). Thousand Oaks, CA: Sage.

Elizur, D. (1996). Work values and commitment. *International Journal of Manpower*, *17*(3), 25–30.

Fischer, R., & Mansell, A. (2009). Commitment across cultures: A meta-analytical approach. *Journal of International Business Studies*, *40*(8), 1339–1358.

Forstenlechner, I. (2008). Workforce nationalization in the UAE: Image versus integration. *Education, Business and Society; Contemporary Middle Eastern Issues*, *1*(2), 82–91.

Forstenlechner, I. (2010). Workforce 'localization' in emerging Gulf economies: The need to fine-tune HRM. *Personnel Review*, *39*(10), 135–152.

Forstenlechner, I., & Mellahi, K. (2010). Gaining legitimacy through hiring local workforce at a premium: The case of MNE's in the United Arab Emirates. *Journal of World Business*, *46*(4), 455.

Forstenlechner, I., & Rutledge, E. (2010). Unemployment in the Gulf: Time to update the 'social contract'. *Middle East Policy*, *17*(2), 38–51.

Froese, F. J., & Xiao, S. (2012). Work values, job satisfaction and organizational commitment in China. *The International Journal of Human Resource Management*, *23*(10), 2144–2162.

Godwin, S. M. (2006). Globalization, education and emiritisation: A study of the United Arab Emirates. *The Electronic Journal on Information Systems in Developing Countries*, *27*(1), 1–14.

Harry, W. (2007). Employment creation and 'localization': The crucial human resource issues for the GCC. *The International Journal of Human Resource Management*, *18*(10), 132–146.

Hofstede, G. (1980). Motivation, leadership, and organizations: Do American theories apply abroad? *Organizational Dynamics*, *9*(1), 42–63.

Hofstede, G. (2001). *Culture's consequences: Comparing values, behaviors, institutions, and organizations across nations* (2nd ed.). Thousand Oaks, CA: Sage.

Hooper, D., Coughlan, J., & Mullen, M. R. (2008). Structural equation modeling: Guidelines for determining model fit. *The Electronic Journal of Business Research Methods*, *6*(1), 53–60.

Hu, L. T., & Bentler, P. M. (1999). Cutoff criteria for fit indexes and covariance structure analysis: Conventional criteria versus new alternatives. *Structural Equation Modeling*, *6*(1), 1–55.

Jöreskog, K., & Sörbom, D. (1996). *LISREL 8: User's reference guide*. Chicago, IL: Scientific Software InternationalInc.

Kamrava, M. (2009). Royal factionalism and political liberalization in Qatar. *The Middle Eastern Journal*, *63*(3), 401–421.

Kapiszewski, A. (2005). Non-indigenous citizens and 'stateless' residents in the Gulf monarchies. *Krakowskie, StudiaMiedzynarodowe (Krakow)*, *2*(6), 61–78.

Kapiszewski, A. (2006). Arab versus Asian migrant workers in the GCC countries. United Nations expert group meeting on international migration and development in the Arab Region. Population Division, United Nations Secretariat. NP.

Kidron, A. (1978). Work values and organizational commitment. *Academy of Management Journal*, *21*(2), 239–247.

Law, K., Wong, C., & Wang, K. (2004). An empirical test of the model on managing the 'localization' of human resources in the People's Republic of China. *The International Journal of Human Resources*, *15*(4), 635–648.

Looney, R. (2004). Saudization and sound economic reforms: Are the two compatible? *Strategic Insights*, *3*(2), 73–76.

Lee, H. W. (2005). The factors influencing expatriates. *The Journal of American Academy of Business*, 2.

Marsh, H. W., Hau, K. T., & Grayson, D. (2005). *Goodness of fit in structural equation models*.

Matic, J. (2008). Cultural differences in employee work values and their implications for management. *Management*, *13*(2), 93–104.

Mellahi, K., & Al-Hinai, S. (2000). Local workers in gulf co-operation countries: Assets of liabilities? *Middle Eastern Studies*, *3*(3), 177.

Meyer, J. P., & Allen, N. J. (1991). A three-component conceptualization of organizational commitment. *Human Resource Management Review*, *1*(1), 61–89.

Meyer, J. P., Allen, N. J., & Smith, C. A. (1993). Commitment to organizations and occupations: Extension and test of a three-component conceptualization. *Journal of Applied Psychology*, 78(4), 538–551.

Meyer, J. P., Herscovitch, D., & Topolnytsky. (2002). Affective continuance and normative commitment to the organization: A meta-analysis of antecedents, correlates and consequences. *Journal of Vocational Behavior*, 61, 20–52.

Meyer, J. P., & Herscovitch, L. (2001). Commitment in the workplace: Toward a general model. *Human Resource Management Review*, 11, 299–326.

Ministry of Interior. *Qatarization website*. Retrieved from http://www.qatarization.com.qa/Qatarization/Qatarization.nsf/en_Index?ReadForm. Accessed on June 6, 2012.

Mowday, R. T., Steers, R. M., & Porter, L. W. (1979). The measurement of organizational commitment. *Journal of Vocational Behavior*, 14, 224–247.

Muthuveloo, R., & Raduan, C. R. (2005). Typology of organizational commitment. *American Journal of Applied Sciences*, 2(6), 1078.

Muysken, J., & Nour, S. (2006). Deficiencies in education and poor prospects for economic growth in the Gulf countries: The case of the UAE. *The Journal of Development Studies*, 42(6), 957.

Naumann, E. (1993). Organizational predictors of expatriate job satisfaction. *Journal of International Business Studies*, 24(1), 61–80.

Palich, L., Horn, P., & Griffeth, R. (1995). Managing in the international context: Testing the culture generality of sources of commitment to multinational enterprises. *Journal of Management*, 21, 671–690.

Putti, J. M., Aryee, S., & Ling, T. K. (1989). Work values and organizational commitment: A study in the Asian context. *Human Relations*, 42, 73–77.

Randaree, K. (2009). Strategy, policy and practice in the nationalization of human capital: 'Project Emiritisation'. *Research and Practice in Human Resource Management*, 17(1), 71–91.

Rees, C. J., Mamman, A., & Braik, A. (2007). Emiritization as a strategic HRM change initiative: Case study evidence from a UAE petroleum company. *International Journal of Human Resource Management*, 18(1), 33–53.

Robertson, C., Al-Khatib, J., & Al-Habib, M. (2002). The relationship between Arab values and work beliefs: An exploratory examination. *Thunderbird International Business Review*, 44(5), 583–601.

Rutledge, E., Al Shamsi, F., Bassioni, Y., & Al Sheikh, H. (2011). Labour market nationalization policies and human resource development in the Arab Gulf States. *Human Resource Development International*, 14(2), 183–198.

Sadi, M., Al-Buraey, A., & Abdullah, M. (2009). *International Management Review*, 5(1), 70–84, 106.

Sanchez, J. I., Spector, P. E., & Cooper, C. L. (2006). Frequently ignored methodological issues in cross-cultural stress research. In P. T. P. Wong & L. C. J. Wong (Eds.).

Selmer, J. (2004). Expatriates' hesitation and the localization of Western business operations in China. *The International Journal of Human Resource Management*, 15(6), 1094–1107.

Shaban, R., Assad, R., & Al-Qudsi, S. (1995). The challenge of unemployment in the Arab region. *International Labour Review*, 134(1), 65.

Shaham, D. (2009). Foreign Labor in the Arab Gulf: Challenges to Nationalization. *Al Nakhla*, Fall 2009.

Stasz, C., Eide, E., & Martorell, F. (2007). *Post secondary education in Qatar, employer demand, student choice and options for policy.* Rand Corporation.

Suliman, A., & Al-Junaibi, Y. (2010). Commitment and turnover intention in the UAE oil industry. *The International Journal of Human Resource Management, 21*(9), 1472–1489.

Wong, C., Hui, C., & Law, K. S. (1995). Causal relationship between attitudinal antecedents to turnover. *Academy of Management Journal, Best Papers Proceedings.* 342–346.

Wong, C., & Law, K. S. (1999). Managing 'localization' of human resources in the PRC: A practical model. *Journal of World Business, 34*, 26–40.

Yunus, O. M., Mazlan, M., Rahim, A. R. A., & Shabudin, A. B. (2012). Islamic work values and organizational commitment: A case study among employees in broadcasting industry. *China-USA Business Review, 11*(2), 161–172.

Chapter 9

Talent Management & Staffing in Central and Eastern Europe — An Analysis of Bulgaria, Czech Republic, Hungary, Poland, Romania & Slovakia

Zoltan Buzady

Abstract

Purpose — This chapter reports the current status of management practices in the Central and Eastern Europe (CEE) region as seen by international expatri-ates. Based on the results and expert insights, we aim at giving guidance to MNE leaders and strategy makers as well as operative HRM staff and other expatriate managers how to best exploit the value-added opportunities in the CEE region by adopting the region-specific talent management and staffing policies and practices.

Methodology/approach — This study is based on the views of 1108 managers on the local management in six CEE countries: Bulgaria, Czechia,[1] Hungary, Poland, Romania, and Slovakia. Respondents were asked to fill in an anon-ymous online questionnaire containing 47 questions plus identifier questions. Also their local managers were asked to fill in the same questionnaire to estab-lish on which of the 47 questions there is significant disagreement between expatriate and local managers.

---

[1]In this chapter, the term Czechia is used to refer to the Czech Republic.

Global Talent Management and Staffing in Mnes
International Business & Management, Volume 32, 189–226
ISSN: 1876-066X/doi:10.1108/S1876-066X20160000032008

Findings — MNEs have been able to successfully capitalize on the economic integration and growth of the CEE region during the past 25 years. A new generation of competitive local managers is now growing into leadership positions, but MNEs need to find a more sophisticated way to retain those in the region in order to be able to exploit growth opportunities in future too.

Practical implications — Because the national cultural differences between the six analyzed CEE countries remain very characteristic and divergent, talent management and staffing strategies and policies of MNEs must be adopted and fine-tuned accordingly. Language and communication difficulties, knowledge of the standards management techniques are not a challenge anymore. Instead local management's soft skills, leadership values and attitudes need to be developed now simultaneously with increasing wages, as the most talented local staff and management is readily relocating into higher-wage countries.

Originality/value — The originality and scholarly interest of this study lies in its cross-cultural, comparative approach. The originality and practical interest of this study is that it gives clear recommendations to MNE and expat managers. Furthermore the presented results have been tested during critical forum discussions with more than 60 CEE-experienced managers, expatriates, and the representatives several foreign chambers of trade and commerce held at the Central European University Business School in spring 2015.

Keywords: Central and Eastern Europe; talent management; career management; competitiveness; leadership; cross-cultural management

9.1. Introduction

Central and Eastern European (CEE) countries are marking the 25th anniversary of the fall of communism and their transition into new forms of society, new economic systems, new ways to organize businesses and corporations. During this period, the CEE region has attracted considerable levels of international foreign direct investments, but also produced organic growth as well. The region has also reaped the benefits of near-shoring from Western Europe, and acquired a considerable market share in global off-shoring activities. Based on these trends, a rather extensive pool of shared-service centers, innovation and development centers, centers of excellence and extended production/assembly units are now located throughout CEE (Economist, 2005). In order to be able to take advantage of the value-added opportunities, a focus on best practices in managing human resource and the local talent pool is vital, as opposed to simply taking advantage of lower wages (and productivity levels) in far more distant low-cost countries (if possible at all). For an integrative study on the institutional and constructive approaches to the topic of knowledge transfer between multinational enterprises (MNEs) and local companies in the CEE region, please refer to Lang and Steger (2002).

This chapter presents the opportunity to prepare a comprehensive and scholarly analysis on the current work practices in the CEE region, in particular with the view to provide recommendations for improving the talent management and staffing practices of MNEs operating in the CEE region.

The ability of MNEs to capitalize on the CEE talent pool, and the roles and competencies of HR managers in CEE-located multinational companies have been previously studied (Kohont & Brewster, 2014; Smale & Suutari, 2011). However, these studies focused only on a single country, thus ignoring the fact that the many countries in the CEE region are culturally highly diverse. The Global Leadership and Organizational Behavior Effectiveness (GLOBE) studies identified a separate Eastern European cultural cluster, distinct from the Anglo, Germanic, Latin European, Latin American ones (Bakacsi, Imrek, Karacsonyi, & Takacs, 2002). It was reported that talent in the Eastern European cluster is associated with features such as making an effort, having willpower, working hard as abilities, being strong-minded as a positive skill, whilst knowledge is associated in general with the ability to learn (Dries, Cotton, Bagdadli, & de Oliveira, 2015). While other studies have focused on countries like Poland (Przytula, 2014), a comparative large-scale research on the CEE region as a whole has been lacking so far.

This particular chapter contribution is based on a study sponsored by Target, a leading headhunting firm in CEE (Buzady, Brewster, Viegas Bennett, & Sanyova, 2015), representing the views expressed by 1108 CEE managers (872 expatriate managers from 55 countries and 236 local managers — see appendix for further details on the dataset) on the particular management practices in six CEE countries: Bulgaria, Czechia, Hungary, Poland, Romania, and Slovakia, on 47 questions related to talent and staffing policies of MNEs.

This chapter is divided as follows. First, we will explore how the three layers of talent management and staffing (organizational, individual, and contextual) are relevant in the context of MNEs operating in the CEE region, next, we present observational characteristics of the whole CEE region, then, we will give concrete analysis of the opportunities and challenges at individual country/national cultural level, present concrete recommendations for talent management and staffing and finally we present the very detailed results of the most interesting statistical results based on the 1100 CEE manager replies.

9.2. Talent Management at different Levels of Context

At the *individual* level Csikszentmihalyi, Rathunde, and Whalen (1997) state that if *talent* is seen as an exceptional ability to show high performance and outputs, the question arises: how can it be developed even further? The first perspective is to modify the circumstances in such way that they become nurturing to the talents of a person. This can be observed in the constant adjustment of educational requirements and learning output re-definitions in educational settings, but also in corporate environment: typically after each major readjustment of vision-mission-strategy, the human resource (HR) department is asked to also adjust the organizational skills base and talent pool.

Second possible approach is to develop talent by influencing the field's ability to stimulate, and reward higher performance. This can be achieved by increasing the budget allocated to a particular talent development program. Third direction is to develop the talent by developing the individuals themselves (Marer, Buzady, & Vecsey, 2015). After all, it is the individual who ultimately has to carry out the task. This approach touches the fundamental question of what boundaries, limitations, or potential a person's physical traits play in defining his or her scope of talent.

In the managerial context, one has to revert to a more generally applicable approach — that is: how best to manage talented people in the given national cultural contexts? What advice could we give to those, who wish to improve organizational performance by best managing, nurturing and enhancing the talent pool of the average local manager in a given country of our study? We recognize the importance of psychological complexity as the organizing principle for making sense out of the multitude of factors affecting the development of talent. Complexity — or simultaneous presence of differentiating and integrating processes — distinguishes the personalities of talented individuals and their approach to learning (Csikszentmihalyi et al., 1997).

Employees have to be recognized as important assets and people full of potential, in order to develop a talent. Therefore, it is important to know what talents are important for an organization and its performance and vice versa people must also be considered as having skills which are useful for organizational performance. Second, talent development is more efficient, if people have learned the routine of cultivating talent; this means talent development becomes more dynamic and more effective each time the process is repeated. Third, the role of top management in talent development is crucial, by providing support and challenge to enhance the development of talent.

To emphasize the third point, we need to further sketch out of the wider, *organizational aspects* of why *talent management* and staffing policies are particularly important in the international business context. Sparrow, Scullion, and Tarique (2014) explain that the current trend is for MNEs to develop and use a global pool of talent, and becoming less dependent on sending expatriates around the global to local business to execute organizational coordination. Viewed in the context of the CEE region, this trend is clearly detectable. However it also creates new tensions on how to execute a coherent strategy across various countries in an integrated yet sufficiently differentiated way.

Figure 9.1 depicts the *organizational framework* of the leadership and management challenge of MNEs related to finding the best *talent management and staffing*

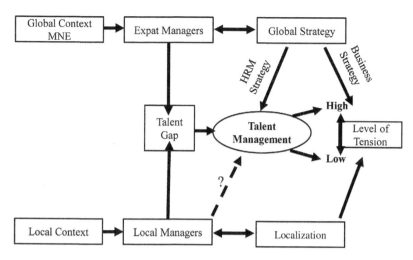

Figure 9.1: Organizational framework of talent management and staffing at MNEs in CEE.

approaches. As widely known, MNEs operate at two levels: a multinational/global as well as a local/regional one. These two levels almost always represent different realities and business contexts. Expatriate managers typically represent the head-quarters' (HQ) global/international perspective, they — with the help of corporate wide management systems — ensure global integration of business activities and they are sent out to the various subsidiary countries and locations to be proactive and positive agents of global strategy.

The local realities, opportunities, and constraints in the relevant business context are represented by managers typically originating from the host-countries. As in most MNEs, the locally incumbent business practices and the national cultures differ significantly from those prevailing at global/HQ-level, the personal and managerial differences between the two managerial levels is often perceived at as a "talent gap." This talent gap, however, is often interpreted as a negative factor for lower organizational performance or agility.

Global strategy, set at HQ-level, direct the overall business strategy goals, but it also closely directs the overall global HRM strategy element, including any aspects of the talent strategy. Global HRM and talent strategy have the purpose of furthering and supporting the global business strategy. It is typical for MNEs to show a clear operational linkage and influence between its overall global strategy, its global HR strategy and the various elements of the talent strategy.

The talent strategy's primary functional purpose is to fill the eventual talent gap between expats and local management. Figure 9.1 also indicates that the influencing channels and input modes and procedures from the local context/level into MNEs' talent strategy are often obscure or maybe non-existing at all. The significance of this however can be immense: An appropriate and differentiated talent strategy can make the difference of high or low level tension between global and local business strategy. In other words, the more differentiated and localized the talent and staffing strategy is the more likely it is that the MNE will find a harmonious way of integrating "glo-cal" business strategies.

This calls our attention to the importance to take local variations into the account. Central and Eastern European countries are often emphasizing to multinational/global HQ and their expatriate managers how different each country's socio-economic and national cultural heritage and ways of doing business are (Buzady, 2014). By integrating those differences into the talent and staffing strategies, MNEs will be more likely to capitalize on the value-added potential of their investments in the CEE region.

Third, we also wish to draw the reader's attention to the *contextual implications* of good talent management and staffing practices in the even wider, more macro-economic perspective. For this we will briefly present the regional and international *competitiveness view* on *talent management* and *staffing*.

Table 9.1 shows the rankings of the six observed CEE countries based on their overall ranking and competitiveness as published in the IMD World Competiveness Yearbook.

The data show that ranking of the analyzed countries are more or less stable. The countries keep their global position, but generally speaking there is a slight movement down on the leader board. As far as the basic country facts are concerned, Tables 9.2 and 9.3 provide information about GDP growth and GDP per capita rates.

Table 9.2 shows that real GDP rate is growing in the last year all across the countries, economy recovering faster after the financial crisis in the region (e.g., compared to Western Europe). Table 9.3 shows the considerable income differences among the six analyzed countries measured in GDP per capita. However, the overall trend across the CEE region is showing a positive growth.

In order to gain an additional perspective, we sought the views of expatriate managers in the six CEE countries to rate the competitiveness level of the given country in which they happen to work.

Table 9.1: Rating of six CEE countries.

	2010	2011	2012	2013
Bulgaria	53	55	54	57
Czechia	29	30	33	35
Hungary	42	47	45	50
Poland	32	34	34	33
Romania	54	50	53	55
Slovakia	49	48	47	47

Source: IMD World Competitiveness Yearbook.

Table 9.2: Real GDP growth rate of CEE countries.

	2010	2011	2012	2013
Bulgaria	0.7	2.0	0.5	1.1
Czechia	2.3	2.0	−0.8	−0.7
Hungary	0.8	1.8	−1.5	1.5
Poland	3.7	4.8	1.8	1.7
Romania	−0.8	1.1	0.6	3.4
Slovakia	4.8	2.7	1.6	1.4

Source: Eurostat (2014).

Table 9.3: GDP per capita of CEE countries.

Purchasing Power Standards in Relation to EU28 Average (Index EU28 = 100)	2010	2011	2012	2013
Bulgaria	43	44	45	45
Czechia	81	83	82	82
Hungary	65	65	65	66
Poland	62	64	66	67
Romania	50	51	53	55
Slovakia	73	73	74	75

Source: Eurostat (2014).

Table 9.4: Overall ranking CEE countries competitiveness based rating by expatriates.

	In 2009	**In 2014**
Poland	1	1
Romania	4	2
Czechia	3	3
Hungary	5	4
Slovakia	2	5
Bulgaria	6	6

Table 9.4 shows that the rankings have changed since the last survey done in 2009. As we can see, Romania moved up and Slovakia went down. In the 2015 Study (Buzady et al., 2015) there is still a considerable variation among the different countries. While in 2009 Slovakia was the second best evaluated country by Brewster and Viegas Bennett (2009), in 2014 Slovakia has dropped to 5th place. On the other hand

we can see that Romania went up from 4th to 2nd position. Poland is still the best evaluated country in CEE region.

9.3. Comparative Analysis of Expat and Local Managers' Views on Current Management Realities in CEE

The current study[2] is based on the views of 1108 managers (about 872 expatriate managers from 55 countries and 236 local managers on the local management in six CEE countries: Bulgaria, Czechia, Hungary, Poland, Romania, and Slovakia). A leading headhunting firm shared with the research consortium its extensive pool of corporate, international, and local firms' contacts developed in the six countries over the past decade. In addition to these, the members of the British Chamber of Commerce in the concerned countries were contacted asking their CEO or HR-Director to fill in an online questionnaire. The time period for this was 6 months in order to ensure that at least 100 responses have been collected from each country. In addition to their views the research also solicited replies from local managers working in the same companies to have a comparative control pool of respondents.

Here are some typical direct quotes and statements, all reproduced directly from Buzady et al. (2015), which were made by local managers, when they were asked about their views on MNE versus local management, and on the policies and practices related to HRM, talent management, and staffing:

> There is a big gap between the corporate multinational culture and the local business culture. Therefore managers who have grown in a local business can hardly be integrated in a multinational business culture. That drives high scarcity in the market. (Local Bulgarian manager)

> Local managers still need to better develop their leadership style. As Czechs, we still concentrate more on hard skills and experience rather than on competencies. Emotional intelligence is severely underestimated in this area. (Local manager in Czechia)

> As I have heard many times that Hungary is a low-cost country it made me understand why the best managers are not expatriated here … most of them feel like this is a penalty in their career. (Local manager in Hungary)

> Polish managers will find themselves in a multicultural environment, adapting well to the market changes. This review mainly refers to the female managers. Still, women in positions of senior management earn less than their male counterparts. (Local Polish manager)

---

[2]The current study is a repeat study of an earlier study published by Brewster and Viegas Bennett (2009). Descriptive analysis of our research sample can be found in the appendices below and more detailed data for research purposes can be obtained from the author upon request. The study was conducted in fall 2014, sponsored by TARGET Executive Search and GfK Slovakia, and is a "Follow up" of the 2009 study realized by TARGET International Executive Search under the supervision of Prof. Chris Brewster. Any statement that describes trends and changes is thus referring to the management analysis compiled in 2009 on the six CEE countries. The 2015 study contained 47 questions, two more than the one conducted in 2009.

I have seen many cases when local Romanian managers developed strong business plans and/ or brilliant solutions and managed to achieve way-above-expected results, showing an impressive combination of corporate approach and entrepreneurial skills. As per my experience, their skills and abilities were at least equal with the ones of expats and international managers. I strongly believe there are many local talents, the real art is to identify them at the right time and place them into assignments/environment where they can really contribute and develop further ... and overcome the Western/US superiority prejudice. (Local manager in Romania)

Local management culture only reflects the broader social, political and cultural environment. (Local manager in Slovakia)

We have analyzed, in what specific domains and topics the view and *opinions* of expatriate and local managers *differed* in each of the six countries.

There were a series of statements on which the local managers in the countries perceived themselves more positively than the expats, some of the statements being quite consistent across countries, as shown in Table 9.5. There is a common tendency (in at least three countries) of overestimating the level of local managers' customer service orientation, and also in the level of their selling skills and creativity. Other areas where local managers' own perception differed to those of expats were: taking initiative, having the required wide enough and strategic view on business aspects, adequately satisfying shareholder needs, and understanding the competitive market. Hungary stands out as having more positive evaluations made by locals versus expats. Also there expats reported hard working norms and not for just showing long hours (termed as "presenteeism") whilst the Slovak managers were seen as to overestimating their soft skills, their capabilities in building good relationships with customers and being flexible.

Table 9.5 shows in which aspects the local managers appreciate themselves more positively than the expatriate managers did.

So far we have described the major perceived and reported differences between the expatriate and local managers. In the following we will give a very brief summary of what major differences can be found between the six countries.

Positive changes in *Bulgaria* are:

("Positive" trend is defined as an increase in the *relative share* of respondents who *agreed* with a particular statement.)

• Business deadlines and timetables are taken seriously in this country
• It is easy to find well-trained managers in this country
• Local managers work well in teams
• Local managers are concentrated and efficient with their time

Negative changes (meaning a *decreasing relative share* of respondents *agreeing* with a statement):

− The business environment here is now less active and dynamic
− It is less important now to make friendships with colleagues and customers
− There is more of culture of "presenteeism" (working long hours "for show")
− There is less strong entrepreneurial spirit among managers here
− Local managers do tend to think that expatriate managers are overpaid

Table 9.5: Statements on which local managers appreciate themselves more positively than expats.

	Bulgaria	Romania	Czechia	Hungary	Poland	Slovakia
Local management is dedicated to excellent customer service	X	X	X		X	
Managers in this country tend to be excellent at selling	X		X		X	
In this country business and commerce are highly customer-service-oriented			X		X	X
Creativity in problem solving is a strong local management characteristic			X	X		X
Managers like to take the initiative in preventing and solving problems	X			X		
Managers like to take a wide, strategic view		X			X	
Senior managers are highly focused on satisfying shareholder needs	X	X				
Managers here understand their competitive markets very well	X	X				
Managers in this country work hard				X		
There is not a culture of "presenteeism" (working long hours "for show")				X		
Local managers are good at dealing with overseas customers and colleagues					X	
It is easy to find well-trained managers in this country		X				
Humor is important in working relationships in this country						X
Good personal relationships with customers are essential to business culture here						X
Managers in this country are very flexible and adaptable			X			
Managers are good at dealing with unexpected situations						X

Czechia, officially called the Czech Republic, showed following positive changes as defined above:

- It is easy to find well-trained managers in this country
- We could recruit better managers if we could pay them more
- Hierarchies here tend to be informal
- Local managers welcome responsibility
- Managers are good at dealing with unexpected situations

The negative changes were:

- The business environment here is less very active and dynamic
- There is more of a culture of presenteeism
- Less local managers do speak at least one foreign language
- Managers here work now in a less planned manner
- Ambitious managers are less admired now

Hungary showed following positive change trends since the identical expatriate study conducted in 2009:

- Business deadlines and timetables are taken seriously in this country
- It is easy to find well-trained managers in this country
- Managers here do place much value on the company they work for
- Managers in this country work hard
- Corruption is not a significant problem in doing business here

Negative changes were:

- It is now less important here to make friendships with colleagues and customers
- Good personal relationships with customers are now less essential to business culture here
- Hierarchies here tend to become more formal

The positive changes in *Poland* according to expats' opinion were:

- Managers in this country work hard
- Managers here do place much value on the company they work for
- Business deadlines and timetables are taken seriously in this country
- It is easy to find well-trained managers in this country
- Managers like to take the initiative in preventing and solving problems
- Senior managers are highly focused on satisfying shareholders' needs

The negative changes/trends in their view were:

- Managers are now less cooperative, but rather individualistic in their thinking
- Business environment in this country is now less active and dynamic
- Strong interpersonal skills in managers are valued less now
- Managers in this country tend not to be less excellent at selling now

The positive changes observed by managers in *Romania* were:

- It is easy to find well-trained managers in this country
- In this country business and commerce are highly customer-service-oriented
- Business deadlines and timetables are taken seriously in this country
- Local management is dedicated to excellent customer service

Whilst the areas in which there is less agreement in 2014 than was in 2009:

- Corruption is slightly a less significant problem in doing business here
- There is less of a strong entrepreneurial spirit among managers here

The reported positive changes in *Slovakia* are:

- Communication with and between managers is not too formal
- It is easy to find well-trained managers in this country
- We could recruit better managers if we could pay them more
- Business deadlines and timetables are taken seriously in this country
- Hierarchies here tend to be informal

The negative changes in Slovakia are:

- The business environment is not very active and dynamic
- Corruption is a significant problem in doing business here
- Good personal relationships with customers are not essential to business culture here
- Bureaucracy is a serious problem in this country

The general findings in our study about the Central and Eastern European region as a whole, based on what the expatriate managers reported are the following:

Social culture as an intangible heritage plays an important role in this region both personally as well as professionally. It comes as no surprise that this did not change from the earlier study. One can find here a justification why most expatriates enjoy living and working in these six countries. Slovakia was the only country where the satisfaction with working and living there went down. In all other five countries the satisfaction has increased, especially in Romania.

On the other hand, the scoring of importance of *making friendships* with colleagues and customers changed. Expatriates perceived this factor as less important mainly in Bulgaria, Hungary and again in Slovakia. Although foreigners evaluated rather negatively the importance of making friendships, expatriates perceived local managers as more flexible and adaptable than in 2009. As previously, there is an opposite trend in Slovakia and the situation is rather worse in 2014.

The conventional rule is that only very large companies can effectively *influence* their relevant business environment in a way it favors their business strategies. For most companies this relationship is inverse. A static business environment allows for longer-term planning and clearer business strategies, whilst a highly dynamic business environment favors organizations with more flexible, hence fuzzy strategic plans and goals.

Our 2014 study respondents reported clearly decreasing level of activism and dynamism in their *business environments* across all CEE countries, except for Hungary, which remained stable to the 2009 data. This observation seems to support the generally negative impact of the global economic crisis on business environments of the region, probably also resulting from a declining EU-accession business euphoria.

A more static and risk-averse business environment normally results in clearer *business strategies*. Our recent study shows that local companies in Bulgaria and Slovakia are the most rigid by not adjusting strategic goals to the changed environment. Companies in Czechia and Romania surprise with formulating their strategic goals even more than in 2009, although they report a decreasing activity and dynamism of the business environment.

Humor, an often ignored, but essential element in social interactions, seems to be a stable and important element of working relationships in all countries. We have noticed, however that it is particularly important element of doing business in Romania, whilst it is also the country where it has become significantly more important during the past five years.

A key decision making factor for international investment decisions is the availability and easy attracting of well-*trained local managers*. Hungary and Poland clearly lead the field in this respect, probably reflecting the first-mover advantage of these countries by having attracted the highest levels of FDI over the past two decades. FDI inflows stimulated the development of internationally re-known business schools and relevant management education, fostering a new class of professionals and leaders at local level. A rapid improvement of management training level has been reported from Romania, Czechia, and Hungary.

Customer orientation is still a critical issue. Although the situation is getting better in all countries, particularly in Romania, still there is least a full half of expatriates who disagree with the statement that business and commerce in the CEE region are highly customer-oriented. A Dutch expat in Slovakia reported that, "Slovak managers are not customer-minded at all. They do what they personally think is enough and that is not much. They do not have any idea about business expectations in Western Europe. Bureaucracy is extreme. Paperwork is done in detail, but this is not efficient and does not solve anything. Lower-level workers are OK, but Slovak Managers cannot motivate them in the right way, because of lacking competence among the managers themselves." Whilst a Canadian expat in Romania said: "There appears to be a lack of a service culture here in relation to 'customer service' and somehow it just does not seem to be expected, nor valued highly enough when great service is actually given. This is not just about tipping, but about attempting to always set, meet and/or exceed customer expectations."

Perception of local managers as dedicated to excellent *customer service support* the positive trend and the improvement of the customer orientation situation in the

CEE region. While in Bulgaria and Romania, we can observe improvement, Poland and Slovakia registered no major change in comparison to 2009. *Organization of business* is still very complicated and not efficient. Though the perception of business in the CEE region as very well organized and efficient has risen against 2009 there is still some room for further improvement. The share of expatriates who agreed with statement is still lower compared to other statements. The same trend can also be seen in evaluation of *responsibility* of local managers. It seems that local managers welcome more responsibility than in 2009 but it is still perceived as a problematic issue. Here two direct quotes to the point in case: "Slovakian Managers should in general 'take' (and not simply just 'receive') more responsibility!" (a Dutch expat in Slovakia). "Most people are 'lazy', disorganized and shun requisite responsibility. Laziness means no or little planning which results in knee-jerk reactions when things go wrong (which they often do) and then time wasted putting things right hence losing time which should have been used more efficiently" (a British expat in Bulgaria).

There is again a low share of CEE managers who like to take a wider, *strategic view* and the improvement is slow. On the other hand, we can see stronger improvement in the perception of managers who do place much value in the company they work for in the whole region, Hungary and Romania in particular. Our current study also supports the general notion that the preferences of *working in a planned manner* changes as one goes further South and East, ranging from Czechia and Slovakia at the top, followed by Hungary and Poland next and Romania and Bulgaria forming the third cluster of countries. This clustering is very similar when respondents were asked about the local managers' concentrated and efficient use of their own time.

Expatriates found Bulgaria and Romania to be most challenging in terms being able to rely on *agreed decisions* to be actually acted upon. Our study also shows that by and large all local managers work hard and "presenteeism" is not a general problem either.

Bureaucracy and corruption is an issue in all the CEE countries. The share of expatriates who mentioned bureaucracy as a serious problem increased in Czechia and especially in Slovakia, where 73% of foreigners disagreed with the statement about corruption being an insignificant issue. On the other hand, in Bulgaria, Hungary, and Poland, we can see improvement but the share of agreement is still very low. Poland is again the only country where more than half of respondents perceived corruption as an insignificant problem. Though Slovakia came second in 2009 (in terms of perception of corruption) in 2014 the situation is completely different. Only 30% of expatriates evaluated corruption as an insignificant problem.

There seems to be no "*gender equality*" problem in the management sphere. On the contrary, expatriates appreciate role of women in business management. The view of an American expat in the CEE is that "Czech women tend to be more hard-working than Czech men; Czech men are very intelligent and good at problem-solving, but lack initiative." Speaking of gender equality, when we compare results to the scores of 2009, there is a slight decline in the whole CEE region except for Romania — the only country with a higher share of foreigners who agreed with the statement that on the whole women in the given country tend to be more effective managers than their male counterparts.

As to *working with other cultures* the results are showing a positive trend — expatriates enjoy living in the CEE region. Expatriates appreciate working with local managers.

In general the positive findings are that the management context in the CEE region is improving. There are still problems that challenge the whole region such as bureaucracy and corruption. But on the other hand, the perception of condition and evaluation of local managers is getting better. The positive trend can be seen also in the possibilities of finding well-trained managers in the CEE region. This statement was evaluated significantly better in all six countries especially in Romania and Czechia.

The following section describes our findings related to *managing talent and on staffing*.

In 2014, more expatriates agreed that better managers could be recruited if they could be paid better; managers suggested the same points in relation to managing talent and creating a staffing strategy.

In general it can be observed that the younger generation of local managers can adjust their working style, especially if leadership training is provided. Whilst it seems difficult to find good managers, whom would qualify in the views of an expatriate as a "leader," it is easier to find someone they would label as a "boss." That is someone who believes that when reaching a certain level of power, he or she just has to give orders, but does not make the internal connection between "being the head" and assuming the responsibility that comes with that position. They also reported that, most local managers are not well-prepared for their future roles and responsibilities. It is unclear to local managers in the talent pipeline what is expected from them in such power position. We observed that there is a lack of expatriation policy for future local managers, although it might be a good policy to train them abroad and to fill the local talent gap.

Interestingly, some expat managers reported that they observed — across the whole of CEE — a clash between the manager generations, age wise: "The old guard is still around and active. They have the main power levers and don't want to give it up, yet. But the younger generation is coming up too and fortunately they are far more receptive to new ideas."

A German expat responded to this aspect that "A high level of jealousy among peers exists; you should be aware of a strong materialistic culture. People are judged by the amount of material things and money they can display; kindness and respect is discounted a as a sure sign of weakness; also is noticed some lack of awareness that value systems of people can be rather different outside of the home countries, such as Poland in our case."

9.4. Detailed Analysis of Statements Made by 1100 + CEE Managers

When asked about the *general business environment,* foreigners in all six analyzed countries agreed that local companies usually do not have a clear business strategy (Figure 9.2). Czechia, Hungary, and Romania reached slightly better results in 2014 compared to 2009. However, Bulgaria stands out, as only 19% of participating expatriates agreed that local Bulgarian companies have a clear strategy. This is well below the average registered in the other five countries.

As Figure 9.3 shows, the perception of the business environment as very active and dynamic is different in all six countries. In Poland and Romania more than two-thirds of respondents agreed (strongly agree or agree) with the statement, while in all other countries the percentage shares are lower.

When we compare the latest results with the 2009 survey, the share of respondents agreeing with the statement shrank, except for Hungary with the same level as in 2009. To look more precisely, there was a significant decrease in Slovakia (from 48% who strongly agree and agree to only 23%), Czech Republic (46% → 28%) and Bulgaria (37% → 18%).

While the evaluation of business as being generally very well organized and efficient reached a better score than in 2009 the indicator is still generally low (Figure 9.4). Results among all six countries differ — Czech Republic, Poland, and Slovakia achieved a higher share of expatriates who agree with the statement that business is generally very well organized and efficient. The lowest share was measured in Bulgaria.

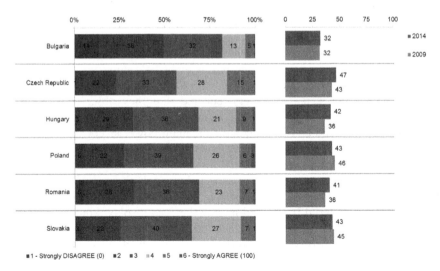

Figure 9.2: Local companies usually have a clear business strategy.

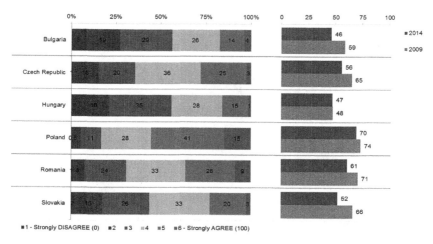

Figure 9.3: The business environment here is very active and dynamic.

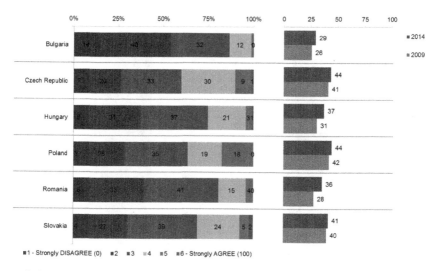

Figure 9.4: Business is generally very well organized and efficient.

Becoming friends with colleagues and customers is perceived as important in all countries, with a slight decrease in Bulgaria, Hungary, and Slovakia, compared to the 2009 results (Figure 9.5). The highest share of foreigners who agreed with the statement on the importance of forming friendships was seen in Romania (91% agree).

In Figure 9.6 we see that even though the survey showed lack of well-trained managers available for hire in all six countries, results in 2014 showed a better

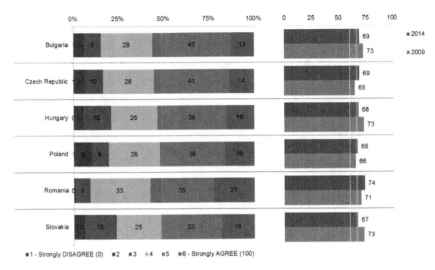

Figure 9.5: It is important here to form friendships with colleagues and customers.

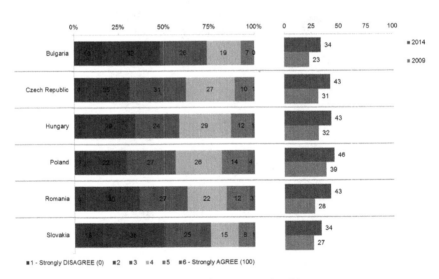

Figure 9.6: It is easy to find well-trained managers in this country.

situation compared to 2009. On the other hand, it is still hard for foreigners to find the right experienced managers. This is even worse in Bulgaria and Slovakia, where approximately 70% of expatriates find it difficult to find well-trained managers.

While in Bulgaria, Czechia, Romania, and Slovakia more expatriates than in 2009 believed that they could recruit better managers if they could offer them better pay, in Hungary and Poland there was no change (Figure 9.7).

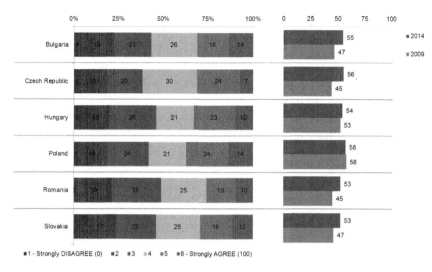

Figure 9.7: We could recruit better managers if we could pay them more.

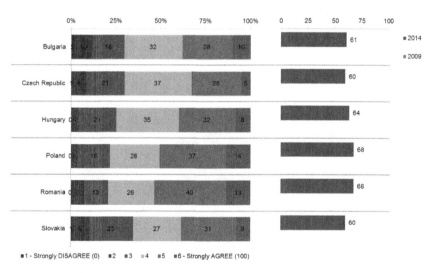

Figure 9.8: In this country, the level of power and hierarchical position of managers tend to coincide.

Figure 9.8 shows that in the CEE region foreigners tended to think that the level of power and hierarchical position of managers tend to coincide. The responses varied from 66% of agreement in Slovakia up to 79% in Romania. This statement was not measured in 2009.

As shown in Figure 9.9, about 60% of the expatriates think that rules and policies are more important than circumstances, especially in Czechia (65%). On the other hand, the lowest level was registered in Bulgaria (52%).

Management style also needs to be analyzed to get a more fine-grained picture on the contextual realities of managing talent and solving staffing functions: Team work of local managers is improving across most countries (Figure 9.10). It is noticeable however that it has the highest level in Czechia though and is lowest in Hungary. The most significant improvement in locals' team work has been observed in Bulgaria.

However, in a similar extent, expatriates evaluated local managers as being rather individualistic than cooperative (Figure 9.11).

In terms of hierarchies, Figure 9.12 shows that still most expatriates consider that hierarchies are formal in these countries, though the situation is improving.

While in 2009, foreigners mainly agreed that managers are unwilling to take responsibility, the situation is getting better in 2014 in all six countries especially in Bulgaria, Czechia, and Romania (Figure 9.13).

While in Bulgaria and Slovakia communication is evaluated as not too formal (77% and 65%, respectively), in Poland and Czechia half of respondents evaluate communication as formal (Figure 9.14).

As illustrated in Figure 9.15, local managers' ability to take a wide, strategic view is still rated quite low, though improving. The best situation is in Poland — 36%, Czechia — 32%, and in Slovakia 30%.

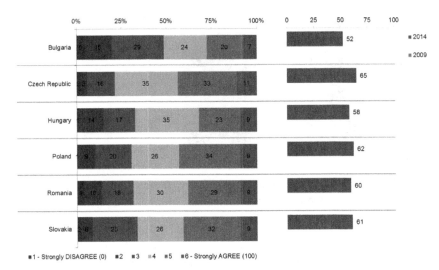

Figure 9.9: Rules and policies tend to be more important than the specific circumstances.

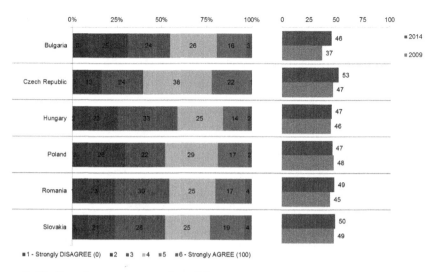

Figure 9.10: Local managers work well in teams.

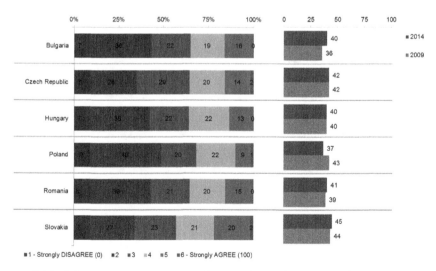

Figure 9.11: Managers are cooperative, rather than individualistic, in their thinking.

The perception of the flexibility and adaptability of local managers is also improving, except for Slovakia; however, it is still at quite low levels (Figure 9.16).

Similar situation in terms of local managers' ability to deal with unexpected situations (Figure 9.17): improving, though below 50%.

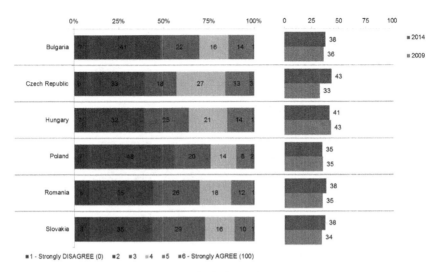

Figure 9.12: Hierarchies here tend to be informal.

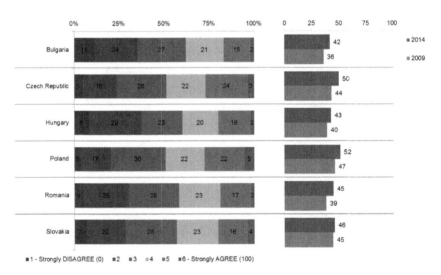

Figure 9.13: Local managers welcome responsibility.

Same situation in terms of efficiency of local managers (Figure 9.18) — positively evaluated in Czechia and Slovakia, while in Bulgaria and Romania the scores are the lowest.

Expatriates perceived strong interpersonal skills in managers as highly valued mainly in Romania and Hungary (Figure 9.19). The situation is different in Poland

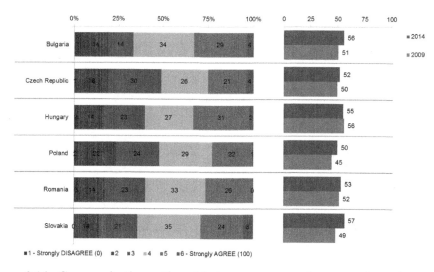

Figure 9.14: Communication with and between managers is not too formal.

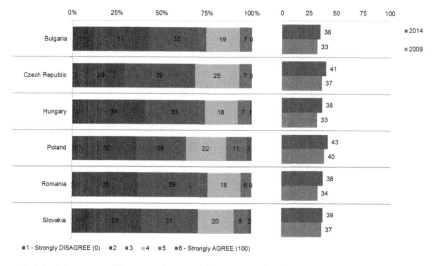

Figure 9.15: Managers like to take a wider, strategic view.

and even decreasing, as 48% of expatriates did not think that strong interpersonal skills were highly valued.

Creativity, on the other hand, is not considered a strength of the local managers in CEE yet, even though improving. In Czechia, Hungary, Poland, and Romania however one half of respondents gave positive evaluation, while in Bulgaria and Slovakia the positive evaluations were below 40% (Figure 9.20).

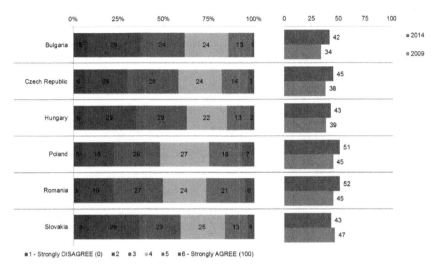

Figure 9.16: Managers in this country are very flexible and adaptable.

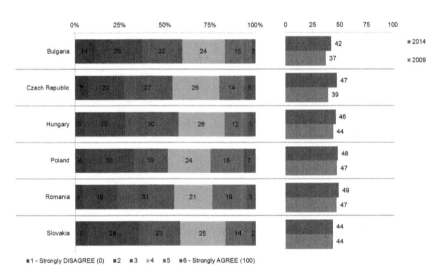

Figure 9.17: Managers are good at dealing with unexpected situations.

An improvement was noticed also regarding the perception of local managers taking initiative and solving problems (Figure 9.21), especially in Poland, Hungary, and Czechia.

As shown in Figures 9.22 and 9.23, CEE managers are perceived mainly as hard working, especially in Poland (84% agreement). However, the issue of "presentee-ism" has not disappeared, even though the perception is improving. About half of

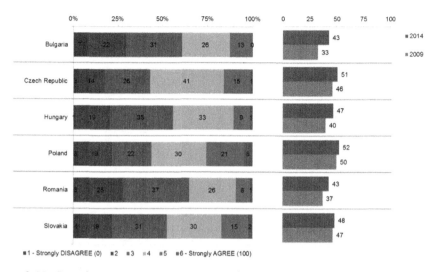

Figure 9.18: Local managers are concentrated and efficient with their time.

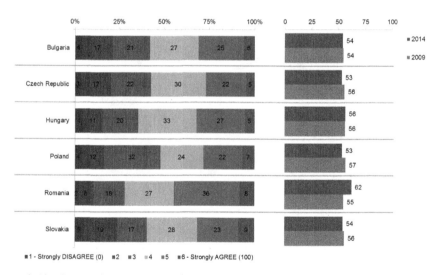

Figure 9.19: Strong interpersonal skills in managers are highly valued here.

foreigners evaluated the local culture as "culture of presenteeism"/working long hours for show.

Regarding the knowledge of the CEE managers on their *competitive markets*, the situation is also improving in most of the countries, with positive evaluations from around 50% of the expatriates (Figure 9.24). While in 2009, 53% of expatriates in

214   *Zoltan Buzady*

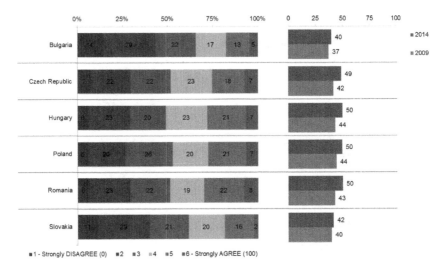

Figure 9.20: Creativity in problem solving is a strong local management characteristic.

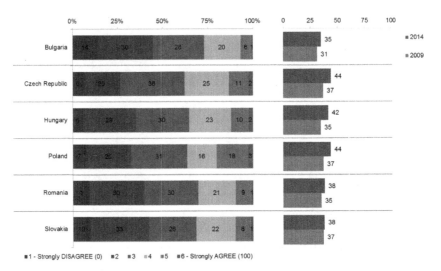

Figure 9.21: Managers like to take the initiative in preventing and solving problems.

Bulgaria disagreed with statement, this share is lower now at 44%. On the other hand, the situation in Slovakia got slightly worse from 54% of foreigners agreeing with the statement in 2009 to 49%.

Expatriates mainly perceived the local management in the CEE region as not dedicated to excellent customer service though the perception is getting better in

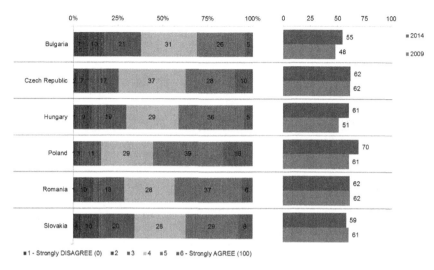

Figure 9.22: Managers in this country work hard.

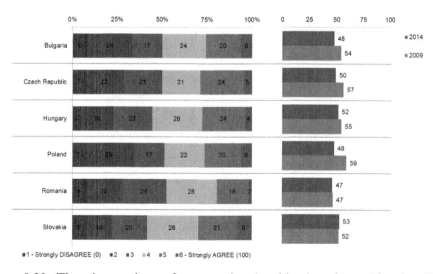

Figure 9.23: There is no culture of presenteeism (working long hours "for show").

comparison to 2009, as shown in Figure 9.25. Three countries showed significant growth in the share of people who agree with the statement and evaluated local managers as customer-oriented: Bulgaria (from 19% in 2009 to 30% in 2014), Hungary (from 33% in 2009 to 41% in 2014), and Romania (from 22% in 2009 to 38% in 2014).

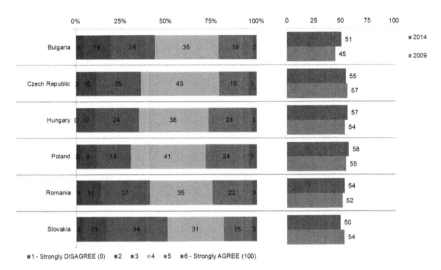

Figure 9.24: Managers in this country understand their competitive markets very well.

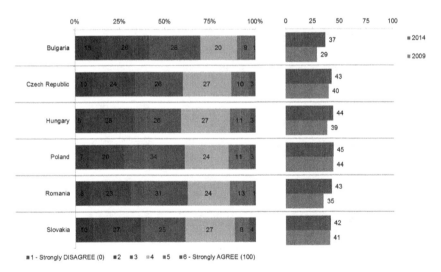

Figure 9.25: Local management is dedicated to providing excellent customer service.

Poland is the only country where more than one half of expatriates perceived managers as having a strong entrepreneurial spirit (Figure 9.26). The lowest share of expatriates who agreed that there is a strong entrepreneurial spirit among managers is in Slovakia — only one in three foreigners.

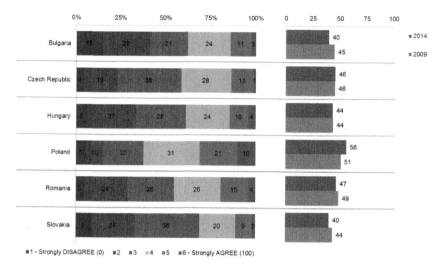

Figure 9.26: There is a strong entrepreneurial spirit among managers in this country.

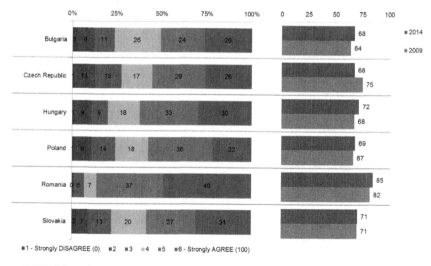

Figure 9.27: Most local managers speak at least one foreign language.

Expatriates in all six countries positively evaluated that most local managers speak at least one *foreign language* especially in Romania with 93% agreement (49% agreed strongly) (Figure 9.27). The only country where the situation got worse in comparison to 2009 is Czechia, where the share of agreement decreased from 86% to 72%.

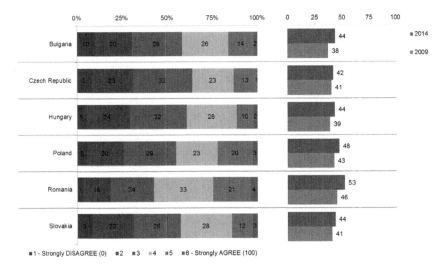

Figure 9.28: Local managers are good at dealing with overseas customers and colleagues.

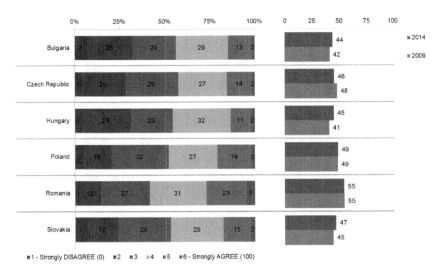

Figure 9.29: Managers are good at understanding and adapting to different business cultures.

Figure 9.28 shows that CEE managers are generally not evaluated as good at dealing with *foreign customers* and colleagues except for Romania. This is the only country where the share of foreigners who agreed with the statement was higher than 50% and the only country with a substantial increase in comparison to 2009.

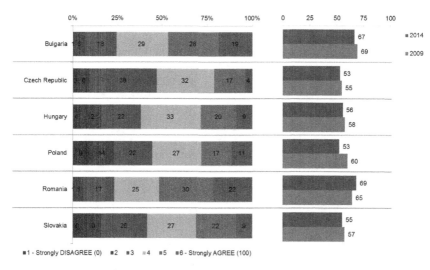

Figure 9.30: On the whole women here tend to be more effective managers than their male counterparts.

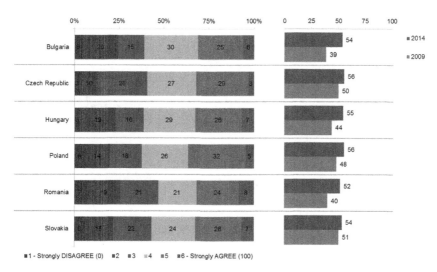

Figure 9.31: Managers here do place much value on the company they work for.

Similar situation is shown in Figure 9.29, regarding managers' ability to understand and adapt to different business cultures, only in Romania more than one half of expatriates agreed with this (58% agreement, 28% markedly). In the other five CEE countries the share of foreigners who perceived local managers as good at

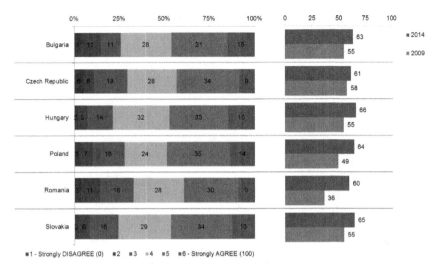

Figure 9.32: Managers in this country are not overpaid for their levels of experience and qualifications.

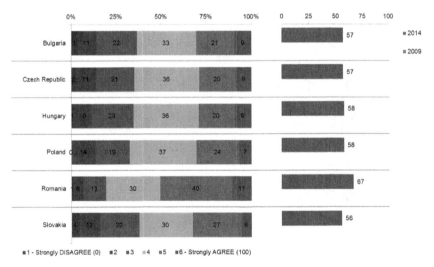

Figure 9.33: Local managers are experienced in working together with foreigners.

understanding and adapting to different business cultures varies from 43% in Czechia to 48% in Poland.

Foreigners in Bulgaria and Romania generally evaluated women as more effective managers than their male counterparts (Figure 9.30); high scores of above 50%

were registered though by all CEE countries. In comparison to 2009, the perception of women as more effective managers than men has declined only in Poland.

While in 2009, perception of company loyalty differed in the CEE region, in 2014 the responses in all six countries are at the same level (Figure 9.31). The situation got better in all countries especially in Bulgaria (from 30% agreement in 2009 to 61% in 2014), Hungary (from 38% to 62%), and Romania (from 36% to 53%).

In general in CEE managers are not considered *overpaid* for their levels of *experience and qualification*, according to Figure 9.32. The responses varied from 65% in Romania to 80% in Hungary, and in all the countries the evaluations improved as compared to 2009.

As shown in Figure 9.33, in Romania expatriates evaluated local managers as experienced in working together with foreigners (81% agreement, 51% markedly); in all the other five countries the share of agreement was approximately 63%, so still relatively high.

9.5. Findings on Managing Talent and Staffing in CEE — Conclusions and Outlook

In *general*, the business context and local management practices in all countries of the CEE region are improving in almost all aspects. CEE countries have a tremendous economic development potential, as the MNEs only started to grow in this region after the fall of the communist period, so only in the last 25 years. However, the influence of the communist period left some legacies behind, common in all of these countries: corruption, bureaucracy, hierarchical organizations, and authoritarian models of leadership, when compared to standards in Western Economies, the home country of most MNEs operating in this region.

On the other hand, according to the evaluation by expatriate managers' competencies, characteristics, experiences of local management/staff are gradually improving, strengthened by new generation of local managers rising into leadership positions. Those people typically gained already the new type of management experiences, often having studied partly abroad, they got socialized in competitive market economies and many of them have gained first-hand work experience international companies operating locally.

We recommend MNEs to further invest in the skill development of their local CEE managers. HRM policies in CEE should focus in particular on enhancing the *leadership skills* among their managers, focusing on *soft and people-related skills*, in order to close the gap vis-à-vis their global operations and organizational standards. Along with the general efforts on HRM policy part, the *organizational culture* plays another crucial part in building, retaining, and promoting stronger local leaders. This can be achieved by encouraging more *egalitarian/informal hierarchical relations*, fostering *personal accountability*, supporting local managers in growing their *communication, people management and self-management* practices. Also, *planning and time management skills* should be further developed too.

Satisfying this *complex set* of talent development needs puts HRM policies in CEE into a new context: whilst in their home countries MNEs rely less and less on co-operations with *established global* business schools in their talent and staff development programs, in CEE *now* is the time for *developing* and building integrated leadership, talent and staff development programs *together with newly emerging, locally leading* business schools and universities.

In this overall HRM process foreign *expatriate managers* have also still maintained their *traditional* role in bringing/bridging in the western culture and models of leadership into CEE.

However, based on our study we can make following *further recommendations* to MNEs for the talent and staffing strategies and practices in CEE:

In the rapidly changing CEE business environment the burdens and work load of expatriate managers, local and global HR staff in talent development should be assisted by tools of *international coaching* done by *internal* staff from the MNEs global, international network, or by *external* experts with requisite business and/or coaching experience and leadership skills from the *neighboring* CEE countries (via business schools/universities/training companies/professional associations and even chambers of commerce). An additional effect of international coaching would be that local managers are also made aware of the existence and relevance of cross-cultural differences within the CEE region. *Cultural intelligence* is an awareness of *added business complexity*, which currently in most cases only the expatriate managers become aware of when arriving as newly appointed heads of a CEE local operations. International coaching would be thus a very valuable and easily implementable policy element for talent and staffing policies in CEE.

After having identified the local talent potentials we recommend MNEs to introduce a system of talent *inpatriation* from the CEE region to the HQ and then to return those persons. Such HRM strategy not only fastens the knowledge transfer and span boundaries, but also facilitates the vital internal exchanges between the various organizational entities and business units of an MNE. The practice of inpatriation is highly attractive to local talent, because after a calculable period of professional development they can return to their CEE country of origin to capitalize on their cultural competitive advantage, their local personal networks and resolve potential dual-career dilemma and/or other personal family plans.

Finally, another important dimension in building and retaining talented local managers in CEE is directly related to the financials, to salaries and benefits: in all of these countries incomes are considerably lower than the locals can earn in more advanced economies. In addition there is still a considerable gap in payment for a similar position between expat and local managers. Currently this system encourages local, high-performing managers to relocate abroad and to take over global positions, rather than remaining on the local CEE market, thus deepening the gap between global and local structures. Clearly this trend is not sustainable and

MNE headquarters budget allocations for HRM in CEE needs to be considerably adjusted in order to capitalize or in some cases not to miss out on the economic growth potential in this region.

Our current study showed the current situation and the dynamics of managing in six Central and East European countries, with a particular focus on HRM and the implications of managing talent and staffing functions, primarily based on the insights of expatriate managers, CEOs and HR Directors. *Further research,* more in-depth analysis needs to be conducted in future to discover internal statistical correlations of existing data or to see if managing talent based on the ways more compatible with the local cultural norms and practices actually result in better performance and knowledge transfer.

References

Bakacsi, G., Imrek, V., Karacsonyi, A., & Takacs, S. (2002). Eastern European cluster: Tradition and transition. *Journal of World Business, 37*(1), 69–80.

Brewster, Ch., & Viegas Bennett, C. (2009). *Can Central and Eastern European management compete?* Austria: TARGET International and Henley Business School, UK.

Buzady, Z. (2014). Breaking with the leadership fantasy: Adopting a more realistic model of drive and motivation. In M. Kisilowski (Ed.), *Free market in its twenties – Modern business decision making in central and Eastern Europe.* Budapest: CEU Press.

Buzady, Z., Brewster, C., Viegas Bennett, C., & Sanyova, B. (2015). Can Central and Eastern Europe Compete in 2015? *Target-Study,* Published by TARGET Executive Search, GfK, Viegas Bennett, Central European University Business School, Henley Business School. Vienna-Bratislava-Budapest.

Csikszentmihalyi, M., Rathunde, K., & Whalen, S. (1997). *Talented teenagers.* Cambridge: Cambridge University Press.

Dries, N., Cotton, R., Bagdadli, S., & de Oliveira, M. (2015). HR directors' understanding of 'Talent': A cross-cultural study. In A. A. Ariss (Ed.), *Global talent management.* Cham: Springer.

Economist. (2005). *The rise of nearshoring, 377*(8455), 86.

Eurostat. (2014). Retrieved from http://ec.europa.eu/eurostat/tgm/table.do?tab=table& plugin=1&language=en&pcode=tec00115. Accessed on November 2014.

Kohont, A., & Brewster, C. (2014). The roles and competencies of HR managers in Slovenian multinational companies. *Baltic Journal of Management, 9*(3), 294–313.

Lang, R., & Steger, T. (2002). The odyssey of management knowledge to transforming societies: A critical review of a theoretical alternative. *Human Resource Development International, 5*(3), 279–294.

Marer, P., Buzady, Z., & Vecsey, Z. (2015). *Missing link discovered.* Budapest: Aleas Inc.

Przytula, S. (2014). Talent management in Poland: Challenges, strategies and opportunities. In A. A. Ariss (Ed.), *Global talent management.* Cham: Springer.

Smale, A., & Suutari, V. (2011). Expatriate perspectives on knowledge transfers into Central and Eastern Europe. In *The role of expatriates in MNCs knowledge mobilization* (pp. 63–90). *International Business and Management Series.* Bingley, UK: Emerald Group Publishing.

Sparrow, P., Scullion, H., & Tarique, I. (2014). *Strategic talent management: Literature review, integrative framework, and suggestions for further research.* Cambridge: Cambridge University Press.

APPENDIX A

Table A1: Respondents' country of origin.

Nationality	Bulgaria	Czechia	Hungary	Poland	Romania	Slovakia	Total
African	0	0	1	0	0	1	*2*
Albanian	0	0	0	0	0	1	*1*
American — USA	5	7	9	9	6	12	*48*
Argentinian	0	0	0	0	1	0	*1*
Austrian	7	11	22	7	9	15	*71*
Belgian	11	3	4	2	9	8	*37*
Brazilian	0	0	0	0	0	1	*1*
British/UK	11	26	23	11	9	13	*93*
Bulgarian	32	1	0	2	3	4	*42*
Canadian	1	1	1	0	5	1	*9*
Colombian	0	0	0	1	0	0	*1*
Croatian	0	1	0	0	0	2	*3*
Cuban	0	0	1	0	0	0	*1*
Cypriot	0	0	1	0	0	0	*1*
Czech	4	57	8	1	7	5	*82*
Danish	2	1	1	5	0	5	*14*
Dutch	6	6	13	6	7	11	*49*
Finnish	0	1	0	7	1	1	*10*
French	13	16	19	15	29	23	*115*
German	9	6	26	10	15	18	*84*
Greek	13	1	4	1	23	5	*47*
Hungarian	0	1	38	2	8	2	*51*
Indian	0	1	4	1	2	0	*8*
Iranian	1	0	4	0	1	2	*8*
Israeli	1	0	0	0	3	2	*6*
Italian	5	4	6	6	16	14	*51*
Jordanian	0	0	0	0	0	1	*1*
Kazakhstan	0	0	0	0	2	0	*2*
Kyrgyz	0	0	0	0	0	1	*1*
Lithuanian	1	0	0	0	0	0	*1*
Luxembourger	1	0	0	0	0	0	*1*
Macedonian	0	1	0	1	0	0	*2*
Mexican	1	1	2	1	1	3	*9*
Mongolian	0	0	0	0	0	1	*1*
Montenegrin	1	0	0	0	0	0	*1*
Nepalese	0	0	1	0	0	0	*1*
New Zealand	0	1	0	0	1	0	*2*

Table A1: Continued.

Nationality	Bulgaria	Czechia	Hungary	Poland	Romania	Slovakia	Total
Norwegian	0	2	0	0	1	1	*4*
Other Europe	2	0	0	0	0	2	*4*
Pakistani	0	0	0	0	2	0	*2*
Polish	1	0	4	36	2	3	*46*
Portuguese	1	2	0	3	6	2	*14*
Romanian	6	6	2	3	25	10	*52*
Russian	0	2	0	1	2	0	*5*
Serbian	3	0	0	0	1	0	*4*
Slovak	0	7	2	1	1	31	*42*
Slovenian	1	1	1	0	0	2	*5*
Spanish	4	3	2	1	6	2	*18*
Swedish	0	2	0	10	1	2	*15*
Swiss	3	0	2	0	3	3	*11*
Turkish	1	0	3	1	8	2	*15*
No answer	1	2	2	4	1	3	*13*
Total	*148*	*174*	*206*	*148*	*217*	*215*	*1108*

APPENDIX B

Table B1: Expats' years of experience in host country.

	Bulgaria	Czech	Hungary	Poland	Romania	Slovakia	Total
Less than 1 year	2.6%	11.1%	1.8%	7.1%	4.7%	3.3%	4.7%
1–5 years	12.1%	11.1%	7.1%	10.7%	15.6%	9.8%	11.1%
More than 5 years	85.3%	77.8%	91.1%	82.1%	79.7%	87.0%	84.1%